Don Drun_____

Don Drummond

*The Genius and
Tragedy of the World's
Greatest Trombonist*

HEATHER AUGUSTYN
Foreword by Delfeayo Marsalis

McFarland & Company, Inc., Publishers
Jefferson, North Carolina, and London

The lyrics to "Woman A Come" by Margarita and Baba Brooks Band in Chapter 10 are reprinted by permission of Sharon Pottinger Gibson/Treasure Isle.

LIBRARY OF CONGRESS CATALOGUING-IN-PUBLICATION DATA

Augustyn, Heather, 1972–
    Don Drummond : The genius and tragedy of the world's greatest trombonist /Heather Augustyn ; foreword by Delfeayo Marsalis.
        p.   cm.
    Includes bibliographical references and index.

    ISBN 978-0-7864-7547-6
    softcover : acid free paper ∞

    1. Drummond, Don, 1932–1969.   2. Trombonists — Jamaica — Biography.   I. Title.
    ML419.D77A94 2013
    788.9'31646092 — dc23
    [B]   2013021934

BRITISH LIBRARY CATALOGUING DATA ARE AVAILABLE

Cover images: Jean-Christophe Molineris, *Don Drummond*. Oil on canvas, 23.62" × 17.72", 2012 (courtesy of the artist). *Background* blue texture wall (Ingram Publishing/Thinkstock)

Manufactured in the United States of America

McFarland & Company, Inc., Publishers
  Box 611, Jefferson, North Carolina 28640
    www.mcfarlandpub.com

For Ron, Sid and Frank

Table of Contents

Acknowledgments

I would like to thank my family, Ron, Sid, and Frank, for putting up with my obsession, my hours spent at my computer, my gabbing on and on about all things ska, and for allowing me to drag you around the trenches of Kingston instead of sipping fruit drinks on the beautiful north shore beaches of Jamaica. Hopefully, we'll get to see those one day, too.

To my mom, for her unconditional support and love, always. To my brother for helping me to analyze situations, assess the best decision, and see the big picture instead of always going with my impulse. To my dad for first introducing me to the music of Jamaica.

To Brad Klein — what can I say? He is a true skamrade, a brother in ska. I am so thankful for his generosity, support, and shared obsession to keep the train to skaville moving forward!

To Zola, Suzanne, Paul, and Faye — their memories were invaluable in putting together the picture of a woman the world should celebrate. Anita lives always.

To Steve Barrow for reading my manuscript and encouraging my work. It is an honor.

To Ken Stewart, Brian Keyo, and P.J. Patterson, manager and past managers, respectively, of the greatest band the world has ever known — thanks for the stories, insights, contacts, and support.

To Carlos Escoffery for sharing his interest with me and helping me to try to get to the bottom of something too buried to be found. Long live the oldies!

To Maryann Karinch and Rasheed McWilliams for their guidance and advice.

To Allyson Baughman, for her passion, expertise, and support. I look up to her more than she knows.

Special thanks to Leovia Taylor at the Registrar General's Department; Sheree Rhoden, Mavis Williams, and Ahon Gray at the Jamaica

Gleaner; Nicole Bryan and Genevieve Jones-Edman at the National Library of Jamaica; and Superintendent John Cornwall at the May Pen Cemetery. Their research was crucial to my project.

To Sister Shirley Chung, Winston "Sparrow" Martin, and the boys of the Alpha Boys Band — they all took me in so warmly, allowed me access to their past, present, and future, and shared their spirits. No book can ever capture that. I will carry this with me, always.

To Patrick Phillips, my taxi driver — even though he was always on Jamaica time — for taking me into some areas not commonly visited. Without him I would not have had access to some critical sites.

To historians Herbie Miller, Bunny Goodison, Kingsley Goodison, Dermot Hussey, and Laurence Cane-Honeysett for fielding my questions and dealing with my very American tenacity. I am humbled.

To Dave Rosencrans, Clive Chin, and Lloyd Daley for their photos and memories.

To Michael Turner for compiling the discography for me. That is something that is just not my forte and is essential, so I am in awe.

To Sandra Mayo for allowing me access to her dissertation on Alpha and her sisterly encouragement. And to Earl Patrick Alexander Smart for access to his dissertation on Bellevue.

To Basil Hylton and Ronald Knight for their stories and helping to put me in touch with fellow Alpharians. They are keeping the spirit of Alpha's past alive.

And to those who shared your personal stories with me. Some were amusing to relive, some were too painful to speak. Without these, this book would not be possible. Telling stories is critical to preserving history, and I thank the reader for believing in me as your medium.

Foreword
by Delfeayo Marsalis

Late one evening in 1985, I was returning to the Brooklyn residence of my elder brothers Branford and Wynton from a sojourn in Manhattan. As fate would have it, the Jamaican taxi driver recognized my slide trombone and proclaimed, "You know about Don Drummond and the Skatalites?" At that point it occurred to me that I had indeed seen in Branford's collection several albums by this particular group, but — not being interested in ska music at the time — had not checked them out. The driver continued to rave about Drummond being one of the greatest in history, which I basically accepted with a few grains of salt until he asserted, "J.J. Johnson went to Jamaica just to hear Drummond, his legend was so strong!" The matter had suddenly become serious business with the utterance of such a proclamation. Johnson was not only my primary jazz influence, he was also one of America's great jazz masters, known for his precision and profound command of the trombone at all tempos and volumes. Would J.J. have traveled to Kingston, Jamaica, solely to hear Don Drummond?

I immediately scoured the library and discovered three Skatalites albums. I listened and was overcome by the pathos and immediacy of Drummond's improvisations, his melodies expressing an adolescent innocence undergirded with the knowledge of an elder. Extroverted, eccentric and self-taught, Don Drummond's trombone style has an earthiness and songlike quality that makes it immediately identifiable. His melodies are so simple, so perfectly constructed and memorable that they are reminiscent of children's songs; each note is placed in exactly the right place at exactly the right time. He managed to consistently maintain certain qualities not steadfastly present in Johnson's style.

At some point in the mid–1990s, interest in Drummond led me to

1

the Brooklyn storefront studio of Mr. Coxsone Dodd and eventually to a few trips to Kingston, Jamaica. I found that many of the older people were aware of Drummond and his music. His celebrity was such that stories were shared with equal aplomb about his extraordinary musicianship as well as his peculiarities. He not only worked the women into frenzies with his aggressive rhythms, but he also would cause many to weep at the sorrow he expressed on ballads. During the 1950s–'60s, Jamaica was a hotbed of musical talent, including the likes of Roland Alphonso, Johnny Moore, Lennie Hibbert and Tommy McCook. Don Drummond, it turns out, was able to channel emotions from gentility to absolute rage through his music with as much authority as anyone who ever played trombone.

Trips to Jamaica were learning experiences on many levels; however, the greatest single lesson for me concerned understanding and accepting the traditions of the Jamaican people. Although they were respectful toward me and happy to assist in my efforts to learn about this musical giant, they still let me know in subtle ways that they were Jamaican and I was not. When they wanted to have private conversations, the language became unrecognizable. If there was even a hint of impatience from me, actions slowed down to a snail's pace. These quirks gave me a sense of how strong nationalism and pride is in the Jamaican people. As a whole, the individuals I encountered had a way of thinking that was centered on honesty, integrity and good old common sense. While they would never admit to the reality as such, these unique qualities of a people, when codified properly, can form the backbone of their art.

Bob Marley gave a voice and hope to all Jamaicans during the '60s and '70s with his songs of political awareness and protest. The individual who influenced Marley the most with songs that celebrated Jamaica and its unique characteristics was Don Drummond. Marley spent a period of time performing with Drummond and, clearly, knew of his brilliance. Marley's voice covers the same basic range of Drummond's trombone and, as further proof, his "Crazy Baldheads" is pretty much Drummond's "Eastern Standard Time" in a minor key! Even without lyrics, the trombonist displayed his socio-political awareness with songs entitled "Man in the Street," "President Kennedy," "Lee Harvey Oswald" and "Reload." Marley was able to take Drummond's music to the ultimate level, internalizing its strongest characteristics and incorporating them in his own style to great advantage.

Whether by Drummond's own design or that of producer Coxsone

Dodd, the Skatalites performed all of their songs with the famous guitar-led ska (*boom-chick, boom-chick*) beat. Certainly, a studied and adventurous musician like Drummond was capable of creating less formulaic compositions, and his desire to do so is evidenced in at least one example, "Far East." This song highlights an awareness of other cultures and musical contributions as it is a tribute to Eastern music in Jamaican terms. One captivating aspect of ska is the degree to which it is specifically localized (from the people) and universal (for all people) simultaneously. While Don Drummond's distinctive sound was strengthened by consistent performance with the same Jamaican musicians, if he had been afforded the opportunity to share experiences with musicians from different cultures (as is customary today), his music could have expanded to even greater heights.

Speculation aside, we celebrate all that Don Drummond accomplished as a great musician and representative for the Jamaican people. Thanks to his ingenuity, ska remains the only genre of music in which trombone plays the lead voice, with trumpet and saxophone playing the secondary harmonies. Don Drummond was a soft-spoken introvert whose life was defined by the trombone and the great music he created with it. Trombone provided his voice in a way that words could not. Don Drummond played music as though it was all he had; or perhaps as though he felt it was all he had. As listeners, we have benefited greatly from his immense talent and unique ability to touch human souls around the world.

This is the definitive documentation of a seminal figure in the history of Jamaican music which is long overdue!

Delfeayo Marsalis is one of the top trombonists, composers, and producers in jazz today. He is a member of the distinguished Marsalis family, along with father Ellis and brothers Branford, Wynton and Jason. Together they earned the nation's highest jazz honor, a National Endowment for the Arts Jazz Masters Award, in 2011.

Preface: The Known and Unknown

There is no great genius without a mixture of madness.
— Aristotle

It is well with me only when I have a chisel in my hand.
— Michelangelo

P.J. Patterson sat at his wooden desk, remembering. Jamaica had been generous to him. Extravagant, even. Politician and lawyer, prime minister, manager to his nation's most talented performers — Patterson's opportunities and blessings stood in stark contrast to the mystifying self-destruction of his countryman Don Drummond. "Have you ever listened to his music?" he asked me in earnest. "I mean, have you ever really listened to it?"

Of course I had. "It's haunting, isn't it?" I replied.

Patterson had seen both sides of Don Drummond. Patterson had served as his manager during the last days of Drummond's reign with the Skatalites, and he had served as his defense attorney during Drummond's grim murder trial. He profoundly admired Drummond as a performer, an appreciation only deepened with time, but still there was emptiness behind his evocative words about the greatest musician his country had ever produced. Patterson never really *knew* Drummond. Then again, no one really could.

It had been decades since my introduction to Don Drummond's music. As a teenager, I first came to know ska music, like many others, through the English incarnation of artists. When I explored the roots of this enthusiastic music, I discovered the Jamaican genre and realized there was much more to ska than a bouncy tune. The music seized me, but the culture bound me. And no one better captured the underlying want, the pain tinged with hope, the ability to survive with raw skill, than the master trombonist Don Drummond. Now, with Don Drummond's music firmly imprinted in my repertoire, I know that my perception of his creativity is weighted by my awareness of more than just the sounds of his horn. I hear his melodies in a rich context — a deeper story of struggle, exploitation, virtuosity, reclusion, idiosyncrasy, complexity, and sheer brilliance. I've heard many of Drummond's songs hundreds, if not thousands, of times, and each time I notice something different, something new — a subtle slide from one note to the next, a trill, a repetition of the theme punctuated by a flourish. His music is so familiar that it feels like a shadow I live within. His story is so familiar that, at times, I almost catch glimpses of him in my own walks through life. Don Drummond, like his music, is haunting.

There are those who have known Don Drummond for years, either as children growing up together at Alpha Boys School, later in life under the spotlights of the stage, or in musical communion in the Wareika Hills. They all say the same thing: they never really knew who Don Drummond was. There is something eternally elusive about Cosmic Don. Those who came before me have typically done one of two things: they made Don Drummond into a myth, into a legend; or they tried to construct Don Drummond by deconstructing him. My challenge as an historian, as a biographer of this mad genius, is, in a sense, unachievable. How can I allow my reader to know Don Drummond if he was unknowable, even when he was alive? My approach was to put together as much of the story as I could, through the words of others, through investigation of the truth, through setting the scene of what the social climate and his environment was like, so that the reader can construct a true sense of the man.

To do this I walked the same paths as Drummond, went to the same fields, stepped onto the same stage and stared into the audience as he must have. But what could all of these quiet things tell me of Drummond? I touched his trombone. I peered beneath his home, through the gaping holes in the fallen cinderblock foundation where old 45s lay in the underbelly, left by long-gone tenants. I walked the barren earth around the room where he slept, now devoid of vegetation and mottled with debris and lost memories. I examined the home from all angles, circling it like a raven on carrion; moved through the doorways of his school, eyes wide, watching for his ghost; combed through genealogy records and articles and online searches and files of loose photos, probing for a scrap, for an answer, for a passageway to follow to its tragically abrupt end.

I thought I might find handwritten leaves of sheet music. None. A photo of his mother or an undiscovered relative. I came close, but none. I felt — and still do feel — my story is incomplete, with much missing data. I wanted so much more. But I sincerely feel this is the best picture that can be constructed of Don Drummond, based on the information we do have, the stories we do have, the music we do have. We can imagine him as he sat beneath the Monkey Tambourine Tree and the complexities of his thoughts. We can envision him as he stood on the wood floor of the Bournemouth Beach Club, the brilliance that produced improvised notes that brought listeners to tears. We can evoke the young boy, barefoot with glasses thick as Coke bottles and suffer his obsession so deep that it broke him. But he is not merely summoned in his music. He is still alive.

What developed as a result of my approach was not only revealing, it also became dreadfully emotional as the tragedy of the story unfolded. In many ways, Don Drummond will always be a myth. But, I realized quickly, after talking to those who are still very much affected by the aftermath of the madness of Don Drummond, that the story is no myth. It is not folklore. The aftermath of his madness is painful. It is reality, even four decades later. Time after time, people who recounted their tales to me, of their loved ones all those years ago, were driven to tears. Their words broke down. They were unable to continue. They were still surrounded by the disbelief, anger, emptiness. Others refused to talk because they wanted to leave the memory where it was, buried. The story became a strange juxtaposition of the unknowable and the too knowable. This story, like Don Drummond himself, is a contradiction of creation and destruction, feelings of awe and feelings of horror.

While researching the story I gained a newfound respect, appreciation, and love, not for Don Drummond, as I already had that, but for Anita Mahfood, better known as Margarita. Little has been written about her. There is only one song by Margarita, "Woman A Come," also known as "Ungu Malungu Man," and certainly this song does little to showcase her talent. In fact, it's a little odd. But, through talking to Margarita's family members, I discovered a woman so beautiful, so courageous, so strong-minded that she not only brought her self-taught talent for dancing the rhumba to the stage, headlining at the top Kingston clubs, she brought her fellow performers' music to the mainstream in a time when such an action seemed impossible. Her defiance of the odds in so many ways is both remarkable and an inspiration. It makes her tragic death even harder to bear when we understand what an astonishing woman Margarita was.

Without Don Drummond's genius, and without Margarita's tenacity, it is easy to argue that Jamaican music would never have flourished to produce the Bob Marleys, Jimmy Cliffs and Peter Toshes.

The only way to truly get to know Don Drummond is through his music. This book, therefore, is a contextual story. It is a painting whose brush never quite touches the subject, yet fills in the space around it to reveal the subject's shape. The image, the form of Don D. is here in these pages, in his songs, in the music he inspired, in the lives he forever changed.

1

Barefoot Boy

It is expected that when Don Drummond was a little boy, like all other children in Jamaica, his mother told him stories of Anancy. "Once upon a time, Anancy was a head-man for a man by the name of Mr. Mighty, who employed Anancy for the purpose of minding some sheep." Anancy, frequently called Brer Anancy to connote brotherhood or kinship, was a spider, or rather half-spider, half-man. He could be a hero or a villain. He triumphed through his astute ways over others, including Bredda Tiger, Bredda Monkey, Bredda Snake. Brought from West Africa to Jamaica during the days of slavery, Anancy was a survivor, a transformer, indestructible. He brought hope to the slaves of their triumph over the oppressor. He was an accomplished creator. He is a Jamaican folk hero, complex, metaphoric, larger than life. When Jamaican children heard stories of Anancy, they realized that, through craftiness, endurance, and tenacity, success was possible. There was hope.

Although there are differences between the fictional Anancy and Don Drummond, the parallels are many. Drummond was a tenacious and accomplished survivor. Drummond was complex, and was neither good nor bad. Drummond triumphed over the oppressor in many ways. Just as Anancy is a symbol, a representative of Jamaican possibilities, so too is Don Drummond.

Donald Willis Drummond was born on March 12, 1934, at Victoria Jubilee Hospital in Kingston, Jamaica. He had a devoted mother, Doris Maud Munroe, and an absent father, Uriah Adolphus Drummond. Virtually nothing is known of Don's father except that he was a laborer who had been born in Broughton, Westmoreland, on May 4, 1908. Uriah's mother was named Rhoda Drummond, also a laborer, with no father listed on her birth records. Likewise, genealogical records with the Jamaican General Registrar Department have no documentation of a father on Don's birth record. On his admission record to Alpha Boys School, however,

Uriah's name is given, along with the comment that "Donald's father has shown little or no interest in him, his mother on the contrary is interested and helpful."

It was not unusual for women in Jamaica during this time to give birth to a child without being married to the father. In fact, it was quite common. Vital statistics from the *Daily Gleaner* reveal that, of the 34,247 births recorded for Jamaica in 1934, 71.9 percent were illegitimate. Many times the father was completely gone from the child's life, as in the case of Don, or the father came around to visit the mother and child sporadically. Frequently, the father had many children with many mothers.

Doris Munroe was born on January 7, 1913, in the parish of Westmoreland, in a tiny village named Flower Hill (current population: 2,000). It is likely that Munroe was the surname given to the family by their slave masters. The surname Munroe is of Scottish origin, so it is likely that the Munroe family once belonged to Scottish landowners. Doris's mother, Hannah Lee Munroe, was a laborer, according to birth records. It is not known when Doris traveled to Kingston from Flower Hill, but it was common for young women looking to make a better life for themselves by going to the city for job opportunities.

Doris was 19 years old when she gave birth to Don. It was a great advantage to have birthed a baby at a city hospital, rather than in a village home, which was more typical of Jamaican women of the time. But Doris's move to Kingston also provided her new family with opportunities, such as modern medical technology, and so Don would have been afforded a comfortable and skilled birth rather than a rural one marked by rituals and cultural practices in the village. Built in 1887, Victoria Jubilee Hospital is still in use today.

Donald was not named at the time of his birth; his mother registered his name legally two full months later. They first lived at 26 Potters Row in South Kingston, the same street where the great Jamaican poet Mutabaruka grew up two decades later. Potters Row was located a short distance away from the Myrtle Bank Hotel, where the wealthy came to play. This palatial hotel was built in the mid–1800s as a bank which was then converted into a boarding house and soon a bustling, modern, government-run hotel. The meticulously landscaped grounds included a filtered saltwater pool, 205 rooms with French doors that opened onto verandas overlooking the ocean, and a tropical garden in the center with a stage on which the West Indian Regiment Band performed twice a week. It is possible that Drummond may have heard these musicians perform on a walk with his mother, but the luxury of the hotel, although nearby geographically, could not have been culturally further from the poverty of Drummond's home in Rae Town.

080202478866/2012 CERTIFICATION OF VITAL RECORD

JAMAICA

Registrar General's Department

Issue Date: 10th February, 2012

BIRTH REGISTRATION FORM

1. BIRTH IN THE DISTRICT OF: **KINGSTON**	2. PARISH: **KINGSTON**
3. NO. **AA 3655**	4. Place of Birth: **VICTORIA JUBILEE LYING IN HOSPITAL**
5. Date of Birth: **TWELFTH MARCH, 1934**	6. Sex: **MALE**
7. Name of Child: **see line 26**	

8. Physician or registered midwife in attendance: nil

FATHER

9. Name and Surname: **********

10. Age at time of birth: nil   11. Occupation: nil

12. Birthplace: nil

MOTHER

13. (a) Residence: **26 POTTERS ROW**

(b) Town/Village: nil   (c) Parish: **KINGSTON**

14. No. of Children previously born to mother (a) Alive: **Not stated**   (b) Still-born: **Not stated**

15. Name and Surname: **DORIS MUNROE ***

Maiden Name: nil   16. Age at time of birth: nil

17. Occupation: **DOMESTIC**   18. Birthplace: nil

INFORMANT(S)

19. Name and Surname: nil   nil

20. Qualification: nil   nil

21. (a) Residence: nil   nil

(b) Town/Village: nil   nil

(c) Parish:

REGISTRAR'S CERTIFICATE

22. (b) Entered by me from the particulars on a Certificate received from: **M S LEWIS**

CHIEF RESIDENT OFFICER

23. Witness: nil

24. Date: **FOURTEENTH MARCH, 1934**   **Signed by Registrar**

Name if added after Registration of Birth

26. Name: **DONALD WILLIS DRUMMOND ***

27. Authority: **CERTIFICATE OF NAMING**   28. Date Added: **ELEVENTH MAY, 1934**

Last line of Vital Data

for
Yvette Scott
Registrar General &
Deputy Keeper of the Records

Donald Willis Drummond's birth certificate.

11

Two blocks away from Don's first home was the General Penitentiary, the same one Black Uhuru sang of, calling it a "warehouse of human slavery." At the time of Drummond's birth, this prison was the principal maximum-security prison on the island, and although it was designed to house 800 inmates, at times it held twice as many. In the early 1930s, street lights were just being installed in Rae Town. Mayor of Kingston, H.A. L. Simpson, even wrote to the town clerk at this time to complain about unsanitary conditions in the neighborhood, including "unpleasant smells," and refuse in the streets. He also complained about the "negligence and indifference to the welfare of the people residing in this district," and asked for "attention to deplorable conditions in Rae Town."

A year and a half before Don was born and lived in his mother's home in Rae Town, a horrific stabbing took place next door. A newspaper article of August 8, 1930, reads, "Blood flowed freely from Josephine Sinclair of 28½ Potter's Row in the Rae Town District, on Wednesday night when, it is alleged, she was seriously wounded by Orville Martin. The cry of the wounded woman attracted residents in the locality and within a short

Don Drummond's first home at 26 Potters Row (photograph by Conrad Raymond).

space of time a large crowd gathered." The tenants, Jonathan Brown and Iris Sinclair, served as a witness to the crime. Iris lived next door to her sister, the victim Josephine, who survived her lover's attack.

For a number of years surrounding Drummond's birth, a tuberculosis hospital was proposed for his neighborhood to treat patients, but sites were selected elsewhere. There was, however, a hospital located near Drummond's first home; it was the same hospital where he would die. Also located nearby was the expansive Bellevue Mental Hospital, then called the Lunatic Asylum, located on Windward Road.

It is not known exactly when Don and his mother moved out of Rae Town, but by the time Drummond grew older they were living at 21 Hitchen Street, a safer neighborhood to the north called Allman Town. Allman Town was located near Alpha Boys School, just east across South Camp Road. Don was baptized a Roman Catholic at the Alpha Chapel. Allman Town was a community of mostly wooden houses with zinc fences; there were a couple of Chinese grocery shops, tailors, and cold supper shops. In the 1930s and 1940s, it was a neighborhood of hard-working people and low crime rates and was considered a buffer between the rougher Jones Town and the wealthier Vineyard Town. Residents had no fear when walking the rather narrow streets of Allman Town. "Don, Rico Rodriguez, and [I] lived there," recalls musician Ronald Knight. "We had a church and a primary school there. We were poor but proud, made ourselves look rich by dressing sharp."

There was a citizens' association, the Allman Town–Woodford Park Citizens' Association, which met frequently to discuss ways to meet the needs of the residents. The organization had a structure akin to a municipal council, with a president, a vice-president, and most likely, a parliamentary procedural method of conducting business. Among the issues discussed at the time were securing a public pay telephone station for residents; utility improvements and the construction of sewers; reconstruction and construction of streets; opposition to the legalization of Peaka Peow, a gambling game played on the street; helpful hints on how to properly raise poultry; construction of a post office; distribution of garbage cans; and inadequate police protection.

Residents of Allman Town were concerned about the increasing crime in their community, but incidents appear to have been rather minor in comparison to the crime in other parts of the city, and certainly mild when compared to crime in the modern era. It is likely that residents of Allman

Town wanted to prevent their community from disintegrating into the higher-crime areas, like the regions to the west, such as Back-O-Wall and Smith Village, or up on Spanish Town Road, or down on the docks.

The then-recent 1929 stock market crash led to an economic depression, bringing poverty and unemployment to the world. With poverty comes crime, and so the residents of Allman Town were careful to keep their community as healthy as possible. In 1933, residents of Allman Town asked the inspector to increase the number of police officers in their neighborhood and in nearby Kingston Gardens. In 1938, in what was called the "Allman Town Shooting Case," a jilted lover shot his ex-girlfriend, wounding her and an innocent bystander who was walking along Great George Street. Other crimes included newborn babies found dead in freshly dug holes. Less serious offenses were "the abusive language used by young women," or the call for residents to keep their goats, pigs, and cows from roaming the streets so the sanitary condition of the neighborhood could be properly maintained. The house at which Don and his mother lived, was at 21 Hitchen Street. Doris worked hard to provide for Don, only child. Fellow musician Eddie "Tan Tan" Thornton recalls, "He love his mother. Love her, love her. She was a nice, quiet, sweet lady. Don used to look after her. I can see them now as I'm talkin' to you, laughing."

Doris Munroe was a domestic, meaning she worked in the homes of the wealthy. Domestics worked for very little pay during an era when men typically worked in the cane fields. To earn her meager salary, Doris washed clothes, ironed, or cooked. As electricity was scarce in that region during the 1930s and 1940s, work was done during the day, or by lamp light. Domestics routinely carried water to the chickens, goats, and pigs, but never on Sunday, which was a day of respect. Allman Town had an abundance of domestic workers who advertised themselves as "decent women," "civil, hard-working young girls," or "a respectable woman." Some even advertised their "light complexion," "fair education," or the ability to complete tasks "without any trouble." Entire pages of the *Daily Gleaner* were devoted to advertising domestic services in the 1930s and 1940s, a time when girls and women had little or no opportunity other than domestic work.

Doris was a devout lady, recalls Clive Chin who visited the family home during the 1960s. "It had a veranda," Chin remembers. "It had a gate and then you go into the yard. It's not a big house. It had zinc roofing and louver windows. That house must have been built in the '30s or '40s.

It had carved-out colonial-style decorations around the windows because that area back then wasn't really regarded as a poor area. It was near Sabina Park." Behind the house was a large area of land known as No. 17 Wild Street. This property comprised 1,800 square feet of land that abutted Don's yard to the north and was perfect for children's play. "His mother would be inside either cooking or working," said Chin. "I've only seen the mother once. She was a nice lady, wear glasses and she seemed to be on the Christian side, a woman who keep herself neat and have them Bible with them."

In his early years, Don attended Franklin (or Franklyn) Town Primary School which was located at 4 Victoria Street, in Kingston. "Franklyn Town was one of many little private schools that was in the open air, outdoors. Normally, a woman teacher used [to] teach basic reading, writing, and sums," remembers Ronald Knight. After attending this school, according to his record, Don went to the Alpha Elementary School. Knight says, "Alpha Elementary School was well organized with qualified teachers and taught religion and was strict. The school was situated next to Alpha Academy High School for girls on South Camp Road below the boys' home." Children typically went to school barefooted, although in a school uniform of white and blue, or whichever color demarcated their school. School lunches during these times cost a penny and included a biscuit and a sweet. Students had a slate they used in school, and a book. But Don wasn't interested in school. He began skipping classes, arriving late, and goofing around rather than taking his studies seriously.

Winston "Sparrow" Martin, fellow student and current bandmaster since 1988 at Alpha Boys School, says, "The reason for Don Drummond to come to Alpha is his mother couldn't take him for his antics. The antics. He used to play a comb. He used to have a comb and a paper and he used to play [like a kazoo] and then people would come out and sit and listen to him, people in the yard where he lived in Allman Town, so he used to do it and that's the reason why he had to come to Alpha. He wasn't a bad boy, but his antics. Sometimes maybe he doesn't want to do anything."

Young children during these times frequently roamed the streets, especially as their mothers had to work as domestics in other people's homes during the daylight hours. They simply couldn't watch their children every minute of the day and provide for all of their needs at the same time. In a *Daily Gleaner* article dated April 20, 1940, the prevalence of children wandering and playing without supervision was noted. "It was agreed that at the May meeting," said the article of the Citizen's Association of Allman

Town and Woodford Park, "attention should be given to the number of boys and girls of school age who roam thoroughfares and also the race course, with boys gambling in gullies. It will be proposed that that the authorities should take steps to check the juvenile evil complained of."

According to Don's school record, he was admitted to Alpha Boys School, the "school for wayward boys," as a result of "truancy." Still, one would need to be recommended for admission to Alpha. "In those days you don't go to the police to come to Alpha, you would come to Alpha through a priest, but after the government start coming into the school, that all changed," Martin says. Drummond was placed at Alpha by "RM Court," according to his record, meaning the Resident Magistrate's Court. This court, which still exists today as part of Jamaica's Ministry of Justice, presides over both civil and criminal matters and includes a number of different divisions, including the Juvenile Court.

On December 10, 1943, Don entered Alpha Boys School. Medical officials were required to oversee an examination of each child recommended for admission. According to Don's record, he did suffer from a physical ailment but was admitted nonetheless. The record states, "This is to certify that Donald Drummond is suffering from an ulcer of the right leg but is otherwise physically fit for admission to the Alpha Industrial School." It is signed by R. Davidson, M.O. Kin., which is likely an abbreviation for medical officer. Don's height at the time of admission was four feet and three inches tall and he weighed 60 pounds. His religion was listed as "R.C." (Roman Catholic). His personal description was that he had a "brown complexion, hair & eyes." The record indicates that parents or relatives were notified of his admission, but that likely was only Doris, and perhaps his grandmother, Hannah Lee.

And so, during a time that the rest of the world saw great unrest and upheaval, during time of devastating battles in Europe and Africa and Japan, during a time of Nazi atrocities too horrific to describe, when danger and poverty and instability were on every doorstep and the fate of Great Britain affected every Caribbean nation under her rule, Don Drummond, a fragile, vulnerable, innocent child, brother to Brer Anancy, left his mother's home to learn how to create, how to endure, how to survive.

2

Upward and Onward

The Alpha story has been the history of kings and queens rather than the
working class people.
    — *Basil Hylton, trombonist, graduate of Alpha Boys School*

Boys stand in the open doorways of the hot cement buildings, their dusty black feet, calloused, dry on the smooth red tile of their classroom floor. Others run for shelter into the dormitories, trade buildings, the dining hall, with their dark blue shirts sticking to their sweaty brown skin. Their eyes look up at the storm. Outside it begins to rain. The rooms turn dark. Above, the clouds, gray and heavy, churn and swirl, then release their burdens into the dirt and pebbles below, slowly at first, and then a torrent. The land is saturated, muddy and lush. Palm fronds and lime trees shift swiftly in the gusty wind. The pavement, where illusion-like heat just rose from the earth now simmers, steams in the cool cloudburst.

Before cars swarmed the streets of the Kingston, before electric trolleys rang their bells and flew through the city on crisscrossing cables, before government yards brought shelter and squalor to the masses, the Alpha Boys School became a fixture in Kingston along South Camp Road. Alpha Boys School was founded in 1880 by Justina Ripoll, better known as Jessie Ripoll, when she and her two devout Catholic friends, Josephine Ximenes and Louise Dugiol, combined their money and bought land to establish an orphanage. They chose 43 acres in south-central Kingston and built an orphanage for girls, a single building, a small cottage. When the doors officially opened, one young girl was given a home and the love and care of three mothers. Their love and devotion to the children of Kingston grew as child after child began calling the school home. In 1883, Alpha Cottage School, as it was then named, first welcomed boys.

Unable to financially handle the orphanage on their own, the three founders joined with a group of nuns from the Roman Catholic Sisters of Mercy in London, who traveled to Kingston to start up the mission in

1890. In addition to growing their orphanage, the three founders also became nuns in the order. Jessie Ripoll was now known as Sister Mary Peter Claver, Josephine Ximenes was now called Sister Mary Joseph, and Louise Dugiol was now Sister Margaret Mary.

On August 20, 1890, the Jamaican government allowed the Sisters of Mercy to register Alpha as an industrial school and began funding the institution which had 12 boys at the time. Over the years, nuns from such countries as England, Malta, the United States, Canada, and Panama, came to serve at Alpha and help guide the students, which numbered up to 700. These sisters assisted in instructing the students in trades they could use to gain employment after they left school. Mark Williams writes in the liner notes to Trojan Records' *Alpha Boys' School: Music in Education*, "Alpha at that time consisted of two industrial schools, one for girls and one for boys. The boys were added to the Sisters of Mercy's particular ministry, and under their care, over the years, Alpha developed trades to go along with basic education." Gardening, printmaking, book binding, pottery, plumbing, shoemaking, tailoring, woodworking, and music were some of the trades taught over the years, many of which are still taught today. Some boys came to Alpha from Maxwell Park, where they were orphaned as babies.

Rico Rodriguez attended Alpha Boys School in the 1940s and says he remembers working several trades while in school. Rico states, "The first job I did in Alpha was in the garden. We didn't have a jet, a jet-type to water the garden. We used to take a paint pan and dip it into a hole for the water. We used to catch the water and water the plants like that. And sometime you eat what you grow, carrot, beet root, the onions and everyting, you know? I used to go to the pottery, too, learn to make brick and pot, with clay, with clay, yeah. And to get that special shine into the clay you have to use horse dung and lead and then when it goes into the kiln it shines in the pot, but I used to be in the garden most of the time." Shortly thereafter, Rico entered the band program at Alpha, where he took up the trombone and became Don's protégé.

Like Drummond, Rico came to Alpha because of his unruly ways: "My mother think that I need some correction, you know? She was working. I used to go down to the waterfront. It was rough. Rough." So instead of going to school, Rico went to the docks to hustle the sailors who came into port. When he got hit by a car and was seriously injured, his mother, deeply concerned about his safety, had him sent to Alpha.

But Alpha boys are certain to point out that their school was *not* for delinquents — that was reserved for a different school. Instead, Alpha helped give direction to boys whose lives may have strayed due to their mothers being unable to care for them financially, fathers being absent or dead, or both. Singer Owen Grey, who attended Alpha while his dad was stationed in the army, says, "Alpha School wasn't for bad boys. No, no, no! It wasn't for the rude boy and bad boy business. There was a place called Stony Hill. That was for the bad boys." Trumpeter Eddie "Tan Tan" Thornton concurs: "Alpha is a great place. They think it's bad boys go to Alpha. There's no bad boys go to Alpha." Thornton was admitted to Alpha in 1945 after the death of his father.

Boys who went to Alpha were required to claim their religion as Catholic. Calvin "Bubbles" Cameron, the great Jamaican trombonist, says that he was never allowed to go to Alpha, although he did try, drawn as he was by the school's reputation for music. As he recalls, "Trying to get to Alpha, they say this church I am from, and I tell them, 'Sorry mon, me cyaan [can not], I am Baptist.' And they say, 'Well if you are Baptist, I don't think Mr. Lennie [Lennie Hibbert, bandmaster at the time] will take you in, or Sister Ignatius, you must come back, but I come back twice and I never see Sister Ignatius and I never see Lennie.'"

Many of the older boys who were lucky enough to attend Alpha Boys School helped to take care of the younger ones. This kind of peer learning was crucial to their success. Trumpeter Jo Jo Bennett, like many Alpha alumni, feels a strong bond to his alma mater, especially because of the camaraderie among students. "That's my second home, or my first home," he says proudly. "I went there when I was ten years of age. Don Drummond and most guys at that Alpha Boys School really grew up within the school, 'cause when I was at that school there were pretty near five hundred boys there, because they had different sections, you know? From babies, to middle ages, like ten, and when they get double figure, ten up, they go to another section for that age group. And when they [turn sixteen] you have to leave school. Older boys take care of the younger boys, and the sisters, too."

Rico, too, remembers the camaraderie at the school: "At Alpha now you have the junior and the seniors, you know? I used to be in the juniors. When we go dinner on Sunday, the mothers put us to sleep and the man who watch us, he said, 'Everybody sleepin'?' No answer. He said, 'Everybody sleepin'?' And nobody answer, and then him come and look and nobody is sleepin', so there was a little difficulty with the watchman."

Most boys who attended Alpha from the 1940s all the way through the 1990s remember their surrogate mother who truly made Alpha Boys School a home. Sister Mary Ignatius Davies was crucial to mentoring, educating, and raising the boys at Alpha, and she single-handedly shaped the course of music with her passion and devotion to her boys. Sister Mary Ignatius Davies, affectionately called Sister Ignatius, and sometimes Sister Iggy, or merely Iggy, was born in Jamaica, in 1921, in Innswood, St. Catherine. While still a child, she went to Kingston, where she attended Mico Elementary School. She eventually became a student at the Alpha Academy, which was the girls' section of the institution. Sister Ignatius became a member of the Sisters of Mercy shortly after graduation. She started serving at the Alpha Boys School in 1939.

If one wants to know Don Drummond then it is critical to know Sister Ignatius, his guide, his teacher, his mentor, his mother. Sister Ignatius filled those roles for all of her boys, but she especially loved Don. Sparrow Martin recalls his days as student at Alpha and how vital Sister Ignatius's tutelage was to the students whom many called "Wayward Boys": "Ignatius was the one who train you, tell you how to play, what to play, and at that time she was a young, beautiful person and she used to teach the boys a lot. She wanted them to be the best. She would teach them how to box because she loved boxing. She would have movies of boxers and she would take us down to the convent and show us these movies of great boxers, Rocky Marciano and Sugar Ray Robinson and all these guys. The guys who do boxing, she would tell them, 'When you look at the movie, you should watch his foot and see his hand how he punches.' She would tell us about the great English cricketers. She would show us how to bat and all this. She like games. She could play table tennis. She would come around and we'd say, 'Sister, can you play a game?' and she'd say okay and she'd play table tennis and we'd try to beat her. She'd smash everything, she always beat the ball, always beat the ball. She would go to football. She show you how to shoot the ball. Everything she would do. If we sit down, she always sit with us, the boys. For spiritualness, she would sit with them."

Sister Ignatius, once described by Pierre Perrone, a reporter for *The Independent*, as "bird-like" because of her diminutive stature, had a great love for music. It was because of her passion for all kinds of music that the band program prospered. The band program at Alpha Boys School was first established in 1892 as a drum and fife corps, and then bolstered in 1908 when a Roman Catholic bishop in Jamaica donated a number of brass instruments to the school. The same year, Walter S. Harrison became a drill sergeant at the school, appointed by the Jamaica Defense Force; he served as the inaugural bandmaster for one year but continued on as drill sergeant through the mid–1960s. As a result, there was a strong connection between Alpha and the military; after graduation from Alpha, boys frequently took positions in the West Indian Regiment, which became the Jamaica Military Band after independence. Music taught during these times was solely classical. But, under the leadership of Sister Ignatius, the band program broadened significantly.

It must have been quite a sight — a petite nun in her full habit, spinning records at a DJ's turntables — but that's exactly what Sister Ignatius did on many occasions at Alpha Boys School. "She build a sound system, we call it Mutt and Jeff. The reason for that, the people who used to play the music, one man was very tall, the other one is very short, so we call it Mutt and Jeff," says Martin. Sister Ignatius bought her sound system from Mutt and Jeff who were sound system operators, essentially modern-day DJs. Mutt was Kenneth Davy and he named his sound system Mutt and Jeff after the popular comic strip of the day which featured a very tall character, Mutt, and a "half-pint" named Jeff. The comic strip was carried in the *Jamaica Star*, one of the island's newspapers. Davy, who was over six feet tall, held the Mutt moniker, and Jeff was better known as Leighton Geoff, a short fellow with an appropriate last name.

Davy attended Alpha Boys School and was a skilled public speaker and debater. After he graduated, Sister Ignatius asked Davy to return to emcee various school events and presentations, including plays, concerts, and sporting competitions. He did this without the aid of any amplification, but around 1956 he purchased a microphone, a small amplifier, and two 12-inch speakers. He quickly moved into providing background music at these events and started hosting sound-system dances at Alpha. As word of his entertainment skill spread, Davy started hosting dances outside of Alpha and he soon found the need to upgrade his equipment to meet the demand. Davy worked his full-time day job in the Alpha Boys School printery, directing the boys in the trade of setting type, inking presses, and printing books that were then bound in the school's bindery. With the blessing of Sister Ignatius, Davy's sound-system upgrade was a project handled by the school's woodshop. The boys learned to produce a custom item under the watchful eye of Davy, whose printery was adjacent to the

Ken Davy with the Mutt and Jeff Sound System, the Alpha Boys' School, Kingston, Jamaica, circa 1959 (courtesy EMP Museum, Seattle, WA).

woodshop. He would frequently leave his shop to help supervise the boys with their table saws, sanders, and hammers. The woodshop, like the printery, pottery shop, the garden and the shoe shop, were not only areas of trade instruction for the boys, they were also revenue makers, helping to offset the operational costs of the school. Making custom items for customers was part of the school's operation, and part of training for the boys.

Davy's friend Leighton Geoff was an electrical technician at Wonards, a large appliance store located in downtown Kingston. Staff members at Wonards, much like the employees of Radio Shack today in the United States, were knowledgeable about all things electrical. They were vital in helping to make the creative ideas of sound system operators into a reality. Davy had the woodshop boys build the speakers into towering cabinets known as "Houses of Joy." Geoff not only built the speaker system, but he also maintained its clarity, continually fine-tuning the sound for precision. Davy now had his sound system, and, with his entrepreneurial spirit, he also had the means of marketing his system, using the printery and free labor at Alpha to send advertisements for his events which touted, "Mutt & Jeff Clear as a Bell." He also used the occasion to promote catering services of his wife, Gloria, since she was a fantastic cook of such local dishes as curry goat and green bananas and rice.

In 1964, after having earned a decent amount of revenue from his sound system, Davy decided to spend more time with his wife and their 11 children. He sold his entire set — equipment and music — to Sister Ignatius, who added the records to her already-large collection. Sister Ignatius had hundreds of 78 and 45 records in her collection — everything from classical music to speeches by Malcolm X. She would regularly send her students, such as Floyd Lloyd Seivright, to purchase records from local record shops, giving him money for the acquisition and a list of her selections. Sister Ignatius recognized the potential of the music for her boys. Of the music that would soon develop in Jamaica and take over the world, largely the result of the talent at Alpha Boys School, Sister Ignatius once said, "I knew it was not going to stay in Jamaica only."

Sparrow Martin recalls his days as a student when they all listened to her tunes: "So she would come on Saturdays and she would have a whole lot of record, you name it, classical, jazz record, pop record, all kind, Latin, American, European music, Cuban music, and mento music, and she would say, 'Okay today we are going to listen to classical music,' and she would take out Beethoven, Bach, and she says, especially to the band boys, 'Listen to your classical music.' Then she'd say, 'Okay, I'm going to play jazz for you today,' and she'd play jazz music. Then she'd play Cuban music. Now we don't speak Spanish but she would take Spanish music from Cuba and she'd say, 'Listen to the drums, listen to the bass, listen to how they play saxophone.' She would sit down with you so you have the interest," says Martin. And Sister Ignatius even took up her instrument from time to time. Owen Grey says, "Our teacher, Sister Ignatius, she was a musician herself because she could play the saxophone, she could play the flute, and she was very strict."

Sister Ignatius had great trust in her boys. As a result, she gave them opportunities and responsibilities, even at a young age. Martin says, "She could say to the boys, 'Now we are going to the beach, and you're going to leave here after breakfast and you walk straight to the beach and make sure to come back,' and there's no one to look over us. And she would line us up in the walkway and we walk down to the beach and we stay

Classroom at Alpha Boys School where Don Drummond once sat for regular curriculum. School motto "Upward and Onward" still appears on the building today (photograph by the author).

there. She says to be back at five o'clock. And we go to the beach, sometimes four hundred of us. Because this school sometimes had six hundred, seven hundred students. Four hundred of us, walkin'. We go to the sea and we enjoy the day and we came right back. Those who can swim helped those who can't swim. She sent us to a movie. She used to send us to the Carib Theater to a movie. I can't remember if it was a Sunday evening, it was such a long time ago, but she would say 'Okay, you are going to a movie at the Carib Theater and you're going to see a beautiful movie and you're going to come back, boys, because remember, school is the next day.' And we would go, sometimes fifty of us, we go up to Cross Roads to go to the movie and we come right back. She would do that."

Boys at Alpha knew to behave because of the strict discipline administered by the staff at the school. Those who tended the garden, watched over the dormitories, assisted in the cafeteria, all were part of the discipline as were the school administrators. And the punishment could be tough, says Dr. Sandra Mayo, assistant professor in the school of education at Azusa Pacific University as well as daughter and niece to two Alpharians, Victor and John Richards. Mayo wrote her dissertation on the Alpha Boys

24

School in 2006 and spent time interviewing Alpha alumni on many aspects of their experience, including punishment, which was a part of the school's culture. She writes that there was "widespread use of corporal punishment at Alpha, which often took the form of public floggings.... At Alpha and similar schools, religion and corporal punishment worked in unison to maintain social control and submission."

Ronald Knight recalls, "Punishment consisted of different degrees. The more serious the offense, like running away or going outside the institution, the punishment would be getting twelve lashes on the bottom from Mr. Baker, or having the head shaved and wearing a flour bag dress with holes cut out for the head and arms, or being locked in a stairwell cupboard for a couple of days."

Martin says that punishment was a way of life at Alpha. He says, "If you are rude, Ignatius know how to deal with you. She is very stern. That means if you do something she call you and ask you and you know you have to get punishment. If you do something wrong, she would say, 'I'm going to send you around and you're going to take your punishment,' and she would give you the strap and you take it around. And you go and say, 'Sister say to give me three,' and give you three, give you back the strap, you say, 'Thank you, Sister.' She was calm, stern, tough heart and calm heart." Rico also recalls the strict discipline that was part of daily life for boys who misbehaved or stepped out of line. His memory involves his time in the garden. He says that there were days when the boys were very hungry and would sneak a bite of a carrot or beet while they worked. "But you can't let the watchman, you can't let the watchman see," Rico said, or you faced the consequences. "You get beat, you get slapped, you get hit. The ones in charge hit you."

Ronald Knight recalls his days at Alpha and how Sister Ignatius's stern ways kept the boys in line: "My recollection of Sister Ignatius was the lectures she used to give about immorality and punctuality, which were more beneficial to me in later life. I can remember two run-ins I had with her. The first one was being called out in the refectory for talking when I wasn't guilty and I got six strokes of the ruler in front of the house. The other time was on a Sunday morning [as] we were lining up to go to Mass and she was examining heads. She said my hair was woolly and unkempt and I was to see the barber after Mass and have a scalp cut [baldhead], now in fashion these days. Looking back now I learned a lot that kept me level-headed to survive in England."

But there was great love for the nuns of the school, and most Alpha boys remember their experience fondly despite the punishment they may have received for being "rude" or sneaking a bite to eat when hungry. Even long after the boys leave Alpha and become Alpha Old Boys, as they call themselves, many keep connected to the school. This is certainly a two-way street. Martin says that Sister Ignatius always stayed close to her Alpha Old Boys and fostered them through their adult years. He says, "She try to arrange for them to go to England to stay at somebody's house. They live in England ten years and come back with their wife and children. She used to say, 'How many children you make?' and you'd say, 'Four, Sister.' She say, 'And those that you don't know about?!' (laughs)."

Martin says it is because of Sister Ignatius's love for her boys that they grew to be successful men. "She would treat you like a human," he insists. "She always have something to give you, some sweet. If you come to the steps and she's up there and you look up, 'Sister?' We don't go up the steps. She come and say, 'What is it now, boy?' and you'd say, 'Sister,' and you'd tell her. She say, 'Don't you know that you're not supposed to do that?' Sometimes she'd say, 'Okay now, go to early bed.' But in those days when I was here, we never sleeping. We had Radio Diffusion, a little radio, and sometimes, late at night, she'd come and open the window and she look to see if everybody here. She was a caring person, very caring. You can't describe her. You can't describe Ignatius. She's a mother. Some say, 'How can you be a black boy and have a white mother?' [I tell them,] 'She's my mother. She's Alpha's mother.'"

It was Sister Ignatius's love for music and her boys that ushered in the age of ska, rocksteady, and reggae. Without her guiding hand, these boys would never have become jazz musicians, they would never have stepped onto the stage or performed in a studio, or go on to create a wealth of music. And there would be no contribution from Don Drummond.

3

The Monkey
Tambourine Tree

Barefoot, he steps into the room, tile floor warm on his dirty skin. The cinder block walls painted bright yellow hold the heat in the hollow band room. It is nine A.M. Framed pictures of Sister Claver, Sister Joseph, and Sister Margaret Mary hang on the wall, their wide white wimples a swath of brightness in each photo. Metal bars with chipped aqua-green paint cross the room's glassless windows, a reminder of the ocean a few miles away. A rat scurries across the floor and into the storage closet where the instruments are kept. He sees the rodent but takes no notice, as common a fixture as the boys themselves who now begin to enter the classroom, their bare feet slapping the smooth surface in a random rhythm. Mr. Delgado emerges from outside through the door-less opening in the wall, a shadow at first with the luminous sun behind him. The boys are ready, assembled in their wooden chairs, empty instrument cases beside them, metal stands in front of them, sheets of music, open, waiting. This is Alpha Boys School, Jamaica's Nursery for Brass Band Music.

Don Drummond was enrolled at Alpha Boys School on December 10, 1943, at the age of nine. It wasn't so much an enrollment as it was an "order of detention in an industrial school," according to the decree. He entered the third form, as it was called. In Jamaica, the school structure is similar to the British format due to colonization. In American terms, the first form is equivalent to the seventh grade, second form is eighth grade, and so on. At the end of Don Drummond's first year, in 1944, his student record reveals he had "good" attendance and his conduct was "fairly good." He stayed in the third form, or ninth grade, for three years, from 1943 through 1946, or from age 9 through 12. His attendance was always good and his conduct was upgraded to good as well. He entered the fourth form, or tenth grade, in 1946 at the age of 12, and stayed for two years

ALPHA BOYS' SCHOOL

STUDENT'S REGISTER

RECORD AND HISTORY

Child Authority No. ....   Card Index No. ....

NAME____DRUMMOND, DONALD._____

Age__9 11__ Birth Place_Jubilee Hospital, Kgn.·__ Date_12·3·32__

Date of Admission__10-12-43____ Height_4'3"__ Weight__60 lbs__
                                        5'8"(1950)   120 lbs (1950).

Date of Discharge___9-12.50_____

Sent by_____R.H. COURT_____

Sent from_____KINGSTON._____

Religion_____R.C.·_____

   If Catholic where baptized?__Alpha Chapel·_____

   Date?_____ First Com.?_____ Conf.?_____

Personal Description__Brown complexion, hair o eyes._____

Private Cash and Property_____

_____

_____

Name of Parents or Relatives_Mrs· Donis Muncos (Mother) Uriah Drummonds (Father)

Address__21 Hitchen St. Alman Town P.O._____

Parents or Relatives Notified_yes· 10·12·43_____

GENERAL REMARKS AND OBSERVATION ON ADMISSION

_____

_____

_____

_____

_____

PARTICULARS OF HOME

(i) Family History and Home Conditions : Donald is an only child, and his mother was in a position to maintain him, but he became truant from school. Donald attended Franklin Twn. and Alpha Elem. Schs.

(ii) Character and Parental Attitude

Donald's father has shown little or no interest in him, his mother on the contrary is interested and helpful.

EDUCATION

Date	Std.	Attendance	Ability	Conduct	House
1. 44	IIÉ	Good		Fairly good	Campion
45	IIÉ	"		good	"
46	IIÉ	"		"	Aloysius
47	IV	"		"	"
48	IV	"		V. Good	"
49	V.	"		" "	"

OCCUPATION WHILE IN SCHOOL

Date	Occupation	REMARKS
11. 12. 43	Light Domestic	Fairly good
45	Gardening	Fairly good
45	Music (Trombone)	Very good
49	Tile Factory	Fair
49	Tailoring	Fair

RECORD OF PROGRESS

Date	Occurrence	REMARKS

Opposite and above: Two pages from Don Drummond's student record (courtesy Alpha Boys School). Note the stated birth date of 1932, which is also found in various other sources but is at odds with his stated age of 9 and with his birth certificate.

before entering the fifth form, or 11th grade, in 1949 at the age of 15. This does not suggest that Drummond repeated grades or stayed too long in a grade. His academic success was typical of this system and therefore cannot be compared to the timelines of other country's schooling systems.

Although younger and older students are combined in classes at Alpha today, during Don Drummond's time the younger and older boys were separate. According to trombonist Basil Hylton, a graduate of Alpha Boys School, the school "was divided into the Junior Home or the 'Club,' and the Senior Home. The Junior Home consisted of four houses." Drummond stayed in one of these houses, known as Campion, for his first two years at Alpha Boys School. Hylton continues, "The Senior Home had five houses. St. Ignatius, St. Aloysius, St. Xavier, St. Peter, and St. Paul." St. Aloysius, also just called Aloysius, was the senior home where Don Drummond stayed for the rest of his time at Alpha. The boys washed their own clothes and had communal showers. The houses competed against each other in sports like cricket and football. Most of the senior band boys stayed together in the same house since they often went out to play within the community, sometimes returning late in the evening. Drummond, too, performed out in clubs during his years at Alpha, to gain experience, exposure, and money for the school. Such performances included an evening at the Holy Trinity Cathedral Men's Sodality Social in May 1948; a garden party at St. Anne's Church during the same month; a half-hour of play on Kingston radio station ZQI one evening in April 1947; a procession at Winchester Park on November 4, 1947, in honor of the Feast of Christ the King; a concert at the Cathedral Rectory Grounds on North Street in July 1949; and plenty of others. The Alpha Boys Band had their own uniforms which were obtained through donations at fundraisers during Drummond's time in 1949. The colorful uniforms featured a red jacket trimmed with gold braid and buttons and gold-seamed black pants.

There were a variety of trades, or occupations, offered to students at Alpha. The term "occupation" is important since "Occupation," later changed to "Music Is My Occupation," became a popular tune composed by Drummond. This term was printed on each student's record and each trade attempted and their success level at that trade was noted on each register. Drummond's occupational record states that by November 1943 he had tried light domestic work at the school and his remarks are that he was "fairly good" at this skill. In 1945, he was transitioned to gardening and was found to be also "fairly good" at this occupation. In 1949, he tried the tile factory and tailoring but was found to be only "fair" at these two trades. Why he even tried these two trades is a mystery since, in 1945, he was sent to the occupation of "Music (Trombone)," according to his record, and was found to be "very good" at this work. Mark Williams says, "For a naturally gifted child like Drummond, Alpha could not have been a more perfect setting to explore and develop his innate talents."

It wasn't unusual for school administrators to move students from trade to trade in order to find their proclivity. And the band program was a popular request for students who may have thought that blowing a horn was less work than tilling the land or hammering wood to form a table. Ronald Knight, a member of the Alpha Boys School Band with Don Drummond, says that Reuben Delgado, who served as bandmaster from 1947 through 1955, before Lennie Hibbert took over the reins, used to select boys to become part of the band. Knight says, "He periodically came down to the garden where us boys was working and picked out who he wanted to join the band. He would look at teeth and lips to see who would be good to play reed or brass instruments. I was chosen to play trombone so I was delighted as I wouldn't have to go gardening so early in the morning and I would get out to play to the public. It was tough learning the trombone, but I managed. We used to have musical theory and reading, played classical, marches, etc."

Finding a place in the Alpha Boys School Band was a bit tough, too, because there were only so many instruments to go around. Don Drummond's protégé Rico Rodriguez MBE remembers, "It wasn't easy to get into the band. I tried, but I get in because I have a few friends in the band, like Don Drummond and Tony Brown and Ossie Hall, a few good friends in the band. They take me in and I decide to do horns, horns. F horns, F horns. I used to play that thing and you just play 'pop pop pop pop,' you know? I did a lot of different instruments before. A little trumpet and saxophones, there were two saxophones. The most things they had at school was clarinet and trumpet. Trombones were full so I didn't go on trombone."

Many students, like Rodriguez, were assigned to a variety of instruments. Eddie "Tan Tan" Thornton, Don Drummond's classmate and close friend, says that finding the right instrument for a student was just a matter of economy. If the school had more trumpets, you played the trumpet. If the school had a saxophonist graduate, then a saxophone was available. Thornton says, "Everybody want to learn music, so there's no space. Everybody want to learn music but everybody want to play trumpet, saxophone, trombone, and tenor. Nobody want to play drums, nobody want to play tuba, the big thing. Nobody want to play it, so I said to myself, 'Shit, nobody want to play tuba? Hey, I play tuba!' After a couple months I get a tuba and blow, '*wu, wu, wu, wu*' [laughs]. So what happens is, luckily now, that's when the blessing come for me. Mr. Delgado come. Don Drummond used to play French horn, [imitating] '*soon come, soon come, pah pah,*' and Sergeant Harris was our caretaker for the school and he used to tease Drummond, [repeats imitation] '*soon come, soon come,*' [laughs]. So I'm in the band and all the guys them leaving now. So when Mr. Delgado come, Mr. Delgado take Drummond off French horn and put him on trombone because the thing is, we know music already, they teach us to read and write and that, so we know method already. He just take me off of that instrument and put us on the next instrument. All you have to do is learn the fingering because you know the music already. All Drummond need was to learn the position of the trombone. Because the guy play French horn he can read music and so forth. He take me off of tuba and put me on trumpet."

Vocalist Owen Grey also recalls that Drummond tried other instruments before settling on the trombone: "Don Drummond tried the saxophone. Then he changed from the saxophone to the trombone and that's what made Don Drummond in Jamaica the number-one trombonist. One time he was trying to learn to play trombone. It's a very hard instrument to play because it's got no keys. The keys are just judging the distance. It's not like a trumpet. Because it take the holy hell out of you, you understand? And I respect that man as a youth growing up to a lad growing up and everything like that." Saxophonist Headley Bennett OD who received the Order of Distinction from the Jamaican government, an award equal to America's Medal of Honor, also recalls Drummond beginning his musical training on instruments other than the trombone: "He used to play different instruments. He start off with what we call the baby trumpet, then he played the euphonium, and then he goes straight to the trombone. He was so talented that when the trombone player leave school the space was open for a trombone and the leader put him right on the trombone."

Rodriguez says that even though Drummond's first instrument wasn't necessarily the trombone, his skill at playing the assigned instrument was apparent even early on. "I was maybe about 12 or 13 when I first met him," Rodriguez recalls. "He was three or four years older. We used to go to the

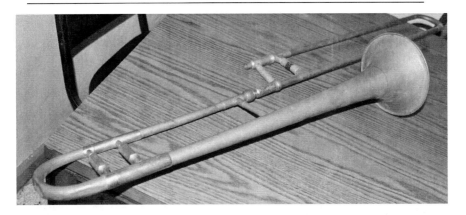

Don Drummond's trombone from his days at Alpha Boys School. The instrument is in the school's historical collection. Two of Drummond's other trombones are in the collections at EMP in Seattle, WA, and the Jamaican Music Institute (photograph by the author).

band room and practice every day. We used to practice scales and reading, reading, reading. He was a nice man. He used to play the euphonium, you know? It shaped like some trumpet, it got a lot of bends in it, like a French horn, like a French horn, the euphonium. And he was very good and he used to start up the band by singing and play the euphonium. He was a good euphonium player, very good euphonium player, par excellence, you know? So the trombone come later."

Bandmaster Reuben Delgado was critical to teaching Don Drummond music, introducing him to the classical music Delgado himself learned to play as a student at Alpha, as well as in the West Indian Regiment, where he built his career before returning to Alpha to teach. Thornton says, "Mr. Delgado was a good man. He was an old Alpha boy. Maybe he was in Alpha in the teens or '20s or something like that, or maybe 19th century or so. He learned clarinet. He was the best clarinet player in Jamaica. So he joined the military band in Jamaica. He was in the military band for all his life and then he leave the military band to come and teach us at Alpha. Sister get him from the military band, so it was like a blessing in disguise because before he came we have a band leader named Buchannan, he was one of the old boys who leave school but he was not a good teacher, didn't teach music for nothin' you know? He was an old boy, too, he leave school and he play bass. He was just a temporary until Sister could get Mr. Delgado. So when Mr. Delgado come, everything change, musically, because we get better and all that and so forth. Mr. Delgado was doing the same music as what the military band was doing. So we was at the top level with all the classical bands in Jamaica, because Mr. Delgado come from the military band and play classical music all the while. He bring all the classical music arrangement, come to the school, so the standard of our music went high, because we were playing Beethoven and Mozart and all those great classical composers. The Jamaica Military Band, all they play is great composers from Germany, Russia, and Vienna. All those American tunes they play in the army, that's what we used to play. So I know all the American tunes. So the boys get a good experience that when they leave Alpha they can play in any band because they can write and they come from classical music, which is the foundation. He was a nice man. He was one of us. He always encourage everybody and he teaches really good, really good. There is no better teacher in the world than Mr. Delgado."

Ronald Knight recalls, "We did mostly classical music and marches, overtures and a medley of calypsos, which we were more than happy to play rather than marches. Mr. Delgado wasn't keen on dance and jazz music. He wanted us to join the Jamaica Military Band instead of going to dance bands. He used to say things like, 'Look how pale and sickly these dance hall band men look.' He went to the Royal School of Music London so he thought we should all be like him."

Williams says that Delgado was one of many former Alpha students who returned to lead the band since the culture of older leading the younger was a tradition at Alpha, and the connection to the military was strong, set in place in the early days at the school. Mark Williams writes, "By the time the 1930s rolled around, Alpha appeared to have set in place a regenerative system whereby past students returned to teach at Alpha, including the bandmasters. Many of the earliest bandmasters from the turn of the 20th century had in fact been musicians in Jamaica's military regiment band — Sergeants Harrison, Knibbs, Beek, Logan. The military band has probably historically been the single largest employer of Alpha musicians upon graduation and this association continues to the present day."

Sparrow Martin says that Delgado's involvement in the military band was important in setting a foundation for the boys when he came to instruct at Alpha. "Reuben Delgado was with the West Indian Regiment," Martin explains. "The Regiment was a set of musician that they choose to play in

Africa and for the queen, where she reign in different countries. They come from Trinidad, Barbados, Jamaica, all these West Indian islands. They change today to Jamaica Military Band when our government change. I was in the military band because when you're in the band and you want to have a steady job you go in the military. Delgado was the tutor for Don Drummond."

Involvement in the Alpha Boys School band consisted of both practice and class, in addition to taking classes in regular curriculum. As Eddie "Tan Tan" Thornton recalls, "We wake up in the morning around seven o'clock. We do our early practice before school because school don't start until nine o'clock. So we wake up early. School go from nine until twelve and we've got two sets of school, you go to school from nine to twelve and from one o'clock down you go to music. So you have one set of boys learn music from nine until twelve o'clock and at one o'clock you have the next set come. I always go to school after one o'clock and from nine o'clock we are practicing. So from nine o'clock until twelve we have practice and at one o'clock we have school now. You can learn any trade you want to learn, bookbinding, printing, tailoring, shoemaking, and gardening, but I love music so I do music."

Rodriguez also recalls the days spent in band class in the 1940s and 1950s with Reuben Delgado: "You go to band practice in the morning and they don't make you play, you know, they just go into theory. When they ask you a theory lesson you got to be conscious for the theory lesson, so most of the time at band practice is on theory. They check you on theory, what is this note lead to another, you know? In the music you have a family, a musical family. There are notes that belong to that note, so theory was very important. You have to know that. You have to know that so there was a lot of attention to theory. Reuben Delgado, he used to teach the sessions. Sometimes when you have time you should go write the answers up on the house staff, you know? This is the ones he would try to ask us, to write it on top of the house staff, and when you go he cannot see you lookin' up, you know? You got to be very clever, you know? He'll say you're not really concentrating, you're only watching what's written up there. Very strict man, very strict man, very strict. One day we were playing a song, 'Ol' Rotten Joe,' you know that song? (Sings) And the drummer wasn't concentrating, and he touched him with his staff, touched it. He wasn't playing with sincerity. You must play the music with more sincerity, more meaningful."

Ronald Knight also recalls that Delgado was a strict bandleader: "Mr. Delgado, the band master, was quite handy with whacking a boy with his baton if a wrong note was played." The boys were careful to study hard and stay in line, learning from Delgado as well as each other. "During the teaching period the older boy would give you a few smacks around the head if you were slow picking things up. We called it swellheading and I think we all had a share of that," says Knight.

But they all agree that Mr. Delgado was critical to their success. "The bandmaster was very good at it, you know," says Rico. "Anyone who come out of that teaching was brilliant. He was the bandmaster, the bandmaster, so him keep the show. Delgado was the man in charge and the bigger ones look after us." Vocalist Derrick Morgan recalls that one of the bigger ones to help look after Drummond was an older trombonist: "Understand that he was trained by another trombonist named Carl Masters, one of the great trombonist ever in Jamaica, but he never do recording. I guess they used to go to that school, Alpha, he was there and he was a hell of a man to Don. Carl Masters, yeah, he's the man who train Don."

And one of the bigger ones for Rodriguez, and many other students, was Don Drummond, who had a natural ability to teach. "He was number one," says Headley Bennett, "and why I come to that reasoning is because when Mr. Delgado want to take a couple of minutes off, for some water or to go to the washroom, he gave Don Drummond the baton. The conductor stick. He used to conduct the band when Mr. Delgado's not there. That's how I know he was so talented." Ken Stewart, manager of The Skatalites says, "Don was certainly a big big influence at Alpha because he was one of the superior musicians from the get-go, even as a young boy, and then I believe that he went on to become a teacher." It was common for the older students to help the younger ones, even long after they left the classroom. Mark Williams writes, "This in-house network would be a continued source of strength once the boys graduated, as one established musician would assist others in finding gigs."

Ronald Knight confirms that Drummond came to teach after he had left school: "I remember him dropping in a couple of times during band practice and Mr. Delgado let him play first trombone. Don Drummond was in the big bands of the day and Mr. Delgado would let him play two pieces which consist of a lot of doubling and tripling of the notes. I never spoke to him because he wasn't the talking type. Quiet man. With me being ten years younger than him, I felt he was beyond me. When Don

(c) The Gleaner Co. Ltd.

The Alpha Boys School Band, led by Reuben Delgado. A young Rico Rodriguez is visible on trombone, at far left. The trombonist next to him, just out of the photograph's frame, may be Drummond, but the date of this photograph is unknown (© The Gleaner Company Limited).

was finished playing, we boys was in awe. We, the other trombonists, felt very inadequate indeed."

Rico remembers Drummond's instruction for the younger boys as well: "I met him in the band and he was an excellent player and he show me things. He was a little bit quiet, you know? A very, very quiet person. You don't know what he's going to do next, you know? Not like a lot of others, he was a quiet man. He don't talk a lot, quiet. He was my friend, my friend. Through the bandmaster and on account of the band, he was a trombone teacher, you know? He write some different things we used to play and so forth, so there is always someone from the band that can teach you something. When he write the music he get you to come and sit with you and play the music with you. He taught me the double tongue and things like that, yeah, different styles. Don was first trombone. And I was a learner, a learner [*laughs*]. I'm a student. I'm a new player in the band at that time. I used to take his stand in his practice. When the band goes

37

out I carry his stand, music stand, carry the music for him. The ones who were more advanced show the ones who were not so advanced. He used to give me some scales to study, one or two scales for the day and he would see how I was getting on. He show me everything. He'd play the scale and show me before so I get the feel, you know? He was tough on me, tough on me. He told me, 'If you want to be a musician you have to take everything seriously and practice.' He was okay with me. He was a friend, a friendly type of person."

So how did Don Drummond develop such musical skill at such an early age? Certainly Reuben Delgado had a big hand, Drummond's classmates and mentors like Carl Masters had a hand, but truthfully, it was Drummond himself who took the opportunity he was given and made the most of it. Instead of playing games like other boys, instead of going to class to further develop his math or reading skills, Drummond spent time, on his own, under a tree, practicing. Sparrow Martin recalls Drummond's discipline for music when they were both students at Alpha: "I came here when I was nine years old and Don Drummond was on his way out. He was a man who liked to stay by himself. There used to be a tree by the band room when I used to be here called the Monkey Tambourine Tree and he used to sit there practicing, or if he not practicing he would be looking at a piano book. He practiced the trombone out of a piano book, because the piano has the melody and the harmony so you practice that and he would play the part of what the piano played. On the piano you have something called the treble section and the bass section so he would play the bass section." A monkey tambourine is a specific style of wood tambourine. The tree that Martin and others referred to as the Monkey Tambourine Tree was also called the Dibby Dibby Tree by Sister Ignatius and others after a slang term meaning bad quality.

Headley Bennett also remembers Drummond practicing and studying under the Monkey Tambourine Tree: "We meet him at Alpha. He never used to play games with us. He just sit under the tree and watch the games. And he used to read a lot. He used to read a lot about leaders, like the Russian leaders and German leaders. He used to read those kind of books. And I used to look at him and tell him that I don't really understand those books. He need the knowledge, you know? But they were too high for him, for his age, you know. He was around 14 or 15 years old and we were the same age. We played cricket, football, baseball. He sat under the tree and watched us. And he always smilin', you know? When we see him under the tree he smiled. He used to practice more than any one of us. When we finished class at three or four o'clock, he practiced every evening when he's not watching games. He practiced very hard, more than us. We were in the band together with Reuben Delgado. He was a very strict band leader. Drummond was quiet. You could not get him to talk too much. He don't want to discuss nothing. You don't have to talk about nothing at all. He used to read a lot, that's how he tried to gain more knowledge." It was during this time that Drummond was fitted for glasses since he was found to be extremely nearsighted. His glasses were very thick, almost like magnifying glasses.

Martin says that Drummond even began skipping classes to practice on his own and the administrators allowed it since he was so skilled at music. Walking the path on Alpha's campus from an area of overgrowth and debris that used to house the old band room, Martin recalls, "When he was going to school, we take our instruments from here and walk to the practicing area. But when we leave the practicing area and come back to put all the instruments away, Don don't put his instrument away yet. He sit down under the tree and practice, so when the bandmaster come in, Mr. Delgado, he would still stay there, with his instrument, but he would have the piano music in his hand."

Drummond spent time studying classical music in the classroom, but on his own he listened to jazz on the radio and he started to compose songs of his own. "Don Drummond didn't want to play classical music, he wanted to play jazz music and he practice jazz music, so a lot of guys do that when they're older, they want to go into jazz, the Louis Armstrong, the J.J. Johnson, all these type of jazz musicians we used to hear about," says Martin.

Delgado left the school in October 1955 when he took sick leave and underwent an operation for an unknown condition. He recovered and continued to perform and instruct into his later years, including a performance with the Jamaica Legion Band in 1975; acting as a judge for the island's Festival Drum Corps Competition in 1968; and he returned for a short time to guest teach at Alpha in 1967.

Drummond's first influence at Alpha was not Delgado, but Vincent Tulloch, who led the band through 1946. According to Williams, "Tulloch was a past Alpha boy who had both [Tommy] McCook and [Wilton] Gaynair as students." Sparrow Martin describes Tulloch as a "'big band man,' and it is perhaps his tenure that signals the beginning of Alpha's incredible blossoming of musical talent." The introduction of big band music into the repertoire at Alpha inspired the boys and made them much more marketable to fit the tastes and trends of the musical scene.

The band started to gain recognition as a source of great talent. On January 15, 1947, Drummond had the honor of performing with the Alpha Boys Band for Alexander Bustamante, who later became prime minister of Jamaica, but at the time served as minister of communications and leader of the Jamaica Labour Party. Bustamante toured the school and their various trade rooms, including the band room where Drummond and his fellow band mates performed two selections for the dignitary. Of his observations, Bustamante exclaimed, "These boys should be taken care of when they leave here. There should be some aftercare, and they should be given all the support possible in these institutions."

Drummond spent a lot of time under the Monkey Tambourine Tree, which no longer stands on the grounds at Alpha. But the memory of Don Drummond as a young child, alone, practicing, reading, is still strong in the memories of his friends and fellow students, even though they may have never really known him well. Jo Jo Bennett was only two years younger than Drummond at the time they went to school together, practiced together, ate together, read together. Bennett says he didn't really know Drummond as a person at all, because he never talked about anything other than music. From those early days, a stray boy on the street became a musician in every sense, every minute of the day, an identity, a group to belong to. "He was kind of a loner," Bennett says. "He stay by himself, you know? But I can see the potential in him." Perhaps Drummond saw that potential in himself and so that vision became the only thing he could see.

On October 31, 1950, six weeks before graduation, Don Drummond left Alpha Boys School to take a residency with the Eric Deans Orchestra at the Colony Club on Halfway Tree Road. His record notes that he "attended the school for seven years, during which time he took courses in gardening, music, tile manufacture, and tailoring. He is intelligent, industrious, civil, and willing. As far as we know it he is honest." Scouted for an open position with the big band, Sister Ignatius ushered her young prodigy into the career she and the others had helped to shape for him. Ignatius once said of Drummond, "Even though he was still in school, he was almost the number-one trombonist in the island. When the band went out on Alpha engagements, a lot of musicians would go and listen to him. Band leaders used to come 'round and listen."

4

Downtown Musician

Don sat on the edge of the curb, his brown, unlaced boogas, rubber and canvas sneakers, touching the dried and hardened mass of runoff from the chicken coops and goat waste along the side of the road. A pregnant woman stood on the corner arguing loudly with an older bearded man who punched her in the face and dragged her into the yard. An ice seller walked by with a red flag tied around the cart's handle. Brick red Hondas, rusty bicycles, sky blue Fiats, short-bed lorries, motorbikes hauling baskets of goods, mules pulling wooden carts driven by shoeless youths, trolleys and their incessant bells, and bus after bus careening at high speeds, wove through the street, moving and stopping, honking, yelling. There was activity everywhere. Don was still. He sat on the side of the road and watched, his trombone in its case beside him. The faces all became the same. The motion became a blur and then was frozen. He arose, stood among the people, the life, spread his arms to his sides to bring it all in, tilted his head back, closed his eyes, and filled his lungs with great puffs of dusty and humid air. His body disintegrated into little dots and disappeared as his atoms floated above his head, mingled with all the atoms in this world, into outer space, returned in a flash into its original form. He was Don Cosmic, ready to take on the universe.

When Don Drummond began working in Kingston's club circuit, just out of Alpha Boys School, a young bright-eyed teenager, the scene was still rooted deeply in the music of America, piped in on transistor radios receiving stations from New Orleans, imported by the wealthy bringing back records purchased on their travels. Giving tourists and locals a taste of Benny Goodman or Glenn Miller was all that was on the menu at club after club in Kingston, so Don, like all the other greenhorns, took his place behind the bandstands that proclaimed the names of their directors. This one, at the Colony Club up on Half-Way Tree Road, was the Eric Deans Orchestra, a 12-piece group led by Eric Deans, who enjoyed

41

A young Don Drummond, far right, photographed with the Eric Deans Orchestra in January 1951 at the Sugar Hill Club. Deans is pictured second from the left; Ernest Ranglin is pictured right of Deans (courtesy Lloyd "The Matador" Daley).

a middle- and upper-class clientele. Deans was a well-known clarinetist who had been directing his orchestra since 1944 and he attracted crowds because of his repertoire of jazz standards. At one point Deans even organized an all-girl jazz orchestra at the club.

World-renowned guitar player Ernest Ranglin recruited Drummond for a position with the Deans orchestra, as well as others. Ranglin says, "I have permission for him to come out of Alpha School for Eric Deans' band. I had to go to Sister to get permission for him to play in the band. We were all young fellows and I took four of them out of Alpha. I took one saxophone player, which is Reuben Alexander, he's not alive now, he's passed; Edward Thornton who used to play with Aswad and all those bands from England; Blue Bogey [Wilton Gaynair], who is somewhere in Germany; and Don Drummond. I was a member of the group, we all were young fellows in the group."

It was common for bandleaders at the time to source Alpha Boys

School for talent for their bands. Just two years earlier, Sister Ignatius had endorsed the placement of saxophonist Joe Harriott to take a position with the Sonny Bradshaw Orchestra. Alpha was a prime source of talent for bandleaders for a number of reasons. Mark Williams writes,

> In assessing why so many talented musicians emerged from Alpha in a relatively short period of time, one must probably look beyond merely the quality and nature of the teaching being given. Instead, it could be a function of supply and demand, and the demand was coming from throughout the island, where past Alpha graduates were finding work playing music in various settings.... The hotel and society club's circuit system may have been an active arm of colonial rule, but it also provided a setting for professional, big band swing and Latin music orchestras as well as well-rehearsed jazz ensembles to flourish.

Eric Deans was only one of the bandleaders of the time scouting Alpha since he was known to groom young musicians into professionals. He immediately secured Drummond, who was joined a few months later by Trumpeter Eddie "Tan Tan" Thornton, Drummond's classmate. Thornton recalls, "Eric Deans was society. No poor people could come there. It's just the lawyer, barrister, and tourist, mostly tourist. It's an exclusive club. You have to have money to go in it. We used to play six nights a week — Monday, Tuesday, Wednesday, Thursday, Friday, Saturday. A lot of American tourist used to come there, every night. In those days a lot of American tourist used to come. It's the club they come to first, they go to Glass Bucket after. Eric Deans was the best band in Jamaica and we play the same music that was played in America — Count Basie, Duke Ellington, Benny Goodman, Artie Shaw, Harry James, everything. The music we played is America music. There was no ska in those days. Nobody know what was ska or reggae."

A decade earlier, in America, the Cotton Club in Harlem was the epicenter of jazz music, with the biggest musicians of the era performing on a regular basis. Duke Ellington and Cab Calloway led their orchestras filled with the most famous entertainers, such as Ella Fitzgerald, Fats Waller, Louis Armstrong, Dizzy Gillespie, Nat King Cole, and Billie Holiday. In 1949, Birdland in New York opened with Charlie Parker headlining many nights, in addition to performances by such artists as Thelonious Monk, Miles Davis, Bud Powell, and Stan Getz, among many others. These were the clubs that Jamaican band leaders were attempting to channel. These were the scenes they wanted to recreate. This was the music they wanted to play.

Every night Drummond performed with his fellow musicians in Eric Deans's orchestra for well-heeled audiences. The ladies present were decked out in white and pink silk dresses and sparkling pearl jewelry; they laughed, nodded their heads to the music before setting down their clinking glasses of Tom Collinses and gimlets, sashaying their way to the dance floor, where they paraded around, hands and arms outstretched to some awaiting male. Their heads tilted upward with delicate pride, the dancing couples held one another in a distinguished display. Drummond had never seen anything like it before. It is said that he even stopped playing when white women would take to the dance floor since he was so unaccustomed to the sight. No amount of musical training at Alpha prepared him for the social disparity.

Laurence Cane-Honeysett of Trojan Records writes of one person's memory of Drummond's first performance for the graceful audience at the Colony Club.

> Who, among those who heard him in those yesteryears, can ever forget when at 2 A.M., pianist Linton struck the E-flat minor opening chord, Donald Jarrett started slightly brushing the snare drum, and the Don slid gently through the tune. "Full Moon and Empty Arms," drawing tears from the eyes of drunk and sober patrons.

Heather Royes, the upper-crust daughter of Dr. K.C. Royes who would later come into Drummond's life as administrator of Bellevue Mental Hospital, recalls that Don Drummond was not someone her kind listened to. Royes says, "I remember the music of the times. Don Drummond would not have had contact with the movers and shakers. We weren't that interested, frankly. He was a downtown musician." Certainly, though, many others in Kingston, tourists and locals alike, found Don Drummond to be a talent that broke through the social divide.

Before each night's performance at the Colony Club, Tan Tan Thornton arrived at Don Drummond's mother's house in Allman Town so the two could ride together to work. "I used to go over there to eat, Thornton recalls. "It was my second home. Because we used to work together and I live at the Alpha Old Boy home on the school compound and pay them to stay there. So Don Drummond and I, we used to ride bicycles to work every night and we leave our horns there in the band room inside the club. We start playing from nine o'clock until two o'clock, three o'clock in the morning, every night. But we do sets. Every cabaret have a show, they sit them and then go home. White people were mostly Americans or white people in Jamaica that had money, like lawyers. All people who had money used to come there. In Jamaica the aristocrats, they call it, they got the money so they can come there. When we get a break we always go to a place name Bruce's for practice."

Tan Tan says that a number of musicians who would go on to great careers worked with them at the Colony Club and it was a training ground for honing the skills they learned in school, especially because they had the opportunity to travel and take their talent to other shores. "I stay long with Deans at the Colony Club with Drummond, me, and Ernest Ranglin, guitarist," says he. "We went to Nassau, Bahamas, and we come back and went to Ocho Rios to the best hotel in Jamaica, Tower Isle Hotel."

One of those trips Don Drummond took with Eric Deans was to Haiti on February 22, 1951. The group traveled to demonstrate the skill of their Jamaican instrumentalists who adapted their playing to the styles then popular in Haiti. Ernest Ranglin recalls that they were appreciated

Eric Deans (© The Gleaner Company Limited).

and respected by Haitian audiences: "Haiti was our first trip abroad. Crowds were very good. We stayed there three months. They went back for a second time but I didn't go that time. Don did. We got a great response from the crowd every time. Eric Deans band was a very good band, you know? Anywhere we go, we were well received." Drummond

45

returned from that trip in May 1951, according to an "After Care" record at Alpha Boys School which also notes that he "reported to the school. The orchestra expects to leave for another W.I. island shortly."

A January 12, 1951, issue of the *Daily Gleaner* recounts this trip to Haiti through the eyes of Eric Deans; it was written by Gertrude Sherman, a society columnist.

> Eric Deans is a happy man. I talked with him yesterday and discovered that he has had much success since he accepted in November last an engagement with a nightclub in Haiti. Haitians treated him and the other members of his band with such extreme hospitality that Eric Deans now says "Haiti is the place for me." Born in Montego Bay on Jamaica's northshore, Eric Deans has been conducting his own band since 1944. He plays the saxophone and the clarinet as well as all other instruments in his 12-piece orchestra, writes his own jazz compositions and variations, and instructs his "boys" during the cease-less hours of rehearsing which form the basis of his performances. Thrilled by the enthusiastic reception accorded his band in the neighboring Republic, Eric has been swift to pick up all the new tunes and twists of Haitian music so as to maintain his place in the esteem of his public. "They love the mambo and our calypsos, as well as the slower dance melodies like 'Mona Lisa' in Haiti," he told me. Eric will take his boys back to a long-running contract at Port-au-Prince's premiere night club which begins in late February and may continue for a year. His patron has plans for sending Eric and his band to the Dominican Republic and Trinidad on tour later this year, after which the amiable young Jamaica bandleader declares: "I think I'll just remain in Haiti where they treat me and my boys like presidents." Finally, Eric told me of the new song he has composed and which has been recorded in Haiti. It is called "Wanderer of Love," and he expects to put it on the musical market just as soon as he returns to Port-au-Prince.

While on that tour of Haiti, Don's grandmother died. According to Laurence Cane-Honeysett:

> There had existed a strong bond between the youngster and his elderly relative who had been so supportive of his ambition to follow a career in music; spending what little money she had on procuring him his first horn. Deans had been notified of the bereavement, but chose keep the information from the young musician until their return to Jamaica, by which time the funeral had long since passed — it was a decision that would haunt Drummond throughout the remainder of his life.

Tan Tan Thornton recalls the aftermath of Drummond's discovery: "He cry, he miss her." Singer Clancy Eccles once said of the death and the fact that Deans withheld this news, "Wouldn't that drive you mad?"

Helene Lee in her book *The First Rasta* claims that the experience of his grandmother's death was Drummond's first mental break.

Mad with grief, he went berserk, smashed his instrument, and was locked up in Bellevue Mental Hospital. When he got out, his friends gave a benefit concert in his honor in order to buy him a new trombone. But he was changed.

Contrary to a belief held by some that Don Drummond left the island at other times in his life to pursue a career in England (or even rumors that he worked for the London Underground but was disturbed by the train's noise and returned home), Drummond never traveled outside of Jamaica other than two times with Eric Deans in Haiti. A search of the United Kingdom Board of Trade's Incoming Passenger Lists from 1878 to 1960 for ships arriving to the United Kingdom from foreign ports outside of Europe and the Mediterranean reveal no listing for Don Drummond, nor do National Archives Passenger lists leaving the United Kingdom from 1890 to 1960. Is it possible Don Drummond traveled to London after 1960? Vin Gordon doubts that strongly: "No, Don Drummond had never been to England. The only place he had been to is Haiti with the band called Eric Deans."

So, while the Jamaican and international aristocrats returned to their homes on the hill or hotels after an evening of dancing and dining, Drummond returned night after night to his mother's home in Allman Town. Tan Tan Thornton recalls one night when the commute to and from the Colony Club didn't go so well: "There was the storm in 1951 in Jamaica [Hurricane Charlie]. We went to work at the club and we knew the storm was coming. They say, 'Okay, there is no club tonight because the storm is coming, to go home,' right? Then we were riding, coming down South Camp Road to go home and then the storm gets worse, but we were lucky, it was just coming, so he [Don] ride over to his house and I ride to Alpha." Without phones to notify them not to venture out, both were fortunate to survive Hurricane Charlie, which killed more than 250 people. The storm even destroyed two buildings at the Alpha Boys School and four students there died.

It was common for musicians to perform for multiple clubs, even playing for one club one night and another the next. Tan Tan explains why Drummond left Deans: "The thing is Drummond was with Deans and Deans and him have problem. Deans get rid of him. I was sad. I am sad even now. Deans get rid of him. Deans love a girl, but the girl love Drummond, so there was friction. Deans love this girl but the girl don't love Deans, she loves Drummond, yeah? And then jealousy coming, right? That's how I see it. Drummond went to play with Sonny Bradshaw."

Sonny Bradshaw and His Seven frequently performed at the Bournemouth Club, or the Bournemouth Beach Club as it was frequently called. This facility, located in the southeast part of Kingston, featured not only a jazz club, but a public swimming pool, so more local, middle-class patrons attended this venue. Advertisements beckoned customers to "wine, swim, dance, and dine." Tan Tan says, "At the Bournemouth Club it was a different crowd." It may not have been high society, but in Kingston, any club meant money for those looking to eke out a living.

Carlos Malcolm, a fellow trombonist who went on to lead his own band after performing with Sonny Bradshaw, recalls how difficult it was to become established in a music career in those days: "In that time music was actually for a certain level of the society. Music was more a vocation. It was something you earned a living out of. If somebody in the middle class say to somebody in Jamaica, 'I'm a musician,' they say, 'Well yes, what else do you do?' When I came into music it was just bending the corner into professional status where someone could earn a living out of music only. Most people playing music in those times had a day job." Malcolm and Drummond practiced together in Malcolm's back yard in Vineyard Town, facing Caxton Park near Duppy Gate.

Drummond didn't have a day job, though; in fact, music was all he had. At Alpha Boys School he demonstrated no skill at any other vocation, not gardening nor tailoring nor printmaking, only music. And his skill was just starting to get recognized by the bandleaders who scurried to hire him, as well as the public who began to talk about him and seek out his name on the bill to attend his shows. Drummond started performing with a number of different bands all over Kingston. Percussionist Larry McDonald says, "People would come down to do shows and they'd put together a band. This could be the Carib Theatre, this could be the Regal Theatre, this could be the Bournemouth Club on a Sunday evening, it could be anywhere like that. It seems like there was always more music going on then than there is going on now. Everybody knew that Don was a tremendous performer. I mean, you just knew that. How tremendous, I don't think anybody knew at that time. Just like with Bob Marley. Everybody knew Bob was a good artist and everything but nobody knew he was this tremendous talent like that. There are no outtakes. There are no weak songs on any of his albums. You're not actually thinking in those terms.

Don Drummond, center, performs for Sonny Bradshaw's band with Carlos Malcolm, immediate right; Rupert Anderson far right; and Rico Rodriguez, left; 1957 (National Library of Jamaica).

Those are more terms for historians. You're just happy you were able to do a couple of gigs with this guy."

There were plenty of bandleaders hiring instrumentalists like Drummond to perform for their bands, in the Kingston clubs and in the hotel clubs on the north shore. Bandleaders like Carlisle Henriques, Redver

Cooke, John Weston, Roy White, Val Bennett, Milton McPherson, Jack Brown, Roy Coburn, George Moxey, Count Buckram and others employed musicians who performed the jazz standards culled from scores the leaders ordered from England or transcribed themselves from Count Basie or Duke Ellington. The jazz and big band artists of America greatly influenced the Jamaican repertoire. Alpharian Tommy McCook listened to John Coltrane and Charlie Parker. Johnny "Dizzy" Moore, also an Alpharian, listened to Dizzy Gillespie. And Drummond was influenced by Bennie Green, a Chicago-born trombonist who performed in the big band style as well as the fast-emerging R&B scene in the States. If Drummond didn't hear these tunes from Sister Ignatius's vast record collection, then he likely heard them from the American radio stations, like WNOE in New Orleans, WLAC in Nashville, and WINZ in Miami. The island's only radio station in the early days, ZQI (which became RJR in 1950), didn't play jazz during the one-hour-a-week broadcast initially, moving to a whopping four hours a day. This station mostly played news, war updates, BBC relay broadcasts, or local classical music. It is no wonder, then, that audiences longed for the American trends which they learned to perform on their own for the American audiences who paid money to hear it.

Before Carlos Malcolm played trombone he played piano with a small group called The Vivian Hall All-Stars. It was then that he met Drummond. Malcolm says he saw Drummond's talent right away: "Vivian Hall was a very talented trumpeter and Drummond was playing trombone there. I noticed an unusual aspect of him as a musician. I'm an arranger also. He was playing a third below the first trumpet, which is usually played by the second trumpet, and the rate at which he was playing was quite a fast tempo. I noticed that even before I actually engaged him in conversation, I noticed his dexterity with the piece. So after we broke for a few minutes, I walked over to his stand to look at the music and I saw he was transposing the second trumpet part because he was in the treble clef. He was transposing the part and playing it an octave higher, and at that rate, he just blew my mind. Trombone is written in the bass clef and it's different for the treble clef, so when you transpose in the bass clef and you have to play an octave higher also, and he was doing it very accurately. Right then I knew he wasn't just a garden variety musician. We became good friends after that."

Clive Chin, whose father, Vincent Chin, recorded Don Drummond on his Randy's label, says he, too, noticed Drummond's unusual methods while he practiced: "One of the things I remember, and it was so amazing to see was, looking at the music that he was practicing from, the score sheet was upside down. In other words, he was reading the score sheet literally upside down. I'm not saying that he had turned it upside down by mistake. He was actually practicing upside down."

Others note his skill in those early days as well, including one who has patterned his style of playing after Drummond, Vin Gordon, a trombonist also known as Don Drummond Junior. According to Gordon: "Don Drummond took over the scene with a different style of music, a different trombone style. Don Drummond played the more staccato kind of music, staccato, Latin-kind of music, playing the trombone in a Latin style." BB Seaton, the great Jamaican vocalist who was a member of the Gaylads and appeared on the same bill as Drummond from time to time, comments, "There was something about it. When he took his solo, it was so rhythmic and full of notes, some notes that people wouldn't think of to play and chord formations. He was unique in that aspect. I think he was the best trombonist to come out of Jamaica."

Saxophonist Headley Bennett, known affectionately as Deadly Headley, remembers playing with Drummond in those early days: "I was one of his personal friends because I used to go by his house in Kingston and we sit there and tell one or two jokes, you know? And we used to practice and he used to tell me how to play along with the music. He helped me a lot. I went to his house in the morning always and at that time his mom went to work, so him alone. And he used to ride his bicycle around and have lunch with his mom. We used to go by the beach in the evening hours to look at the people swimming and things. Let me tell you something. He was ahead of most musicians. He never used to communicate too well with the other musicians, because there was something about him that they never like. He wouldn't talk as an associate. He was a conductor. I remember on one occasion one of those professional guys in America came on tour and they used to use the band in Jamaica to back them up. I don't remember the name, and he played with the Sonny Bradshaw Orchestra and they say that he is one of the best, the best trombone player in the world. He was rated I think number two."

By 1954, Drummond began headlining his own band, the Don Drummond All-Stars and the Don Drummond Four and he wrote his own songs. One of those songs, "The Message," was even banned by venues because it drew riot-sized crowds. Musician Neville "Brammy" Bramwell, who performed in clubs with Drummond during these days, recounts that on one occasion when Drummond performed "The Message" at the Carib Theatre, he began blowing his horn from the balcony and made his way down to the stage in a dramatic display for the audience. The crowd nearly rioted with excitement over the incredible performance and those who listened from outside of the theater, which was packed to capacity, pushed for a chance to get inside to catch a glimpse of the exhibition. The iron fencing outside of the theater was bent by the feral multitude.

Drummond continued to make guest appearances with other ensembles, such as Baba Motta, Lester Hall, Roy Coburn and his Blue-Flames Orchestra, Sonny Bradshaw, Vivian Hall, Tony Brown, and Kenny Williams. He performed at such locations as the Colony Club, Bournemouth Beach Club, Silver Slipper, Ward Theatre, Carib Theatre, Palace Theatre, Little Theatre, Regal Theatre, Tropical Theatre, Queens Theatre, and Majestic Theatre. Don Drummond was all the rage. One 1955 advertisement for his gig proclaimed, "You'll get more than your money's worth when you join the fun at Bournemouth. Dance to the strains of Don Drummond and the All-Stars." Others that same year told readers that Drummond was a "musical treat," who promised "a night of gala entertainment with one great little band."

A review in the *Daily Gleaner* on November 11, 1955, read that the annual "300 Jazz Concert," held at the Carib Theatre and featuring the Don Drummond Four, was a huge success due to the rising popularity of jazz. Journalist Clifton Cuthbert stated, "If McNair [Harold "Little G"] was the show's featured star, there was one other slight young man with a large horn who, in one opinion, should have got top co-billing. Maybe Don Drummond suffers from the usual under-rated fate of stay-at-homes. With his big-toned trombone he played a 'Lady in Red' and 'Man I Love' rich in ideas and long variation. He seemed the least derivative player of the evening, an impressive feat for one so young."

In 1956, great American jazz singer Sarah Vaughan came to perform at the Tropical Theatre, and the Glass Bucket in mid–July. Don Drummond played trombone as part of Vaughan's musical backup and Vaughan was so impressed with his playing that she said he likely ranked among the top five trombonists in the world. In 1959, when Drummond performed at a concert at Sabina Park, the great American jazz pianist Dave Brubeck stopped in the middle of a performance, thunderstruck by Drummond's ability to improvise. He and guitarist Janet Enright were the only two Jamaican musicians invited to perform with Brubeck.

Don Drummond was experiencing success, playing show after show at venue after venue, and many of the names and faces of those he played with were the same each night. Performers like Foggy Mullings on piano, Janet Enright on guitar, Lovelack Brown on trumpet, Clu Johnson on bass, Bobby Gaynair on tenor sax, Jack Jones on alto, and Julian Iffla & Totlyn Jackson, "The Girls with the Voice," as they were billed. There were comedians Bim & Bam who were "elected by all parties as chief ministers of fun," according to advertisements. And there were dancers, like Pam Pam & Gloria who did the jitterbug. Then there was one dancer who appeared on the same bill as Don as early as 1955 in per-

Don Drummond performs on stage (© The Gleaner Company Limited).

formances like the Constellation 300 at the Rialto Theatre, and at the same theater again one week later with the Calypsonians and the usual cast of characters. It's likely he never noticed her, as he was always too focused on his music, writing, practicing. Plus, she was a young girl then, just entering her teenage years. But she would continue to perform, year after year, on the same bills as Don Drummond. She would continue to dance, her ruffles shaking, her hips swaying, her long hair flowing, luring the crowds to see the "exotic" dance in the "Latin Quarter" where she performed at Club Havana and loads of other places. She was Margarita, the Rhumba Queen.

5

Rhumba Queen

O chestnut-tree, great-rooted blossomer,
Are you the leaf, the blossom or the bole?
O body swayed to music, O brightening glance,
How can we know the dancer from the dance?
— William Butler Yeats

Margarita — Jamaica's No. 1 Torrid Rhumba Dancer
— From an April 1960 advertisement for
The Glass Bucket Club, owned by Bob Webster

Sparkling Native Floor Show featuring Desir & Rahma in their sensa-
tional dance on broken glass, and Marguerita, "exotic dancer."
— From a July 9, 1955, advertisement for the Glass Bucket

Margarita, sometimes spelled Marguerita, was born Anita Selema
Mahfood on June 14, 1939, to a businessman, Jad Eid Mahfood, and his
first wife, Brenda May Virtue, a white woman from Jamaica. Brenda gave
birth to four daughters by Jad — first Monira, then Conchita, third Anita,
and, finally, Janet. Anita's father, Jad, also had two other children with
two other women, neither of whom he married, and one of those children
was born while he was still married to Brenda. Despite the many tragedies
that would shape their lives growing up, the four sisters stayed very close
to one another. Even when they married and moved away, they still
returned home as often as they could to be together. Their personalities
may have been as different as night and day, and they may have tussled
with each other from time to time, but the girls were a strong unit, a rock
in the storm that was their lives. Monira was the oldest and a voice of reason, Conchita didn't want to get involved with the antics of the girls, Anita
was a troublemaker, and Janet was an academic and a gossip who instigated
Anita.

Jad, immigrated to Jamaica in the 1920s when his father, Eid Mahfood, sent for him and his two brothers, Murad and Saleem. They came

from Beirut, Lebanon. The family name was originally Mahfouz, but immigration officials misunderstood the pronunciation and wrote it as Mahfood, a common mistake committed by clerks at immigration posts. Jad was raised in Kingston and his family was well known as a business family with resources and class status since they were light skinned and wealthy, although the Arab community never accepted Jad's decision to marry a white girl. Jad quickly learned the Jamaican patois, calling his foes "bumbaclots" and "rasclots" like his Jamaican brethren, albeit with an Arabic accent that garnered even more respect from those in his large presence.

In 1947, Jad Mahfood applied for a fish shop license at the Victoria Market, and although his building was found to be in order by constables, he had previously been selling fish "all of the time without a license," according to a report in the *Daily Gleaner*, and so his application was refused. Nevertheless, Jad went on to establish a thriving fish shop located at a depot on the Torrington Bridge called Mahfood's Fisheries. They supplied fish for the soldiers, the military bases on the island. "They are one of the richest people in Jamaica, the Mahfoods," says Suzanne Bent, Anita's daughter. "Everybody will tell you that." Zola Buckland Sergi, Conchita's daughter, says that her mother frequently worked in the shop, although none of the other girls did with any regularity, nor did their mother Brenda. "He used to pull my mom out of school to

Jad Eid Mahfood (courtesy Zola Buckland Sergi).

work in the fish shop," Zola recalls. "She was just a teenager but he told her she had to work. My mom loved her dad and she was really good with money, so she could help."

The fish shop was located in an enclosed store in the building owned by Mahfood. It was a very successful business and helped to establish the Mahfood family in Jamaica. Jad used his wealth to invest in buildings and land near the shop and furthered his business. But the estate was dealt a terrible blow, as recalled by Jad's son Paul: "My father was from Lebanon, Beirut, and his ancestry is somewhat difficult [to trace], but there is strong origin that extends to the Persian periphery, all the way back centuries. He was living in a very large house in a place located on Antrin Road. It was a huge house, over ten thousand square feet. Anita, Conchita, Monira, and Janet were living, well I wasn't living there for long — four years. What happened was, he owned a very large and profitable fishing depot. It was located somewhere south of Cross Roads. It was a huge block of stores and condo buildings and he owned about a quarter of that, and his store was there. He was well known. He wasn't much of a talker, but when he said something it made sense and people would listen in the accent he spoke. He was a very kindhearted man. He had a very profitable fishing company, and being so successful, we don't know today how it happened, but his entire fishing store burned to the ground and it was believed that it was done by arson, maybe because of competition in business since he was so successful. The case was never settled."

Paul Mahfood says the loss of the family business was especially devastating for his father, who was deeply rooted in his Arab culture. It was a blow to his ego, his manhood, his worth as a person. But then, there was even more tragedy. Continues Paul: "In addition to that was the difficulty with his wife. My father wanted a son. My father was a very kind person but he wasn't, in the loving sense. He was never abusive, he just wasn't that kind of person. Some people are like that — they can raise a family, provide for the family, but they're not the romantic type and when they get hit with issues, such as your store being destroyed and then you can't get a son and then you have economic issues, it's hard. Then it affects you much more and you're noticeably troubled and then you turn to drinking beer, and that's what he did, and he smoked like a chimney. I can just see the [stained] color on his fingers. He became a drinker and a smoker."

When Jad would drink, says Sergi, he forced his wife, Brenda, to drink as well; if she refused, he hit her until she submitted. "When Brenda didn't drink, she was very nice," Sergi explains. "She was always a wonderful lady. She loved poetry, she loved to recite. She was a classy woman. My grandmother never drank but he forced her to drink and she became an alcoholic and was not very nice at that point. If he wanted to have a drink, and it was rum, he would pour her one. She said she didn't want it, and he would slap her. He forced her to drink. The girls loved their mom, but when she drank, they didn't like her much."

Jad's abuse continued when the relationship produced no boys. Paul recalls the huge impact this had on Jad's family because of his Arabic culture: "My father got the first child, which was a girl. Okay, the second, a girl. And so, traditionally, they need to have a son, you know, the Arabic way. Anita was supposed to have been a boy. He wanted a son so desperately. With Anita, because she was the third born, he was upset she wasn't a boy, so he would take her to places, like the movie house or expose her to boy things and so she became a tomboy. It wasn't as overbearing as you might expect, but to him it seemed like he gave up on the idea that he would have a boy and as time went on, the fourth child was a girl. I remember Anita as a tomboy, somewhat in your face, she would be confrontational, she was aggressive, but she had a heart. If you would back off and talk about something that was upsetting to you she would try to represent you and defend you. She had a way about her. If you were against her, she would stand against you. If you were with her, she would stand with you. If you did something wrong and you called on her, she would back you up and try to help you, so she was reasonable in that way." Jad called his little daughter not by her given name, Anita, but by his nickname for her — Sonny Boy.

Sergi says that Jad was cruel to Brenda: "He was abusive with their mother and he was from Lebanon and [in that country, men] were the boss. He said he was going to take his four daughters back to his home country and marry them off. He wanted to marry them all off in the Middle East." In addition, Jad was a gun aficionado. He was said to be skilled at shooting his pistol and could hit a coin tossed into the air with his shot. Paul explains, "He was a marksman. He had different guns and was very talented. He would keep his guns in the home he had. He would refill ammunitions, shotguns, handguns, and so on. They were quite available to anyone."

On October 10, 1948, Anita's desperately unhappy mother attempted suicide with one of Jad's guns. The attempt was witnessed by a young

Anita and Conchita. "They watched their mom shoot herself in the head," says Sergi. The *Daily Gleaner* headline read, "Suicide Attempt Draws Fine for Unlicensed Gun." The article stated,

> Because his wife attempted to take her life with it, Jad Eid Mahfood of 22 Lucas Road was charged with having an unlicensed revolver in his possession. Yesterday, he pleaded "guilty" to the charge and was ordered to pay a fine of 2 pounds. Alternative of serving thirty days imprisonment at hard labour was imposed by His Honour Mr. Neville A. Clare, presiding in the Kingston Petty Sessions Court. Mr. B.L. Myrie, Deputy Clerk of Courts, told the Court that the revolver was used on the morning of October 10, by the defendant's wife, Brenda.

Paul attempted to explain Brenda's actions: "For whatever reason, depression set in and his wife began to drink heavily because of the depression and then one day decided to blow, to kill herself because of all this. It turned out she screwed up her own suicide and she disfigured her face. So now an attractive woman looks ugly and that didn't sit well with anyone at all. So now she recovered, of course, surgery, but she had significant scars, didn't look so good, so that even made it worse. So she stepped off a curb in front of an oncoming truck and killed herself."

Actually, the story of Brenda's suicide is even more prolonged and heartbreaking. As Sergi explains, "She jumped in front of a truck, but that didn't kill her. She was hospitalized and her pelvis was shattered. She fell out of bed trying to get out and that is what actually killed her." Conchita was pregnant with her first child at the time of her mother's death on Mother's Day, May 9, 1954. Anita was just 14 years old.

Shortly after this series of catastrophic events, the four young girls, now motherless and raised by an emotionless and abusive father, found themselves thrown into another calamity by the presence of a new family member, Patricia Carmen Dacres, Paul Jad Mahfood's mother. Paul explains, "My father doesn't know how to raise a family because he's not that kind of person. He provides, but the emotional side of it wasn't there as expected. And he has his own issues. He never married again, but when my mom came into the situation, my mother is about the same age as Janet, so she could've been one of his daughters. He was never married to her but my mother was physically abandoned by her mother. He discovered her along the lot because there were residential apartments along with stores and she went to see her mom there, but her mom basically turned her out. He found her sleeping in abandoned offices on the same lot and he decided to take her into his house. She couldn't go back to her step-mother because she was a witch, so to speak, a very wicked woman, very bad, so he took her in and had her stay in the rooms of his daughters. Well, it turns out that the girls got jealous of her, not knowing why this had to happen. Their mother died a few years ago and [they asked,] 'What's going on here, there's this young pretty girl, you know, what's he up to?' So Anita, being the ring leader, of course, and Janet being the gossiper and the one that basically stirs up trouble, my mother got picked on quite a bit because she's staying there, she's not paying anything and she's young like they are and so they would pick things and fight with her and Anita would be the one to fight her, wrestle her and beat her up."

Sergi corroborates Paul's account: "The girls didn't like her much. She was taking over the house and she was their age." And that situation got even worse when Jad found out about the way Patricia was being treated by the sisters.

Paul says, "So my father learned about this because they would cover things up and they would threaten her not to say anything to him, but when he came home he saw, on one occasion, bruises on her neck. He asked and everybody was quiet and he suspected something was happening and so he went to Anita because he knew what her behavior was and eventually it was discovered, so he moved her into his room and, of course, that's when things happened and she became pregnant with me."

Keep in mind that Jad had already fathered another child, a girl, with another woman while his wife was pregnant with Conchita. Paul says, "It appears that my father, during the time that Anita's mother was pregnant with her second child, Conchita, impregnated another female that was living in the neighborhood."

As time went on in the Mahfood family, dynamics only worsened with the addition of Paul to the household. Jad Eid Mahood finally had his boy. But there was another boy in the family who created another layer of jealous emotions for the already-troubled girls. By this time, Conchita had married and given birth to a son who was very much in the family picture. Paul explains: "My second sister, Conchita, got married and gave birth to a son and his name was Ramon. He was two years of age when I was born. Before I was born and when Anita was no longer a tomboy, my father felt, 'Well, I guess this is going to be my surrogate son. The only son I will ever have.' So he would then favor Ramon. And that was wonderful because that is what Conchita wanted and so he treated him as if he were a son and grandson. When I was born, all hell broke loose because now that attention, it totally evaporated and it went all to me because now, for the first time, he had a son. And he had a son from my mother, who was only fifteen at the time and it created a lot of envy and jealousy and hate and so, eventually, my mom left. I was about three years old or so. She was too young anyway and he was older than her but I was his prized possession, his pride and joy, no one could touch me. Now here's the problem. When I was a baby, I was told by my mother and others in the neighborhood that, on one occasion, when my father was gone, and Anita was the ringleader in leading it, Anita took me from my mother for the whole day, so she was crying the whole day. I don't know where they hid me but I'm told I was also crying. They didn't feed me. They hid me to spite her and give her a hard time. Their father was then coming home at a certain time and they would bring me around. Anita would tell her, 'Don't say a word to Daddy, or else,' so she wouldn't say a word at all, and so that went on for a little bit, not for long. And then on one occasion, I was about one, I think, and Conchita's son was at least two years older than I am and he wanted something that I had and I was told that he got a hold of me and was basically bouncing my head off of the wall, a very physical thing on me. Conchita saw it, everyone saw it and was basically having a good time of it, I'm told, until Anita said, 'That's enough of it, stop it,' and she couldn't take any more of it, so initially she was looking at it and then she stopped it."

All of this turmoil had taken a toll on Patricia, who was essentially forced out of the home. Paul, however, stayed after his mother moved out. "My father wouldn't have it any other way," Paul says. "You see, I was his only son. He never had a son before and he would kill anyone, even his daughters, if he ever found out what they did. To the day he died, he never knew that they did those things. My mom left when I was three, going on four. Anita was still there for a short time, and Janet. Monira was gone to England, Conchita was close by with her husband and she went back and forth. So anywhere my father went, he would take me. Movies, you name it, I saw it — Westerns. I was the only one he would take."

The four girls may have simply been continuing a cycle of abuse they witnessed in their home. They saw their father abuse their mother, and they, too, experienced abuse periodically. Sergi says, "He would beat Janet on the bottoms of her feet, not her body, because she had cerebral palsy. With my mom, one day he saw my mother coming down the street and my father was on his bike next to her. They had been on a date. And my grandfather drove up in his car. He reached through the window and she had long hair. He grabbed her by the hair and pulled her home, driving down the street, pulling her by her hair. My father saw her being dragged and asked him to stop and my grandfather pulled a gun on him. He was tough with all of the girls. They weren't allowed to date and anything they wanted to do, they had to hide. When the girls ended up in a relationship where they were abused, that's how they were made to feel growing up, so they stayed in those abusive relationships. They grew up seeing it. When my mom was sixteen, if she and my dad had a fight and she came home, her dad sent her back and told her that was her husband."

Jad Eid Mahfood never recovered from the destruction of his business. He never rebuilt the store to its former glory, although he did work enough to make a living for his large family. Paul says, "His other family members had other businesses. One of the cousins of his, Khaleel, had a huge fishing industry, and after the arson, it was suspected that maybe he had something to do with it, but it was never proven. They felt somehow they would help him out so they would rent a small shop and he would actually buy from them and he was diminutive at that point. It's like he was a lame person, not the same person. After that arson, he was changed and then when his wife killed herself he was so devastated he never married again. From time to time, every few months or so, he would bring a woman in, and I never knew what the reason was, but then she would leave the very same night or the next day. And from hindsight, you know what that meant."

These tumultuous and tragic family events coincided with the difficulties Jad had with Anita, who did not wish to work in her dad's fish shop, but instead longed to dance. Norma Faye Chin, Anita's best friend later in life recalls, "The family didn't approve of her dancing but she usually do it because she get paid to do it. He had a fish shop and he wanted all of the girls to be working in the fish shop with him, which they didn't like that after a while." Sergi says that her grandfather didn't like Anita dancing, but her sisters, thick as thieves, tried to keep the secret.

Anita had an exhibitionistic personality, magnetic, charismatic, beginning very early in her life. Sergi says, "She sang, she danced, she played saxophone, she could do anything. She had a mouth. She would speak up. She was funny, too. Once we went to a tea party at church and you had to pay a lot of money to attend. They had little sandwiches and crumpets, British stuff. My mom paid for us all to go but by the time we got there,

there was not much left. My aunt Anita took a bag from her purse, went over to the table dumped the whole tray of sandwiches in the bag. Then she took a bag from my mom's purse and dumped the whole tray of desserts in her bag and she took them home and divided them up for everybody! She was extremely outgoing and loving."

Anita Mahfood, circa 1950s (courtesy Zola Buckland Sergi).

It was this charismatic personality that brought Anita to the stage despite the admonishment from her father. In 1952, at the tender age of 12, she won first prize on *The Vere Johns Opportunity Hour* with her natural, self-taught skill of dancing. She would win competitions week after week. Vere Johns was a Jamaican postal worker who became a newspaper reporter, writing a music column each week for Jamaica's *Star*, but he soon entered the world of radio and stage production. After living for a short time in the United States and developing the concept of a talent show as a way to help a local theater boost its attendance and sales, Johns brought the idea—which had been the brainchild of his second wife, Lillian Margaret May—to Jamaica, when they returned to reside there. Johns's talent show took place at the Majestic Theatre, Ambassador Theatre, and the Palace Theatre in Kingston. The Palace Theatre was an outdoor venue with seating at a price to fit anyone's budget. Guests could reserve a premium box seat, or a wooden chair with a cushion under a roof, or they could sit out in the open air, but in full view of the stage, which was flanked by orchestra pits at the base of a large movie screen. When the theater needed to supplement its movie income with another revenue stream, it held a talent show, and at these events, many artists—dancers, instrumentalists, vocalists, comedians, even bicyclists—received their first taste of show business. Ten acts appeared on each bill and admission was less than a shilling. Vere Johns auditioned performers each Tuesday and Thursday at three P.M.

Winners were selected solely on audience approval — whoever received the loudest applause at the end of the night won the show. Needless to say, this form of selection allowed plenty of opportunity for corruption, such as packing the house with one's own supporters, or paying off people to clap for a chosen artist. After the artists performed, Vere Johns stepped onto the stage and held the cash prize of two pounds over each person's head until the audience responded with the appropriate level of applause. Sometimes after a performer won, audience members approached the winner in a threatening manner to demand part of the spoils. If a performer won or came in second place, they returned the next week to perform again, so the corruption continued. Like an early version of *American Idol* or *X Factor*, winning the popular talent contests assured success on the entertainment circuit. The competition was entered into more for the exposure than the money. Those who got their start through the Vere Johns Opportunity Hour include Desmond Dekker, Alton Ellis, John Holt, Laurel Aitken, Bob Andy, Derrick Morgan, the Wailers, and countless others.

In order to perform without being caught, Anita chose a stage name, Margarita, so her father wouldn't see her real name in print advertisements. Recalls Suzanne Bent: "I guess she did that to hide it from the Mahfoods, that I believe, because at that time it was not becoming of a woman. But she wanted to be her own person." And hide her dancing she did, until Anita's father found out from his friends. When Anita won a competition at the Glass Bucket, her father was there to see it, unbeknownst to her. She was found out, but there was nothing he could do to stop her.

Pianist Herman Sang grew up in Kingston's Bournemouth Gardens area near the Mahfoods and says he remembers Anita as a young girl: "We actually lived about four homes away from Margarita Mahfood, so we knew her growing up as kids. She was a beautiful girl. We didn't go to the same school they did, but we were always on the beach so we had to walk past their home to go to the beach. She was a rhumba dancer." Anita and her sisters attended a school called Alpha, but this one was much different than the Alpha Boys School. Anita's school, called Alpha Academy, was a girls' high school and was for girls from elite or middle-class families. Sergi says, "Aunt Anita and my mom [Conchita] really did not enjoy school much, but her other two sisters did and did very well in school."

Winston Smith also recalls growing up near the Mahfood family: "Margarita used to live next door to me in Kingston when she was a little girl before she got into dancing on a road that is notorious for sound system music. I was living across from the sound system place. She was living down the street from me and she would climb under the fence and come out into the street at night to look for her fellas. She was a rudie. I think her father didn't want her to get into this dancing, rhumba dancing. And she ran away."

Anita did, in fact, run away, rebelling against the abuse and turmoil of her home. She was following her own dream, speaking her own mind, celebrating her own spirit. She began dancing at clubs all over Kingston and she made her own costumes as she was skilled at sewing. Faye Chin says, "We danced together. We were in a group on stage. She used to do rhumba; I do creative dancing, limbo dancing. It's Alan Ivanhoe Dance Troupe I was in. She was an individual dancer and whenever they're having performance like pantomimes or the theater used to have *Opportunity Hour*, she would dance there. She was a terrific dancer and she taught herself to dance. We became friends and we really became close and we were friends for a long long time until she passed." Saxophonist Herman "Woody" King remembered her as "a great rhumba dancer. The clubs would want her. Of course, she had to go. That's how she earned her living and she enjoyed it, too."

Margarita, the ultimate performer, always began her dance the same way with the same air of anticipation. As the spotlight hit one area on the center of the dance floor, the music began and Margarita was in the corner of the room, out of view. She sauntered to the center, ruffles rushing through the tables of men and women who turned their heads to see her passage to the light. When she came into full view, the rhythms of the drums at their height, the audience was captivated, fully immersed in her powerful magic. She was auditioning for her dream. One day she wanted to dance on the stages in the United States, but she had to make a name for herself first.

Margarita appeared with the same circuit of performers, as did most Kingston entertainers of the day. She first met Don Drummond in the 1950s at the Bournemouth Club when they appeared on the same bill together. Ads appear in the *Daily Gleaner* in June 1955 for Drummond and "Marguerita (Rhumba Dancer)" together on the same bill with others, including Pam Pam & Gloria, jitterbug dancers, with whom Margarita frequently performed. Margarita performed at the Ward Theatre, Club Havana, Club Baby Grand, Club Adastra, Carib Theatre, Glass Bucket, Rialto Theatre, Ritz Theater, and Queens Theatre, and she frequently received top billing. She played the role of a dance club dancer in the documentary, *It Can Happen to You*, which was filmed by the Jamaica Film Unit in the 1950s. On November 23, 1955, she performed in a show called *The Sundown Serenade* at the Ritz Theater with Bim & Bam, Danny Hyacinth Clover, Wonder Brothers and Did & Don't. This type of billing — with a theme for the show — was a common feature for clubs in an attempt to attract tourists. Another was at the Ward Theatre on Christmas morning 1959 for a show called *Chrismania*, which featured, among others, The Jiving Juniors, Lascelles Perkins, and music by Ken Williams and his Club Havana Orchestra. Margarita also performed that same morning at the Carib Theatre for a show called *Xmas Morning Revels*, featuring a similar lineup with the addition of Vere Johns and Mrs. Vere Johns, and music by Frankie Bonitto and His Orchestra. Artists frequently performed in multiple shows all over the city for Christmas. The clubs themselves also tried to capture themes, and Club Havana, where Margarita frequently performed, advertised itself as "Jamaica's Latin Quarter."

Dr. Aggrey Irons, administrator at Bellevue Mental Hospital in the 1970s and an avid music fan, recalls the days when Margarita danced at Club Havana. He says, "Everybody went there. It was on the way to the airport, on the road from Bellevue, actually, on the opposite side of the road but closer to the airport. People from all walks of life used to go there. As you can tell from the name, it was reminiscent of the era when the Cubans used to have exotic and exciting nightlife and Club Havana was supposed to recreate the goings-on in Havana, Cuba, in the days of Batiste, pre-revolution, so it was a wild and wonderful place with much dancing and merriment and much like that song 'Copacabana,' it was like that. That was Club Havana, like the Copa. I have been [there], much to my parents' regret."

Heather Royes, daughter of K.C. Royes, administrator of Bellevue during Drummond's incarceration, recalls a time when she herself went to see Margarita perform at Club Havana: "I do remember her reputation because all the so-called middle-class boys wanted to sneak over to see her dance. Club Havana was like the Forbidden Garden. I did see her dance at Club Havana on Windward Road, which was quite risqué at my age. Some boyfriend smuggled me in. He said to me, 'Do you want to go see Margarita, the Rhumba Queen?' And I said, 'Sure, but I couldn't tell my parents,' but I went. It was full of middle-class men and some ladies, and it was just like a different world. I was fascinated by Anita Mahfood. All we knew was there was this dive on Windward Road, as it was to us, because we were at Bellevue, we lived there, it was a huge estate. I remember we went to a lot of parties with soca and stuff like that, but you didn't go to Club Havana, or at least *I* wasn't supposed to go to Club Havana."

Paul says his sister's personality was a perfect match for an exhibitionist entertainer: "She was very physical and she could also be very seductive. She had that charm about her. She had a nice way about her. She could get things done. She moved around quickly and she [was] down to earth."

Margarita was incredibly popular in the clubs, truly star quality. She was beautiful and had long, flowing, wavy hair. She had an ethnic look that was a part of every race, in a sense, both dark and light at the same time. She was remarkably talented as a dancer, and she had a personality that was captivating, alluring, and glamorous. Jamaican vocalist Derrick Morgan agrees: "She was beautiful. A very nice girl to be around. Slim, trim, well-trimmed girl. Everybody like Margarita." Singer Marcia Griffiths lived near Margarita when she moved to the Rockfort neighborhood. "The first time I saw Margarita was at a bus stop," she recalls. "I went to a bus stop, waiting there, she was there and I was overwhelmed with this woman's beauty, you know, how beautiful she was. I always admire her. That was the first time I see her and then I kept seeing her after because sometime we take the bus together. Eventually, after seeing her that first time at the bus stop, I spoke to her. Nothing in depth, just talking woman to woman, talking and encouraging her in whatever she was doing. We were both young at the same time. I saw her dance once. She was a fantastic dancer. She was a great dancer. She was a hip dancer more, you know? She really had it going for her. Really had it going for her, with her beauty and being able to dance, she was talented. She was a woman I really did admire. She wasn't tall. She wasn't a tall person, maybe five foot five, five foot six. Long hair. Very, very pretty girl. Very, very pretty girl." Anita's friend Norma Faye Chin says her beauty was definitely not only skin deep. She had a good soul and was a true friend to Chin, who was a loyal friend in return to Anita as well. "A very very beautiful person she was," she says. "On the outside she was a very beautiful woman; inside she was a friend. If you tell her something, it remains there. She's a very genuine person. She likes to dance and she attract, because she was so pretty and petite and beautiful shape, people attract to her a lot."

Margarita had a love for both dance and music. Her favorite song

Margarita, Anita Mahfood, in her rhumba costume (© The Gleaner Company Limited).

was "St. Louis Blues," sung by Lavern Baker, remembers her sister Conchita. Margarita's ability to dance was astonishing and was the perfect accompaniment to the music of the time, jazz, ska, and mento with cymbal, drum, and percussion. Musicologist Herbie Miller says, "At times it was not clear if she was dancing to the band's music or the band was playing music to her moves." He contends that some of the songs she danced to were favorites of the day, like "Peanut Vendor" and "Siboney." He says her dancing was sensual, not vulgar. She never would allow herself to be touched. The term used to describe her form of dance is many times called "exotic," which is very different from the colloquial term used in the U.S. today. In the '50s and '60s in Jamaica, exotic dance was the dance of foreign countries, like the rhumba, cha-cha, and bolero. The rhumba is an Afro-Cuban dance which had been a craze for decades in the U.S. and Europe. It became popular in Kingston during the '50s and '60s when the Cuban population only made it more a sensation. Certainly, Margarita's fluid-looking ethnicity gave her dance more credibility and appeal. Her costume was a typical rhumba costume, frilly and ruffled to punctuate the motions of the dance, a bikini to accentuate the curves of the dancer. Herman Sang explains, "I'm sure you've seen a Spanish dancer. The back of her costume would have a frilly mini-skirt thing. It wasn't vulgar or anything like that. A part of her routine was to dance the limbo, so she had to get down close to the ground with her legs wide open and go under the bar. But she was a nice girl." It was this costume and this dance that made the confident Anita so provocative, and her daughter, Suzanne, clarifies that such assured-ness in these times was misunderstood by some: "They label her as a pros-titute because they're not used to seeing a woman. It was all men, there weren't that many women out there. Women were nothing to them back then."

Margarita came to the stage to express herself, and to escape. She came to escape her abusive home life and the horrific events that wracked the family. But, like so many environments where abuse is prevalent, the cycle of abuse is not so easily broken. Suzanne Bent says, "Her father, being strict and so on, wanted her to have a certain type of company and she chose the company she chose, and that's where everything went wrong." The company she chose at a young age, even though she had previously dated Lester Williams, trumpeter with the Eric Deans Orchestra, was Rudolph Bent, five and a half years her elder. They were married by Jim Russell, registrar of births and deaths in Kingston, the same Jim Russell who married thousands of couples over four decades at the post, including none other than Bob Marley and Rita Anderson, in 1966. Anita, with her love for sewing, made her own pink wedding dress. Anita and Rudolph shared a home on Stillwell Road in a prosperous neighborhood north of downtown Kingston with fellow boxer, Emilio Sanchez. Bent says that her mother met her father after she went to one of his bouts. But Bent didn't save his fights for the ring alone — some who remember the couple in those early days say they frequently saw the two physically fighting. When Anita was 20 years old she and Rudolph Bent had their first child, Suzanne Diane, on October 23, 1960. Two years later they had Christopher Robin. But the two children didn't make a difficult marriage better — it only made their relationship more complicated and dangerous.

Paul Jad Mahfood says his father didn't get involved with this relationship: "She was the only one of the four girls that chose to move out into the world, getting involved with a male that was non–Arabic or non–white. She was the first to marry a black person, and that was Rudolph Bent. He was an abusive person as well as he had a drinking problem and he

Anita Mahfood holds her daughter, Suzanne Bent, in the early 1960s (courtesy Zola Buckland Sergi).

abused her physically. My father didn't say much. I never heard him say a word about that. But he had his own thoughts and I don't know what he thought about it. And no one ever mentioned it because he didn't speak much. He would speak more to me than he would speak to them. He was okay with what she would do except he didn't want her to be hurt and he didn't want her to be penniless. He did for her what he could. He told her to make something of her life and she did what she wanted anyway. As long as she was okay and she wasn't having any problems, she could handle it on her own and he was alright with that. I don't know that he heard about the abuse. It was after the fact and it was not told to him or anyone else, but he learned about it from Janet after the divorce. Anita didn't want to put her troubles on the family. She knew that my father had his own problems. She went off, had these two children, got a divorce from this guy, and then went on alone into the music world."

6

The Dark Destroyer

British Honduras may have been a world away from Jamaica, but the two areas shared much in common. The tropical climate lent itself to rich natural resources, which meant that capitalizing off of those resources fed the rich and starved the poor in each commonwealth. There was terrible widespread unemployment and poverty among the working classes in both Jamaica and British Honduras. Marcus Garvey's Universal Negro Improvement Association sought to empower the oppressed to engage in government to take back control of their lands. Political parties were organized around approaches to labor in both places. And both Jamaica and British Honduras were colonized by Great Britain until each argued for and won their independence.

The people of Jamaica and British Honduras (which wasn't known as Belize until 1973 in anticipation of independence, even though independence didn't come until 1981), also shared a love for boxing. In Jamaica, Sister Ignatius shared films of the sport's greats demonstrating their technique. Local theaters screened fights, including one between Rocky Marciano and Don Cockell. The Jamaica Boxing Board of Control (JBBC) was established as early at 1929 by Jamaican national hero Norman Manley, one of the leaders responsible for negotiating Jamaican independence. (Manley served as president of the JBBC during its infancy.) Alton Ellis even commemorated prize fighter Bunny Grant in his 1963 song, "Dance Crasher." Grant was the first Jamaican boxer to fight for a world title and was extremely popular and successful in the early 1960s. In British Honduras, social clubs frequently hosted boxing tournaments. In Belize City, as early as the 1930s, spectators packed the city's biggest arena, Birds' Isle, to watch various matches featuring the likes of welterweight Fitzroy Guisseppi, lightweight Ludwig Lightburn, and middleweight Rudolph Bent.

It is no wonder then that Rudolph Bent, like many other professional boxers, fought in both countries. Bent was born in Belize City, British

Honduras, on October 13, 1933. A troublesome child, he made life difficult for his mother, who had six other children to care for. Rudolph Bent's daughter, Suzanne, says simply, "He was a bad boy. His mom told me they tried to keep him home and he would get in trouble and they even stripped him naked and he still left the house. They even put his sisters' dresses on him, [but] he'd still leave the house and he would fight. So they put him in a group home and there's where he learned to fight."

Bent was a natural. Tall and muscular, he quickly learned the skills necessary to become a champion. He fought his first professional fight on July 13, 1952, against Jimmy Pollard in Belize City. "He must have been a teenager when he started boxing and fighting," Suzanne surmises. "He was a champion in Belize as a young teenager. He's a champion. He's in the Hall of Fame in Belize and Jamaica." In Belize, he fought Selvin Campbell, known as Satan Flynn and His Satanic Majesty. He also had memorable match-ups with Kid Barquerito (Emilio Sanchez) and Black Bill (Humberto Rejon).

Bent left Belize for Jamaica in 1955 to continue his career. Managed by Abe Ziadie, Bent was incredibly successful throughout the 1950s and 1960s, fighting such opponents as Pete Riccitelli, Roy Lee, Rupert Bentley, Sugar Boy Nando, and Sugar Ray Solomon. While at one of these fights, Rudolph Bent met Anita Mahfood, who had come to see the celebrated boxer. The two soon became a couple. When they had their first child in 1960, Suzanne Diane, it was only then that Rudolph married Anita. Two years later their son, Christopher Robin, was born. The family was not a happy one. According to Suzanne, "My dad was mean to my mom ... [and] to myself and my brother. He raped my mom.... That's the truth."

In November 1961, Rudolph Bent and fellow boxer Jimmy Beecham, also a middleweight, traveled to Peru and Colombia for bouts. Because Bent was frequently gone from their home, Anita was always on the move to try to get away from him. During the periods of time when he was gone it was calm and peaceful, but when he returned, the beatings returned as well. Norma Faye Chin, Anita's best friend, recalls, "What happened was she was married to a no-good, Bent, and he used to beat her a lot. When he used to hit her, she would take the kids when he was gone and she would bring them up to my house, in Harbor View, where I was living at the time. And she would leave the kids with me and she would come back days later or weeks later or months later because she was moving from place to place where he couldn't find her." The children also stayed with

Conchita from time to time. "When she divorced Rudolph Bent, the boxer, the children came and lived with us for a while," Sergi says.

Bent's boxing career lasted for many years, and luckily for Anita, he was frequently on the road. There were many times though when he fought in Kingston, typically at Sabina Park, challenging greats from around the world. In a letter to the *Daily Gleaner*, published Thursday, December 19, 1963, Rudolph Bent wrote the following challenge to a fellow boxer, coining his own nickname for himself, a nickname that now has a layered meaning.

> The Sports Editor Sir,
>
> Will you please grant me the favour of publishing this letter in reply to Hugh Serville's challenge.
>
> I guess that Hugh Serville should remember that we were to fight once but the promoter cancelled the match because the public protested against the match. Since then he has acted as my sparring partner on many occasions. Nevertheless, after I am crowned Middleweight Champion on February 1, 1964, I will be very happy to give him a fight, if only he can find a promoter to promote us, or if not I will be happy to fight him at any gym at any time.
>
> Rudolph Bent
> (The Dark Destroyer)
> (Welterweight Champion of B.H.)
> Kingston, December 16, 1963

In 1962 and 1963, Bent, the Dark Destroyer, fought almost exclusively in the United States, and it wasn't until 1964 that he returned to Jamaica for some bouts at the National Stadium in Kingston. Every time he returned, Rudolph Bent beat his wife and their children, a cycle of abuse he learned from his own mother, Rhoda Mejia. In addition to being a wife beater, Bent was, in his daughter's words, a "womanizer and he had been abusing my mother as well." There were some who had witnessed this abuse directly, like Emilio Sanchez, a fellow boxer and coach who shared the same address as the Bents. Herbie Miller recorded Sanchez's memory of the aftermath of one particularly brutal beating.

> One morning Margarita showed me some marks where Rudolph hit her. "Him beat me up, see, Ruddy beat me last night." But she was laughing like it was a good thing. I said, "Rudolph beat you and you just take it like that, laughing. Wha'happen, you like it?" But she just kept laughing like a mad woman. You know she sometimes acted like she was half mad. Margarita was a carefree girl, nobody could tame her.

Anita sought a divorce from Rudolph in 1964 and obtained a decree nisi, which is a legal waiting period so objections to the divorce can be heard. During this time, Rudolph took the children and had them sent to British Honduras to be raised by his mother. "He just put us on a plane with one of his girlfriends," says Suzanne. According to public records in the *Daily Gleaner*, the divorce was finalized in November 1964, although sister Conchita says it was final one week before Anita died.

By 1965, Bent's boxing career was starting to wane. Not only was he old for a fighter at this point, but he also likely had other things on his mind during an eventful year. An article in the August 30 issue of *Daily Gleaner* bore the headline "Lee beats Bent all the way."

> Tall, young Roy Lee became the new Jamaica middleweight champion at the National Stadium last Saturday night when he beat former holder Rudolph Bent in every one of 15 rounds for the title. But Bent, the tough old campaigner who said "don't write me off" before the fight, showed fighting instinct second to none in the local ring and went down the victim of gathering age rather than inferior skill. Lee was too fit, too young, and too strong for the former champion and starting with the second round when a savage right forced Bent to take the mandatory count of eight, the fight became a one-sided affair with Bent riding the numerous blows as his major defensive tool.

Perhaps Bent's most famous moment in his boxing career came on October 20, 1965, when, at the age of 33, he fought against Boxing Hall of Famer Sugar Ray Robinson in Robinson's final fight. Robinson, who was 45 years old at the time, won his 174th and final victory in a third-round knockout of Rudolph Bent in Steubenville, Ohio. Bent had just come off of a 13-fight losing streak when Robinson won. Robinson's purse for the fight was $500. It was not Bent's last fight, but his string of losses definitely signaled the end of his career. In 1972, having not won a single fight since 1965, Rudolph Bent lost his last bout. His career record was 39 bouts won, with 16 of those knockouts; 53 bouts lost, with 15 of those being knocked out; and four draws for a total of 97 fights and 776 rounds boxed.

Later in life he moved to the Bronx and became a houseman for the New York Hilton Hotel, doing cleaning, maintenance, and other general work before he retired with a gold plaque.

Suzanne says that her father (who turned 78 in 2011) suffers from "punch drunk disease," or dementia pugilistica, a neurodegenerative disease that affects boxers or other athletes who suffer routine concussions.

Rudolph Bent (© The Gleaner Company Limited).

Rudolph thinks he is 33 years old and that he is still married to Anita, but he is actually married to another woman who had 11 children, none by him. And Suzanne, a woman whose strength and compassion is beyond comprehension, cares for her father in his last years, despite his lifetime of abusing the family. "I just do the best I can," she says humbly.

7

Ska Authentic

Man hab cow him look fi milk.
— A Jamaican proverb meaning,
"He who pays the piper calls the tune."

Upside-down plastic pennants on a string connect rooftop to rooftop through every street in downtown Kingston. The morning's tropical deluge stops. The sun emerges and the airliner touches down at Palisadoes Airport. Princess Margaret, representing the Queen of England, and her husband, the Earl of Snowdon, appear from the plane, walk delicately down the wheeled stairs marked BOAC where they are greeted on the steamy tarmac by Prime Minister Alexander Bustamante in his top hat, and the governor, Sir Kenneth William Blackburne in his plumed helmet with ceremonial sword at his side. White gloved handshakes, camera flashes, and then a nonchalant hand in the air, greeting throngs of smiling faces as her car drives past. She feigns interest while donning her pink dress with white polka dots, strings of pearls, and bonnet of tulle flowers. At the National Stadium, in a demure voice full of grace and dignity, she tells the audience that the youth are the future of Jamaica. As midnight approaches, the spotlight on the Union Jack goes out and re-illuminates on the Jamaican flag. Fireworks proclaim to all around, this is an independent Jamaica. Things are different now. Three hundred years of British reign are over. It is an age of progress and prosperity. Out of many, one people.

On August 6, 1962, Jamaica finally became independent from Britain. It had been a long, but respectful, struggle against the colonizers. Aided by a new constitution in 1953 that brought more power to the island, establishing a chief minister and seven other ministers, Jamaican politics began to get a foothold on their own governance. In 1958, against their will, Jamaica became part of The Federation of the West Indies, a move that Britain had long wished to make, combining the Caribbean islands they colonized into one political unit. The islands of Jamaica, the Cayman

Islands, Turks and Caicos Islands, Barbados, Antigua and Barbuda, Saint Christopher-Nevis-Anguilla, Montserrat, Dominica, Saint Lucia, Saint Vincent and the Grenadines, Grenada, Trinidad and Tobago were now part of the West Indies Federation, a group of three million people.

Elections were held for the Federation in March of 1958. Jamaica's Norman Manley representing the People's National Party (PNP) and the newly formed West Indies Federal Labour Party (WIFLP), and Jamaica's Alexander Bustamante representing the Jamaica Labour Party (JLP) and the newly formed Democratic Labour Party of the West Indies (DLPWI), led their parties in the race. A small group of Trinidadians also formed a party and ran for seats in the parliament but did not win any. The Federation's parliament was then dominated by the WIFLP who won the majority of the seats in the election, and the prime minister of the Federation became Sir Grantley Adams from Barbados.

But the Federation was short lived. It only lasted from January 3, 1958, until May 31, 1962, because it was a group comprised of many islands, known as provinces, with their own cultures, their own political ideals, their own identities, and their own economies. It was a situation akin to struggles found today in the European Union which led to their debt crisis. In 1961, Jamaica put forth a referendum asking to be removed from the Federation, citing that other provinces in the Federation were draining their wealth, they had a disproportionate number of seats in parliament in relation to the population, Trinidad's capital Chaguaramas was the seat of parliament instead of Kingston, and the geographic location of Jamaica in relation to the other provinces was isolating. The nationwide referendum passed with 54 percent of the vote and Britain agreed to discuss the option of succession with Jamaica. Manley and Bustamante flew to England to meet and negotiate their independence, which was granted, a tale chronicled in the calypso-based Lord Creator tune "Independent Jamaica."

Jamaica had won their freedom. They were finally free. Free from the slave trade that wracked the country since the British inhabited the island in the mid–1600s and made their fortunes from the exploitation of men, women, and children brought from Africa; free from the political oppression of the British colonizers who controlled every facet of Jamaican life, from trade, to law, to development; free from the poverty that sent good men to the grave, or so they thought.

Jamaica was a hopeful place after independence, ignited by the promise of their potential. Huge celebrations took place all over the island as every Jamaican took to the street to dance and make merry with their fellow neighbors and strangers alike. They were all one people now. Banners and flags flew from the façades of every building. Women prepared feasts of rice and peas, ox tail stew, and ackee and saltfish, now the national dish. Parades snaked through the streets.

But life wasn't all that optimistic for those who called music their occupation. Despite night after night of packed houses in the nightclubs and virtual celebrity status in the music circuit, drawing a decent wage was tough for instrumentalists who had to split their take sometimes 10 or 15 ways with all of the performers on stage. Even those like Drummond who likely were promised a larger slice of the pie had hard times making ends meet. Plus, as the 1960s came to Jamaica, so did different musical trends as the island's transistor radios picked up frequencies from America's newly emerging rhythm & blues era. And Jamaica's own radio era was picking up steam as well as their broadcasting systems expanded island-wide.

Graeme Goodall came to the island of Jamaica in the 1950s, hired by Radio Jamaica Rediffusion (RJR), a commercial broadcasting company with stations throughout the British Commonwealth and specifically the British empire. Goodall had made a name for himself in England working for the International Broadcasting Company/Universal Program Corporation which produced programs for Radio Luxembourg and other independent recordings. Goodall, or Goody as he was affectionately known to his friends, took a position in Jamaica with RJR to engineer the island's first commercial FM service, which he did in 1954. "It was a time in Jamaica when you couldn't buy FM transmitters and we put it in basically as a studio transmitter link, an STL from Kingston, which is where the studios were, into Montego Bay," Goodall says. "It was a double hop across the island and it just worked out that it was a wonderful system and people started buying FM radios from the United States that were definitely better quality, and at the same time they had a network of amplifiers made by the parent company. So that is kind of how it all started."

It wasn't uncommon for a tenement yard landlord to have a transistor radio where yardies gathered around to hear the latest tunes from America. Artists like Jimmy Reed, Bill Doggett, Lloyd Price, Earl Hines, Nat King Cole, Billy Eckstine, Jesse Belvin, and the Moonglows were massively popular in the Kingston streets. The songs that came crackling through the radio, into the squalor of the zinc-walled yards, into the dormitories at

Alpha Boys School in clandestine nighttime listening sessions, into the homes where the domestics worked peeling cassava and washing floors, were doo-wop, toe-tapping tunes with a blues spine and a free-spirited feel.

Not only was American music popular on the radio, it was also popular at sound system dances. Throughout the 1950s and into the 1960s, sound system operators and their selectors, or deejays, played their records on hi-fis or more powerful systems, like the one built by Mutt and Jeff. One of the first sound system operators was Tom the Great Sebastian, or Tom Wong, who played his records at Slipe Road at the Torrington Bridge. Other operators included Nick the Champ, Count Smith the Blues Blaster, Bells, King Edwards, Skyrocket, V-Rocket, Admiral Comic, Prince Buster, and Lord Koo's the Universe. But the two most popular sound system operators were Clement Seymour Dodd, better known as Sir Coxsone, nicknamed after a famous British cricket player, or Downbeat, after the name of his sound system; and Arthur Reid, better known as Duke Reid or The Trojan, after the make of his imported kit van he used to shuttle his equipment.

Sound system operators like Coxsone and Duke Reid had one goal in mind from the start all the way through to the end of their career, and even beyond — make money. Coxsone and Reid, the two fiercest competitors who literally mashed it up over the rights to the crown, both had interest in drawing more business to their family's liquor stores. Get people to come listen to music and dance and you get them to drink, was the business model of their operation. Graeme Goodall says, "People don't realize that the sound systems were the ones who drove the whole record business and what drove the sound systems and the record business was literally every one of them were liquor distributors. If they could get the crowd in there they'd sell more liquor and that's where they made their money." And making sure people heard their music for miles around ensured they would flock to the yard, so speakers were strategically placed to project to the biggest space possible. The DJs who worked for the soundmen, such as Blackie who worked for Coxsone, were showmen, playing the crowd and dancing the coolest moves, such as shuffling their feet, smooth like an old school stepper, a different dance for each song.

Duke Reid was a tough man, a former Kingston police officer for ten years during a time of terrible police corruption. Reid and his wife, Lucille, owned a liquor store called Treasure Isle Liquors which they built after Lucille won the Jamaican lottery. In an effort to sell more liquor, Reid began hosting dances at the corner of Beeston Street and Pink Lane in the early days and then on Bond Street and Charles Street. Reid was flashy and attracted attention everywhere he went. He frequently wore a crown and a red cape trimmed in ermine, bandoliers crisscrossing his chest, and two guns at his side, a shotgun on his left hip and a .45 on his right hip. Sometimes he even arrived at his dances being carried aloft on a gilded throne by his posse. He was known to fire his guns into the air at his shows in a display of his prowess as well as when he liked a song. He was also known to occasionally play with a live grenade. He had a radio show on RJR called *Treasure Isle Time*, and on his shows, as well as at his dances, he always played the most current American hits he purchased on his trips to the United States.

The younger Coxsone Dodd, whose parents were good friends with Duke Reid, also had a family liquor store to promote at the corner of Love Lane and Beeston Street, and so he combined that effort with his love for jazz music that he developed at a young age. While working in his mother's restaurant located at Lawes Street and Ladd Lane called Nanny's Corner, which later turned into a liquor store, Coxsone heard his mother's radio play the biggest hits from America from the likes of Louis Jordan, Dizzy Gillespie, Charlie Parker, Fats Navarro, Sarah Vaughan, Lionel Hampton, and many others. When Coxsone traveled to the United States to pick sugar cane in the Southern states during the early 1950s, he returned with boxfuls of records, speakers, a turntable, and receiver that he shipped back to Kingston. Since he was also skilled as a carpenter, learning to build from his father who helped to construct the Carib Theatre and other theaters on the island, Coxsone built his own "Houses of Joy," or giant speakers for his Downbeat sound system. His sound was so popular that on any one night he would have up to four sound system dances in operation at different locations throughout Kingston.

Sound system dances were hugely popular with the masses who longed to escape the poverty and oppression that was rife in Kingston in the 1950s. When Duke Reid, Coxsone, or any number of sound system operators had their selectors spin the latest songs from America, hordes of people packed the indoor dancehalls, like the Cho Co Mo, Red Rooster, or the Pioneer, as well as open-air locations that were fenced in to contain the crowd. Whoever could attract the most people sold the most liquor and made the most money, period. DJs began toasting over the records to add flourishes to the music and entice people to the area, and Count Machuki was the first to demonstrate this skill. Count Machuki (Winston Cooper), began toasting for Tom "the Great" Sebastian and then came to work for Coxsone, punctuating the tunes with wisecracks, phrases, and vocalized peps or ska skat. Toasters served to attract and keep the crowd.

Competition was fierce, so fierce in fact that "representatives" from each sound system's entourage were known to raid the competitor's dance, destroy his equipment, and literally break the needle from his turntable. Groups of rude boys, or gangs of thugs, were also known to align themselves with a sound system operator and defend his turf from opposing rude boys. "They used to play contests among one another," says Derrick Morgan. Keeping the integrity of one's own musical selections was critical so the competitor's spies wouldn't also play the same song, stealing the crowds to attend their dance instead, selling their drinks to the paying people. Therefore, sound system operators scratched the names from the labels of their coveted songs typically using a coin, or better yet, they made songs, exclusive songs, one-offs, specials, all their own. But that new endeavor required a recording studio, and key to that process was Ken Khouri and Graeme Goodall at Federal Records, the recording studio utilized by all early producers before the Marley family bought the structure in 1981 and renamed it Tuff Gong Recording Studio.

After his three-year contract with RJR was up, Goodall left Jamaica to return to his native Melbourne where he worked in television for only four months before Jamaican administration phoned him, asking him to return to help them install a government broadcasting system — not as competition to Rediffusion, but as an adjunct. "They said, 'We need you back here to put it all in,'" Goodall recalls. "I flew PanAM back to Jamaica and worked for the Jamaica Broadcasting Corporation." He built a concert studio and even used his own intuition and creativity to advance the industry. "I converted the men's lavatory into an echo chamber, which was quite interesting," says Goodall. In addition, Goody built a "primitive studio," as he says, in the back of a furniture store on King Street, owned by Ken Khouri, who at that time was in a franchise business importing music from Mercury Records in the United States and bringing it to the island. Khouri previously had a record label, Times Records, which distributed calypso tunes. Goodall says, "The only other person who was making records at that time was Stanley Motta and you couldn't really call it making records, although I guess it was making records because he was cutting the record disc, but Ken Khouri wanted to do something a little bit better, so I advised him. He got a mic recorder, a tape recorder, some microphones and I threw a studio together for him and so he started making records. Ken Khouri and his wife, Gloria, they were the principal owners of Federal Records. Actually, it started off as Records Limited up on King Street.

"I remember when I said to Ken Khouri, 'We got a problem here. We've got to get some echo in here somehow.' He said, 'What does that require?' I said, 'Well I could design an echo chamber. I could modify the equipment,' which I did. I rebuilt a lot of it to make it a lot more professional and I said I'd design an echo chamber and tag it on the back there. He said, 'That sounds good.' All the walls were a different angle from one another. The Jamaicans that we got to build it refused totally to build it. And I remember one of them talking to Ken and they didn't figure that I could understand. They said, 'It's not right, Mr. Khouri, it's not right. We cyaan build it because all the walls dem different' [laughs]. I figured it all out, these guys were used to putting up walls vertical, floors and ceilings horizontal and everything at 90-degree angles from one another. And Ken said, 'I don't know what he's doing but trust me, you've got to do it his way.' So we built it that way and I think that was one of the primary things because when we started adding reverb it brought it into a completely different era. And that was the start of Federal Records."

It wouldn't be long until this studio was utilized by producers all over Kingston, but they weren't using the studios to rehash American rhythm and blues tunes. They were making music all their own, a music called ska. Bass player Lloyd Brevett says, "When we started, we never started in ska, we started in jazz. We were in separate bands in Jamaica. Big band, we started. I was fourteen when I started to play in a big band. It was jazz and ballads. We started to play rhythm and blues, but jazz was still with it. We started to change the beat. We started to play ska, but we never really name it. But we play ska. Guitar, 'ska, ska, ska.' One guy come to the studio used to say, 'What'up, Skavoovie?' That guy was Cluet Johnson, bass player, joking guy. 'Wha'up, Skavoovie?' He came there so regular and talk Skavoovie, that together with the guitar, 'ska, ska, ska,' that name the music ska. Yeah. That is it."

Sound system operators like Coxsone and Reid soon saw their opportunity and they added another title to their name — producer. It was cheaper to get records from the island's wealth of talent instead of traveling to the United States, plus it was popular with the people who longed for their own identity as a culture. Laurence Cane-Honeysett writes,

The transformation from promoters to creators was one of necessity, rather than any overriding ambition to produce records. The shuffling style of raw American Rhythm & Blues favoured by Jamaican audiences was fast becoming obsolete, a trend that contributed significantly to the scarcity of "exclusives"—records so obscure operators could almost lay claim to them as being their own. In such an environment there was little option but for men such as Dodd to begin producing their own "specials." The local club and hotel circuit provided a ready-made pool of talent from which entrepreneurs could cherry-pick suitable musicians, while frequent talent contests gave a platform for up-and-coming singers.

Producers combed the clubs for talent, like Don Drummond, enticing them with the promise of more work. But Coxsone made an offer of more than just pay to Drummond. During the days that Drummond performed on stage at clubs, he never made enough money to buy his own expensive trombone; instead, he always rented or borrowed someone else's. Coxsone bought Drummond a new trombone, but of course, took the cost out of Drummond's pay. Drummond and other instrumentalists were paid by the day, by the hour, for their musical occupation. No royalties were offered in those days. But money needed to be made, so musicians like Don Drummond began a new phase of their careers. Vin Gordon says, "In Studio One we used to work so hard. We used to do about fifty or forty songs for the day. All these people from all over Jamaica came down there. They came down and audition on a Sunday and then Mr. Dodd would say, 'You come tomorrow, you come tomorrow,' and five or six of them would come tomorrow and they'd get Jackie Mittoo to make the bass line and he'd tell you what to play and he'd just get these guys on the track, you know? We used to do forty songs a day, and it was disciplined. We'd have to punch a clock to come in and we used to punch a clock to go out, because Coxsone Dodd was very smart. He wanted us to be like family there, that's why the music sound this way today from Studio One. Coxsone wanted everybody to be a family so he made sure he pay us salary. He treat you like you working in a factory. That's why he get so much music because he wanted to know that your mind was on the music. You work Monday, you work Tuesday, Wednesday you take off, Thursday you come back, you pick up your pay on a Friday, you don't work on Friday. No royalties. He didn't give us any royalty. Nothing at all. That's a bad thing, too. That's very bad 'cause so many songs I did and I don't get royalties for them because I was so young and I didn't know, I didn't know. So many songs. I was a little boy then. It was hard but it was a learning point, still."

The producers' studios were very much a factory, churning out song after song to attract crowds to the dancehalls where the crowds craved hit music. Carlos Malcolm says, "You see, between the end of WWII in 1945, when the U.S. armed forces withdrew from Jamaica, and 1960, when children born during the war years became teenagers now craving American blues from New Orleans which flourished in Jamaica during the war years, Jamaican producers turned to covers of American blues and other recordings to supply the demands of the market, blatantly ignoring copyright restrictions. Sound system record producers flooded the seven-inch RPM 45 records market. Much of the Jamaican early ska music repertoire consists of instrumentals that are mostly covers of American and other popular music."

Goodall says that producers like Coxsone and Reid used the studios at Federal Records because it was the only one around in the early days and at Federal they could have an acetate cut quickly for a dance that night. "There are no other engineers, there are no other facilities," he states. "There was no Studio One studio. Eventually Downbeat did actually build a studio, but that was well into it and he only really built it because Duke Reid wanted to build one too." Studio One at 13 Brentford Road, which had a one-track board, didn't open until October 1963. Duke Reid's recording studio didn't open until 1966. Until then, both producers used Federal Records like the rest and used their prior locations as audition space and for liquor sales. Producers in those early days were like film producers — they sponsored the production, organized those involved to make it happen, and paid for it up front to reap the rewards on the back end for the life of the song since there was no such thing as royalties or artist copyrights. Goodall continues: "At Federal Records they came because here was a place where they could walk in with an artist, and originally the session people were the Caribs, and they hung around for a long time, but then it was people like Stanley Notice, Ribs; Drumbago on drums; Jah Jerry; 'Easy Snappin'' Theophilus Beckford on piano; Charley Organaire on harmonica; Lester Sterling on tenor sax; Rico Rodriguez on trombone; Don Drummond on trombone; Baba Brooks on trumpet — so all these musicians built up a nucleus of studio musicians and it was funny, they tended to get into their days and I can't remember what day it was, but let's say Duke Reid was Tuesdays, Coxsone was Wednesday, maybe Smith 'Hi-Lite' was on Monday, Lloyd the Matador was on Thursday, that sort of thing. They came in on their particular days to cut discs and everything was left to me because they could pick a tune with a vocalist but I was the one who had to go in and talk to the vocalist about how they would sing and how they would project."

Vocalist Owen Grey says that Don Drummond performed for his hit song, "On the Beach," which was recorded for Coxsone in 1959. It was Drummond's first recording. Grey recalls, "He had played for a few records for me when I was with Studio One. He played all songs I did for Studio One. The biggest song that Don Drummond plays on, and if he was alive he would tell about it, the best solo on a record, that instrumental, the best solo that he did was mine and it's called 'On the Beach,' for Studio One, 1959. Lester Sterling took a part of the solo and he [Drummond] took the second part." While "On the Beach" was the first song Drummond played on for Coxsone, Drummond's first solo single was "Don Cosmic," a song named after Coxsone's moniker for Drummond.

Grey describes Drummond's creative process for "On the Beach" and explains how recording was very different than today's advanced technologies. "So I was sittin' with him because of the little bit of musical knowledge I had from Alpha. I do a little bit of keyboards at that time. There was a place called Champion Hill and that's where we used to rehearse. Now for Studio One, before you go into a studio you have to rehearse so it takes up no time because in them time you got two track or one track. You can't lay no tracks and come back. You got to do it direct. Not like now — you lay down a track and you go over it and go over it because there are so many tracks you have to play around with it, but there weren't all those tracks back in those times, so you got to be in it to win it. And I was hummin' something in a musical theme for the solo and Don Drummond says, 'Listen, just listen to this.' And I listen to him, he's a very knowledgeable boy, and when he finish his solo part, he play '*da da da da a dum, da da da da dum dum dum....*' It was beautiful and he always say it was the best solo he has ever taken on a record, and that's 'On the Beach.'" Grey's lyrics even give credit to the man behind the curtain, Coxsone. "I was dancing to the music of Sir Coxsone Downbeat, on the beach," sings Grey.

Rico Rodriguez says that Drummond did a lot of work over the years for Coxsone: "He used to record with Coxsone, a lot of recording for Coxsone. They have a good relation." But Drummond had mixed feelings about this change in his career, says Rodriguez. In Lloyd Bradley's article, "The Graduates," Rodriguez says that "Don Drummond wasn't so keen to play with the bands. You play music like Stan Kenton, Lionel Hampton,

Basie. He know it's okay for earning, but not for developing. When Coxsone was recording, because he know Don was a good musician he look for him, and Don wasn't so happy about that either—he thought they were just trying to use him because of his ability. He didn't enjoy all those recordings he did, that's why so many of his compositions and his solos sound sad or mournful—they're all minor keys. It wasn't music like he and I used to play every day. We'd play melody and harmony, his own compositions and songs he used to write off songs, like 'Old Black Magic' and 'Night and Day' in his style. It was progressive jazz. That's what he felt he should be doing, not playing stock arrangements."

"People don't realize, but the trombone in the end was bought by Coxsone," says Goodall. "I remember vividly a session when Don was acting up and Coxsone went and took the horn away from him and said, 'It's my horn. It's my horn,' and Don was almost in tears. 'Let me play.' And Coxsone said, 'Listen, I'll tell you when I want you to play and what I want you to play, it's my horn.' And Don finally realized there was no point in just hanging around, he needed to blow his horn and he behaved himself for Coxsone."

Coxsone's demands came from his desire to make money. A hit ska record could sell as many as 50,000 copies. It was a booming success. But time equals money, especially in a rented recording studio, and with the goal of getting 10 to 15 sides down in a day, musicians and engineers had to get it right. Recording in only one take was critical and the recording studios did no editing in those days. They simply didn't have the technology or the equipment, and the artists were there for one reason — to produce. "The magical thing about those days was," recalls Charles Cameron, the harmonica player known as Charley Organaire, "it was a mystical thing with us, man, because most of these songs that we recorded then, we learned that right there in the studio and we ran that thing down once, maybe twice, and the next time it ran through it's recording because you hear it and you memorize the chord conversion. Sometimes there are things that happen where I would say it is somewhat mystical because we, between nine o'clock and five o'clock, we would do about fifteen cuts. Because we got paid by the side. We got two pounds a side. It was paid in sterling at the time because the British were ruling then. No royalties. They know what they wanted, so they selected the artist and they selected the song. They select and we played."

Drummond frequently was told by the producers what they wanted him to play. They were the ones paying the cash for the work and they demanded a certain kind of product. Carlos Malcolm, trombonist, band-leader, and musician extraordinaire, recalls one of the times that Drummond was given such an assignment by Coxsone and he chose to make it his own: "I can remember on one occasion that really gave me a view into where music was created in those times, where it was actually going. There was such a demand for new music by the operators because they operate with new music every week because it is a measure of what they are going to take in at the gate because the people not hear it before they go to the dances. We stopped at the South Camp Road bus stop which is half way between both our homes. We used to stop there and converse and then I turn back and go home and he leave into Allman Town. And he said to me, 'I have a session tomorrow with Coxsone and he want me to do a few tunes. Do you know this tune?' And he started humming this tune. I said, 'Oh yes, that's the "Trolley Song" from *Meet Me in St. Louis*, the Judy Garland song.' And he says, 'Well Coxsone want me to record it.' And then I hadn't seen him for about a week and then one morning I turn on the radio and I heard this trombone, and when I heard the trombone, the first few parts, I said, 'Oh, that's Drommie.' We used to call him Drommie. I said, 'That's Drommie.' And then I began to get a glimpse of the melody. (Sings) 'Ding ding ding went the trolley,' but it was slow. That is recorded at about one hundred twenty beats per minute. This one drop right down to about eighty. It wasn't until they reach the bridge of the tune that I realize it was the 'Trolley Song.' And why I didn't recognize this was the chords were all wrong, but I could hear him on the melody. And I said, 'Well, well, well.' Then I realized this guy was an unusual person. He had taken the thing completely out of its composed context and put it into a new format that I barely recognized it. It turned out to be one of the great Drummond hits that people associate him with and it is called 'Further East.'"

But when Drummond could write without the input of others, and even the times when he did work on assignment, he was deeply influenced not only by the American rhythm and blues stations picked up on the island, but the Radio Havana Cuba, which began broadcasting internationally in 1961. The influence of Cuban music on Drummond's repertoire, culled from radio as well as from fellow musicians Tommy McCook, Roland Alphonso, and Rico Rodriguez who were either born in Cuba or had Cuban lineage, is evident in the titles of some of Drummond's songs, like "Fidel Castro," and in the flavor of others, like "Don D Lion."

Drummond was incredibly prolific during this time in the studio. Carlos Malcolm says, "Drummond's present discography is just of portion of a small 'library' of originals he would share occasionally. The pieces were scribbled on pencil-drawn musical clefs in a blue-covered exercise notebook with the portrait of Queen Elizabeth on the back and mathematical time tables on the inside back cover." Every day the studio was open for work and even though contracts with producers were signed by instrumentalists, promising to do exclusive work for that producer alone, they were never honored. Whoever paid got the work. Vocalist BB Seaton recalls his time in the studio with Don D: "One of my favorite songs is a song called 'Green Island.' I remember when they were playing that, and a song called 'Far East' you know that's a classic song. Sometimes Coxsone give each song a title, sometime Don did, but I think that 'Far East' was a song that Don actually gave the title to. Songs like 'Guns of Navarone' he played as well, but that was a cover song, right? But he wrote a lot of instrumentals, 'Confucius,' many of them," Seaton says. One of the biggest hits at the sound system dances was Don Drummond's "Man in the Street."

Herman Sang, a piano player during the early days in Jamaican music, remembers Don Drummond and other session musicians in the studio. He says that there were many studios recording at the time and most of the songs were improvised on the spot: "These guys were professionals. I remember a session we did, the Jiving Juniors, 'Over the River,' we did 'Oh Pretty Girl,' 'Sugar Dandy' was done later on. At the end of each recording session, I don't know if you're familiar with this Jamaican word or phrase, *brawta*? *Brawta* means that somebody is going to give you a little extra, alright? So Coxsone would say, 'Okay, give me a couple of instrumentals,' and it was nothing we would rehearse or anything like that. I started a riff and the horn man would come over and play the riff and then they would play the melody, the solos, and then back into the riff, and that's how a lot of the instrumental songs were done. You'd have, way back in the ska days, 'Eastern Standard Time,' 'Man in the Street,' 'Guns of Navarone' was later on, 'Milk Lane Hop,' 'Occupation,' 'Ball of Fire,' all of it came out of sessions like that, right?" Karl "Cannonball" Bryan concurs, "Most of the time we just improvise. The guy who create the song maybe he tell you what he want you to play and you have to play that, or else you just come in with something and he say, 'Keep that.' In those days they say, 'Take one,' and the red light came on and the music was free.

"Maybe I should explain what a session looked like. Coxsone had a piano down the road. His mom had a bar and we'd have auditions and we'd audition about ten singers in a day, and then with Coxsone we get together and choose who was right for the studio. And that was on a Tuesday and the studio session might be on a Wednesday or a Thursday. I remember, Bob's kids kid me about it now, but we actually turned down Bob [Marley]. The group at that time was just one of many groups around, right? He didn't have any of his hits yet. We turned him down but another session he came back and he sang 'Simmer Down.' Depending on who could come into the studio and who wasn't working, the core group was all those horn men. On guitar we had Jah Jerry, and before Lloyd Knibb joined the group we had Drumbago. And that core group played for most of the other producers because during that period Duke Reid had to start doing some recordings because Coxsone had some songs that he couldn't play. Coxsone alone had them. That was the thing during that period. Coxsone actually wasn't thinking of producing the records, he was just playing off of his own sound system and it developed after that. And so we had Beverley's Leslie Kong, he was another producer and Derrick Morgan, we used to do some sessions with Derrick Morgan, Desmond Dekker — 'Shantytown,' 'Israelites,' Toots & the Maytals. Prince Buster, he had a little feud going with Derrick Morgan — 'Hard Man Fe Dead,' 'One Hand Wash the Other,' 'Judge Dread,' 'Wash Wash,' and of course, 'Oh Carolina.' I do all those sessions. Nobody wrote any parts, actually. We didn't do rehearsals. I wrote down the name of the song, the key they were playing in, I wrote down a couple of the chord progressions, but when we went into the studio themselves, sometimes some of the singers would sing an introduction which the horn player would play, or guitar player would play, but most of the times there was no intro and it would jump right into the drum beat and right into the song. So during a rehearsal right before the cut, the horn people would come up with the backing. Nobody actually sat down and wrote anything. We would improvise right there and then. Sometimes ten or fifteen singers for the day, and at the end about three or four songs were instrumentals."

According to Sang, after the songs were recorded in the studio, they then made records at Federal Records so the producers could play the tunes on their sound systems or, in the case of Duke Reid, on his radio show. Sang says, "After the session I would go back in Coxsone's van. We actually

Don Drummond with Coxsone Dodd at Studio One (© The Gleaner Company Limited).

stayed after the session and some musicians stayed back with us, so Graeme Goodall did what they called a soft wax. It's a vinyl LP-sized disc and that was used for making the master. So all the songs we did for that day were put on this disc and Coxsone was able to take it if he was playing at a dance that night and everyone would hear it. We would discuss and talk about the songs while driving back home and Coxsone would tell me about Don because he had more dealings with him at first."

Saxophonist Headley Bennett, O.D., says that Drummond was the best instrumentalist for Coxsone, performing on hit after hit: "Oh Lordy, he was one of the number one at Studio One. We used to record together, both of us at Studio One. He used to write the arrangement and he said, 'Play this?' and I said, 'Sure,' but he gave me the trombone part to play off. He gave me the trombone part but I didn't know how to play off the trombone part and I used to play a third below the trombone, and that was alto and I could read the music. I was fortunate to play on about three of his songs, one of them named 'Man [in] the Street,' and 'Garden of Love' and more. He used to just tell us what to do. He conduct the rhythm and the horn section and he give us sheet music to read. If you play it and you don't play it right he took the music from you and go to another level. He didn't talk much. He just stare at the music and that way you don't bother him." According to musicologist Vaughn "Bunny" Goodison, O.D., Drummond may have given those sheets of music to others to play, but he himself never used them. "He gives them the music, but he has none," Goodison recalls. "He plays around them. That's how bright his mind."

Almost anyone who ever played with Drummond or met Drummond has a similar recollection — he was quiet. He didn't talk much. Ken Stewart, manager for the Skatalites, agrees: "Everybody used to say the same thing about him, that if you didn't talk about music then he really didn't have anything to talk about. He was not a conversationalist or small talker. He would not sit there and shoot the shit with you. If you wanted to talk about music, then fine, but other than that, maybe money. Yeah, he was a big stickler about his pay, I know that. There was some kind of altercation between him and Tommy because he used to get paid right after the money came out and he was very conscious of money."

Grey recalls that when Drummond was in the studio it was strictly business, so there was really no chance to get to talk or vibe off one another or get personal. That kind of music was left for other places, like the Wareika Hills. "He's in the studio when you go to the studio, tunin' up his trombone," says Grey. "He don't talk much." Jo Jo Bennett concurs that Drummond wasn't much for talking, and that he could be difficult: "He got hooked up with this record producer, Sir Coxsone. He was the one that got ska music really going in Jamaica and live music players, especially horn players. I run into Don in the studio now and then. Every time the producer call on him to take a solo he would kind of hesitate and then in about two or three minutes say, 'Okay, I'm going to do it.' He was kind of stubborn, too, you know? Instead of doing his solo, he just pack up his horn and leave. He wasn't really a people person. He stay by himself, a strictly loner. A good loner." Marcia Griffiths, member of the I-Threes and solo vocalist, says, "Don Drummond used to be at the studio, same place where I used to record. Don Drummond was exceptionally talented. He wasn't a person that spoke a lot but often times he would hail me and come to the studio, do whatever he has to do, and he's gone. He wasn't a man that talk a lot. He just did what he had to do. He was very, very different, you know?"

Even though musicians during this time played in the halls and studios, they also continued to perform on their own. One such site of musical congregation was at Bridgeview, the title of a now-famous song by the Skatalites. Professor Carlos T. Escoffery of the University of West Indies recalls his days as a child at this hot spot: "It was a popular hangout on Sundays, and if one wanted to be seen and heard in Kingston on a Sunday afternoon, Bridgeview was the place to be! A bar across the road used to be patronized and music came from its jukebox, or sometimes from a little sound system that someone might set up. It was something else. On any given Sunday, almost any Jamaican singer or entertainer, especially those based in eastern or central Kingston, would 'pass through' — even the Don himself. To tell you the truth though, Don D. was a bit reclusive and strange and wasn't as gregarious as most of the other musicians of the time. I used to see him walking up and down the place, always in his characteristic felt hat. I have never seen him without a hat! He had on his characteristic 'banlon' shirt, and often with his trombone, which he rarely seemed to be without. The most I ever got out of him when I said, 'Hi Don D.,' which he was commonly called, was 'Hail, youth!' And that was a long conversation for him! In fact my mother used to scold me and warn me not to go near him as everyone knew that he was a madman!"

Drummond's episodes of despondency became more and more frequent, and many of his fellow musicians say they started to see him change from just being quiet, into something more serious, something strange. Good friend Winston Smith says, "He was the only musician that I ever saw who came to the bandstand with his instrument in the case all put together, sat down in front of everybody, open the case, take out the instrument, dissect it, pull the chamois from his pocket, shined the parts one by one, put them back together, got up and walked away without playing a note. Most of the times, it was my job to go bring him back. Some of the times, I wasn't able to. But there are the times when he would go through the same ritual and when he got to the part where he would put his lips together and made that funny wiggle, you knew he was going to blow."

BB Seaton also recalls some unusual episodes while recording with Drummond: "I remember one day we were in the studio and they were doing an instrumental and I went into the console room with Coxsone and when Don Drummond had to take his solo, his hand was moving, pushing the instrument, you know, the way you play a trombone, but there was no sound coming from the trombone. So Coxsone started to look at the board and checked some wires to see if something was wrong and he tried and tried and nothing happened so eventually he went inside and he saw Don Drummond was just moving the horn. He was not blowin' to get any sound from it. We burst out in laughter. We were shocked. This is the great Don Drummond."

Sometimes Don Drummond would disappear and Coxsone would send others to look for him and bring him back to record. Sparrow Martin remembers that Drummond was very productive in the studio but there were times he just vanished: "He start working at Studio One and he work at Duke Reid, the Trojan, and he played there sometimes and do recording. But he would play and would go away, sometime for days, and he would come back. But when Don play, everyone came. He would just come in and start to play and the musicians start to file in until they stop. And he would do recording."

Graeme Goodall remembers similar episodes in the recording studio: "I always knew Don as a session musician. He was very difficult and, remember, I'm trying to get this put down on a tape so it can be recovered and put down on a disc. And Coxsone and his man Bim Bim, Allan, they knew what went out would probably be successful in the sound system. Don worked almost exclusively with Coxsone. But I had a lot of trouble sort of getting him to understand me, and I had a lot of trouble getting to understand him. I remember Don had a solo in this particular song and I was in the control room and there was nothing coming out. I looked around and there's Don in the corner blowing his horn into the corner, turned around facing the back into the wall, and so I stopped the recording and I said, 'Don, this is where I want you blowing the horn, into this microphone here. I can't hear you. I know it's going to be good, but I can't hear,' and I'm getting frustrated. He didn't say a word but he gave me a strange look. The others said, 'Yeah, that's Don. That's Don.' Tommy McCook is saying, 'Goody say 'ere, he want you to blow solo into 'ere,' so, okay, we started all again, and Don is playing into the bass line and, of course, we used the bass line as a rhythm orientation, and so it came the time for the solo and nothing happened, and I looked and Don Drummond had opened the door and gone up the passageway and was playing in the passageway. It was his way of saying, 'I'll play when and how and where I like,' and that's the sort of thing that went on." Sparrow Martin says, "When [Drummond] gets upset he would just pack his instrument and leave. Pack his instrument and walk away."

Herman Sang recalls Drummond's unusual behavior as well, but says it may have been the trombonist's attempt at self-medication. "I didn't have a chance to meet Don other than when he came to the studio," Sang admits. "He was withdrawn, if that's the right word. He kept to himself, but whenever he was ready to play, he jumped right in. Whenever we were doing the instrumentals, he would come over to the piano and he'd ask me to play a rhythm then he would start playing the trombone melody part. If he didn't like it, he would say, 'How about trying this?' I noticed that he had this brown bag, a paper bag with something that looked like a one-pint little bottle and he would bring it and put it beside the piano, like on the ground where the piano was. And whenever we had a break he would come over and open the bag and nobody really knew what it was. Maybe it was an energy drink! (laughs) But I always remember that."

According to Drummond's "After Care" record at Alpha Boys School, a note is made in April 1961 that he "has not been mentally well, but is recovering gradually. Plans to continue music." Saxophonist Herman "Woody" King says that Drummond's recovery came because he began seeking medical attention for his bouts of mental illness. Drummond first committed himself to Bellevue in 1960 for a three-month stay. King says that Drummond's difficulties started during a fundamental time in his life: "When it got to the time when he first went in Bellevue, they started making local recordings, making recordings of local music, one of the promoters went in there and got him to get him in the studio, which was Coxsone Downbeat. Coxsone got him out, bought him a horn and then he started turning out local songs and he start to get back some more respect. But in 1955 there was this great saxophone player named Wilton Gaynair and they used to play together in bands, but Gaynair was migrating to England. He receive some money and he had been in music longer than Don. He was an older person. In those days you could just buy a passage on a ship from Jamaica to England. You don't even have to have a visa or stuff like that. Don didn't have that type of money. If he had been able to migrate at that time, he would have been a world-class musician. But after Gaynair left, Don had to stay here and face the situation, which was getting less and less work, the electronic sound system coming stronger, so that was a crucial time in his life."

And when Drummond returned to his career after his stints in Bellevue, he returned with the same level of expertise and proficiency, delighting crowds and reviewers alike. Dermot Hussey in his radio show *Requiem to Don Drummond*, which aired on RJR in 1969, features Coxsone Dodd's recollection of his first meeting with Don Drummond:

> When I first met Don Drummond person to person, close up, at Federal Records, I was in my session. He came into the audition for my session as a vocalist. What he had to sing wasn't really ready for commercial purpose but I heard at that time that he really had some musical inclination. I hadn't realized that it was Don Drummond, really, that I had known and seen on stage at places like the Carib. Well after speaking to him I realized who the person was and that he had been in Bellevue and he was seeking some form of acceptance in the field, so I then thought of getting him a trombone to see if he had that sort of stuff that I heard at the Carib Theater early, maybe a couple of years before. Well, I got me a trombone and gave it to him and found out he was in perfect musical condition. As a matter of fact, he seemed happiest playing his music with his instrument in hand.

Hussey reviewed a performance that Drummond gave during a Sunday jazz concert at the Lucas Inn in 1962 after returning to the stage from a Bellevue stay. In his column, "Jazz Beat" for the *Jamaica Gleaner* Hussey wrote,

> It was also the return of the masterly trombonist Don Drummond and during the course of the afternoon and evening, he could be heard in every conceivable sort of tune and mood.... Carlos Malcolm and Drummond in the company of Cecil Lloyd, piano, performed several numbers that were striking for their unflagging warmth and intelligence. Malcolm, nerved by the presence of Drummond, by and large was in springy form, and rarely did he ever fall back on his stockroom of phrases.

Carlos Malcolm says that Drummond's condition was not mental illness but the result of struggling to make a living: "I hope you are not fishing to say he was crazy or anything. You hear all kinds of stories, and I just chuckle. That was not his character. He was just a reserved person. A lot of guys didn't realize what went on in his mind. If he was mad, he was mad meaning angry. He was angry with not receiving after putting in so many hours of practice and practice and perfecting his art. He then goes to the studio and they offer him a few dollars for his recording, which is what's happening in that timeframe."

And Coxsone was so desperate to make money off of musicians like

Drummond that he frequently drove to Bellevue Mental Hospital, where Drummond checked himself in for help, and retrieved him to record for the day. BB Seaton recalls, "Don Drummond played on my first record I sung, and it's a track called 'Only You.' And it was a magnificent solo, and it was being played in the dance hall over and over. And everybody used to fight, and by fight I don't mean physical fights, you know, to get Don Drummond to play on their sound. And that's how he was. He was a guy who had been trained. Most of the time we were going to get him to do some work, I'm talking about in the sixties, we used to go down and get him from the asylum. We used to drive the van and go pick him up. He was classified as mad, so to speak. Many people didn't understand him but I think he was a fantastic musician and he used to write most of his songs that he came into the studio with, on his music sheets and everything, so the other musicians could participate and play the track. Clement Dodd would pick him up in his van he drove. Coxsone was a guy who drove his van all of the time." Seaton never interacted with Drummond in the studio though and says he was "very very very quiet. He used to wear a hat and he used to put it on the back of his head when he was playing."

But Drummond's mental condition was likely something very serious. His behavior became very erratic and Derrick Morgan recounts one time in the early '60s when Drummond performed in a resort town two hours north of Kingston: "I know once he and I were working together in Port Antonio and he was playing for The Sheiks band. He used to play in The Sheiks band. And when The Sheiks start playin' the rhythm for him to start blow, he didn't blow. There was something wrong. He take off his spectacles and put it down and start wee wee on the stage. He start pee from the stage instead of blowin'. That show that his head wasn't that good. He urinate on the stage instead of blowin'. I remember that."

Malcolm says that Drummond's difficulty came from not being able to play the sorts of songs he wanted to play. Even though he could compose to a degree, it was ultimately the producer who had a say in what was made and what was paid. "He had reached a level of proficiency that his environment could not contain him and I think he was disappointed and disillusioned at the fact that he created all this stuff and didn't have the resources to record it," Malcolm theorizes. "He was actually at the mercy of people like Coxsone, the sound system operator and impresario. Whenever he went to the studio he used to have a little book in his back pocket, and if he didn't have a manuscript he would draw five lines and notate whatever he had composed. And when he get to the studio, Coxsone would say, 'Well I pay for this studio, you will play what I tell you,' and he would. Coxsone would record Mongo Santamaria and put in an introduction and call it 'Jack Rabbit,' but it was actually composed and written by Mongo Santamaria. He just change the name of an already-created work and that is really how most of Jamaican music is redone already-created material, because there are so few original creators of music. The Johnny Cash recording 'Ring of Fire' got to Jamaica in late 'sixty-three and Clement Dodd included it in one of his studio sessions in early 'sixty-four and renamed it 'Music Is My Occupation.' 'Latin Goes Ska' was actually a mambo composition, named and recorded as 'Patito e Che' by the great Cuban 'Rey Del Mambo,' Damaso Perez Prado."

Even though Drummond was difficult, the product was stellar, so producers like Coxsone and other musicians dealt with his eccentricities and Drummond reinterpreted the demands of the producers into his own sound. "I planned a session that we started by doing mostly instrumental," says Dodd. "I got him to sign a contract for musical backing and solo works and that lasted for six or nine months. Then at that time he got goofy again and went back into Bellevue. He spent about, I'm not too certain, nine months or a year, but on his return he seemed to be in normal condition because when he is in the right mood he is more jolly. On Don's second return from Bellevue we thought of making an instrumental and named it 'That Man Is Back,' [also labeled as 'This Man Is Back']."

Goodall says, "Don was anything but friendly to me and for years I always thought that it was the 'white man' syndrome. I thought he was being difficult with me because I am white. Then, in later years, I realized that he was like that to virtually everyone, including the other session men. He was difficult with the other musicians, the producers, and that was just him. Thankfully when I did get it, it was great. There's no argument about that. When he got to do something and lay it out on tape, it was absolutely out of this world. Whether Don would turn up for a session or not, that was another thing. But I didn't have to worry about that. That was the producer that had problems with that. But Don was a loner, an absolute loner. If you looked in his eyes or looked in his face you could tell he was a loner. Even with the other musicians he was completely isolated. They respected him but he had an attitude towards the world. When the musicians come together and they take a break underneath the guinep tree outside and talk to one another, Don was always out in left field. It was almost like he had no common ground with them. I can picture him now even though it's been fifty years. Rico left and other musicians, they traveled up to Canada, Miami, but Don was locked in."

Did Drummond's mental struggles prevent him from traveling to realize his full potential? No advertisements for Drummond's performances appear in the *Daily Gleaner* from 1957 to 1961. Could this be due to the advent of the recording industry? Possibly, but it could also be a reflection of Drummond's mental struggles and subsequent hospitalizations. In 1962, a "Benefit Jazz Show" was held for Don Drummond at the Regal Theatre to help support him and his return.

Even though Drummond wasn't able to leave the island to pursue his career or bond with musicians in the studio on a personal level, he did join with fellow musicians in an effort to have more creative liberties. He may have been motivated by the promise of having a little more to show for his talents, a little more than meager pay at the end of the day. He may have wanted a little piece of the recognition he deserved, the headlines, the airlines, the chance to live without struggling for once, like those artists from America enjoyed, the J.J. Johnsons and the Frank Rosolinos. In May 1964, Don Drummond became part of the most talented group of musicians ever to have played on the island. Don Drummond was a member of The Skatalites. But his mental difficulties continued to plague him, and in fact, with self-medication techniques and the rudimentary treatments offered at the hospital, his condition only became worse.

8

This Man Is Back

He takes his trombone from its case, pulls the chamois from the back pocket of his khaki pants. He tenderly strokes the bell of his horn, moving the cloth back and forth with enough pressure and fervor to take the tarnish from the brass. Over and over, he rubs the smooth curves, glides long and hard over the trombone's slide. Finally satisfied with the glistening finish, he slips his brimmed hat to the back of his head, flips the chamois over, closes his eyes and wipes the sweat from his brow. "I'm ready to play," he says.

Prepared to make their own way, the Skatalites formed in May 1964 after years of playing together, on stage, and in the studio. They had played as session musicians for Coxsone Dodd, for Duke Reid, for Prince Buster and others, and now they would try it together to see if any more recognition and money could come their way. They were a group of the most talented musicians the island had ever seen, each a master of his own instrument. Bandleader Tommy McCook's name may have appeared on the front of each bandstand when they played, as Tommy McCook and the Skatalites, but he was merely the group's organizer and the group's administrator of sorts, and each of the group's musicians was equally a leader in aptitude and ability, each a virtuoso.

Skatalites drummer Lloyd Knibb says, "We used to play in a big band on Coney Island, a twelve-piece, fourteen-piece band and we was all together in the same group all the time. We were a certain set of musicians, a certain set. We knew everything that happened and go from band to band, go from one group to the next group, to the next, same set of band."

Skatalites saxophonist Lester Sterling recalls the days when the band first came together. He says that the group was formed due to discontentment: They were tired of playing cover tunes for wealthy tourists; they were tired of putting twists on calypso and show tunes; they were tired of generating compositions that weren't inspired by what they listened to —

jazz and drums from the hills and innovative music. Sterling says, "When we reach teenage days, we all meet, young musicians, talkin' and make arrangement to practice together. We have jam sessions. Don Drummond was there back then. Don Drummond used to play with us as a kid, and Roland, Jah Jerry, Ernest Ranglin, all these practiced. This group of guys used to meet and talk about jazz. We weren't the guys that talk about calypso. We talk about jazz. And we talk about jazz bands."

The Skatalites' first official gig was at the Hi-Hat Club in Rae Town. They later performed at many clubs around Kingston, such as the Silver Slipper Club, the Yacht Club, Club Havana, the Blinking Beacon, Wicky Wacky, and the Sombrero Club. They also performed throughout Jamaica, at clubs in Montego Bay, such as the Wooden Spoon, Cellar Club, and the Embassy Club, and 18 miles away, in Falmouth, at Good Hope and Club Calypso. But they had a residency at the Bournemouth Club in south Kingston, performing regularly on Wednesday, Friday, and Saturday nights, as well as at the Orange Bowl on Sunday nights. Dancers from the circuits — like Pam Pam, Madame Pussycat, and Margarita — performed at the shows. The Skatalites even appeared at the Independence Day Parade in August 1965, shortly before their breakup. Don Drummond was absent from that performance on the Cable & Wireless float, a truck bed covered with silver, gold, and red foil and garland along with the wooden band stands, demarcating Tommy McCook and the Skatalites. The musicians on the float, followed by young boys on scooter push carts, repeatedly played "I Should've Known Better," later known as "Independent Anniversary Ska," which was a cover of the Beatles tune.

Members of the original Skatalites were Jackie Mittoo on piano; Lloyd Brevett on bass; Lloyd Knibb or Arkland "Drumbago" Parks on drums; Jah Jerry Haynes or Harold MacKenzie on guitar; Tommy McCook and Roland Alphonso on tenor saxophone; Lester Sterling on alto saxophone; Don Drummond on trombone; Johnny "Dizzy" Moore, Rupert Dillon, or Baba Brooks on trumpet; and vocalists Lord Tanamo, Tony DaCosta, Doreen Shaffer, and Jackie Opel. Others, like saxophonist Karl "Cannonball" Bryan or guitarist Lyn Taitt, filtered in and out as needed.

Lloyd Brevett, bass player for the Skatalites, says that the formation of the band was a natural progression: "We play for all the record artist, all the artist. Jimmy Cliff, Prince Buster, Bob Marley, 'Simmer Down,' that's Bob Marley played by the Skatalites. All the artists then. Derrick Morgan — any artist in Jamaica at that time. Lloyd Brevett, Lloyd Knibb,

The Skatalites. Don Drummond is not pictured with the group as he excused himself from the shot, not liking to have his photograph taken, says Clive Chin (© The Gleaner Company Limited).

Tommy McCook, Don Drummond, Roland Alphonso, Jah Jerry was the guitar player, and Sterling, Ska Sterling and carried on, carried on from that time. And then Tommy McCook come out and join us. It was known as ska. We are the instrumentalists. We are the true ones. We started very, very early. We have a lot of different tunes, not only ska beat. At that time we were young, in our twenties. Tommy McCook was the elder. Every day we were making tunes. He decided we need a little of the action. Don Drummond was the highlight of the band." Drummond continued to work as a solo artist for such producers as Leslie Kong, when he recorded "Dragon Weapon." He also performed with the Skatalites live at clubs around Kingston and in the studio for numerous recordings.

The Skatalites recorded for various producers but they sought to get better wages than they earned as solo artists. Two producers known for offering fair wages were brothers Justin and Duke Yap, who ran the Top Deck label. Justin was introduced to the Skatalites by Allan "Bim Bim" Scott, Coxsone's assistant, who knew the musicians personally and suggested that Yap record them. During a recording session that lasted all night at Studio One in November 1964, Yap recorded some of the Skatalites' most classic tunes, all written by Don Drummond. He arrived for the session with five songs already written — "Confucius," "Chinatown," "The

Reburial," "Smiling," and "Marcus Junior." In the liner notes to *Ska-Boo-Da-Ba*, the re-release of Top Deck's Skatalites sessions, Yap recalls his thoughts on Drummond for writer Steve Barrow: "I admired Don Drummond. I call him maestro. He takes over. He's in charge. He knows what he's doin', he very professional. And when you hear my recordings with Drummond, you listen, you know that he took charge." He admits that it was difficult at first to deal with Drummond because of his idiosyncrasies: "I remember when I drove Bim down town ... we drove to his home. First of all, I didn't go in — Bim Bim went in and talked

Don Drummond performing, circa 1964 (courtesy EMP Museum, Seattle, WA, and Clive Chin).

to him first. I remember one time he took off! Just went down the road and come back with his answer — it's ok! Whatever he had to do, you know?"

Musicians respected Yap because of the way that he ran his business, unlike the other producers of the time. "It wasn't the fact that they really love Justin," says Clive Chin, "it was the fact that Justin used to pay them the right money and make them very comfortable. Make sure them have them smoke, them food, them drink, and after they finish, they got paid. With Coxsone, Coxsone used to just have them as session men and Coxsone himself wasn't in on most of the sessions. It was mostly the engineer and he would come in after, listen to the tracks and then pay them after." The Skatalites also recorded for Chin's father, Vincent, known as Randy. "I think they felt more comfortable around my dad and you know who else used to pay well too is Leslie Kong," Clive recalls. "Leslie used to make sure them get proper pay. Musicians as a whole would rather work for someone who they know they're going to get their money from as opposed to someone who tell them come back and you come back and they're not there. It's frustrating."

Yap, Chin, Coxsone, Reid and Beverley did whatever they could to get Don Drummond to lay down tracks for them, as did dancehall owners. Drummond was the main attraction for the Skatalites for a number of reasons. First, he was well known in Kingston, having played for the previous 15 years on the club circuit and for the previous five years in the studio, even though some of this time was spent in the mental institution. His tunes were hits and many who came to see the Skatalites were doing so to see Drummond. And for good reason. He was responsible for directing the sound of the Skatalites, even though the official leader was Tommy McCook. "[Drummond's] compositions provide the basis for many of their greatest works," says historian Lloyd Bradley.

Dr. Aggrey Irons, an administrator at Bellevue who had the opportunity to see Drummond perform during his years with the Skatalites says, "He was quite the impresario and, of course, I'm sure you've heard about his long instrumental solos. He would just keep going and going. His hat was his kind of trademark. There was no doubt as to who Don Drummond was, when you saw him on the stage and he always stepped up to the front. 'Eastern Standard Time' or any one of those, he really took to the stage. He was quite the showman and very individualistic. I remember him well. They used to play at the Carib Theater, many concerts were held there, morning shows on a Saturday at ten o'clock, and on public holidays. Those were the places the Skatalites used to play, featuring Don D. The crowd responded in raves! They used to stand up and shout and shout for more. Yeah mon, he was quite popular." Karl "Cannonball" Bryan recalls, "When we were in the Skatalites, everyone would get around him. Sometimes he don't play, he just take out the trombone and shine it up and everybody, 'Oh! Don! Don!' But he did a lot of songs, original instrumental that Jamaicans love."

Vocalist BB Seaton elaborates on the subject of Drummond's musical creativity: "He was in the Skatalites and when he would come in with his song for the recording, something he wrote, he would then explain it to some of the musicians because sometimes it's just so intricate that it wasn't so easy to play it, in terms of the timing sometimes, so he had to explain it to the guys who were in that verse." Eddie "Tan Tan" Thornton concurs, "All that music is Don Drummond's music. He write most everything. Most of them was jealous of Drummond. Yeah, because Drummond was very talented. He's a deep guy, he don't mix with nobody, mon. He was like my brother. I don't lie to you. I pray for him every day. I got his picture in my wallet, walk with him every day."

Drummond's music, because it was based in jazz, was the ideal format for working with a large group like the Skatalites. The typical jazz form of theme and variation was a natural for the band, and Drummond brought his own special touch to fill in that shell. Ken Stewart says, "He had these kinds of haunting melodies. Most of his songs were in a minor key which tend to be a more sad kind of a mood for music and Don had a way of putting in a melody of his, and Knibb's drumming complemented and took away some of the sadness of the song. The song would have this haunting melody, a sad melody, and Knibb would do his little cymbal work and it was more of a happy thing, so the way they complemented each other, all of the musicians — Don was an inspiration to all, especially the soloists in the band, and they would expand on what he had played. He'd solo first a lot of the times and they'd expand on it. But as far as a writer, he was by far the most prolific writer of all the Skatalites, and the chief writer. Most of the other songs, unfortunately, that the Skatalites play were either plagiarized or stolen from Mongo Santamaria."

Carlos Malcolm says that Drummond's compositions came from his own mind, his own heart. Although the producers demanded copies of the hits, and so many of Drummond's tunes are versions of other songs, Drummond somehow made them his own. Malcolm says, "Drummond was Drummond. He didn't sit down and listen to a bunch of jazz records and go imitate anybody. That's why he was so unusual, from my perspective. He had his own harmonies and his own way of expressing what he conceived. It was not along the pathway of logical harmony, what we know — diatonic. I am a trained musician and what impressed me most about him was that he didn't listen to anybody but himself." Take, for example, Drummond's composition "Man in the Street." This song, says Jamaican writer Laura Tanna, features "constant crescendos to recreate the assertiveness of country buses and street noises, transmuting the sounds of raw life into music." Without a single lyric, without really knowing Drummond as a person at all, the soul of the city is felt by the listener. It is only through his music that we can ever try to know Drummond.

Don Drummond's skill as a musician only grew stronger during his years with the Skatalites as he was able to blend his talent with the stellar talent of other serious musicians with whom he had played for years. What made Drummond different from an average musician is that he put himself into his music. He played with his whole being. Neville "Brammy" Bramwell once said that Drummond "played soul before soul was a word." People in the audience during Drummond's shows as well as fellow musicians had been known to cry at the beauty and sorrow of his performances. "Drummond reached into the distance somewhere, communicating a sense of longing with his trombone soaked in pain," says Dr. Gordon Rohlehr.

Former Prime Minister P.J. Patterson asks us, "Have you ever listened to his music? I mean, have you ever really listened to his music? His music has a plaintive sound, doesn't it? John Keats, that's who he reminds me of. Keats' poetry and Don Drummond's music, they always, for me, they've always been the same thing. The joy within, it is surrounded by that melancholy feel." Perhaps the ultimate accolade comes from musicologist Dermot Hussey: "Don Drummond was to ska what Bob Marley was to reggae — a visionary musician with an extraordinary sound on his horn and musical insight."

Without Drummond's compositions and mastery of his instrument and the genre, it is likely that ska would have dissolved into the chasm of music's historical relics. In the September 11, 1964, issue of the *Jamaica Gleaner*, in a column called "Merry-Go-Round," an unidentified author, with an affinity for arcane references, writes,

At this stage in the Ska game, it seems a reasonable moment to try and assess who (or which band) is putting Jamaica's home-brewed best most effectively on the map. There seems to be no doubt, according to public opinion, that Don Drummond is away ahead of the field. The reason is obvious. With his slippery horn he has succeeded in injecting some variety into what must be one of the most monotonous and unimaginative rhythms of all time. In our Jamaica of today, the musical menu is liable to be 'oompha-oompha-oompha' from the beginning to the end of an evening. Only by embroidering on the basic beat can a musician hope to ring a few changes — and no one has done it better than Trombonist Don Drummond. Playing either with his own group or with a gifted combo led by Tommy McCook, he has opened new horizons for what had appeared to be a tomb without a view. This is not to say that other leading bands, though imaginatively outclassed by the "Skatalites," had not previously made a palpable imprint upon teenage sensibilities. Byron Lee, a versatile businessman if ever there was one, had already reached the top of our homebred hit parade with a strictly commercial hors d'oeuvre called "Jamaica Ska" and a rehashed version of an old Russian folk song, "Sammy Dead," and Carlos Malcolm, who ought to have known better, but understandably not wishing to be left either out of the rat-race or off the band-wagon, clipped in with two or three commercially successful numbers. But to paraphrase Oscar Wilde, there was always this little tent of blue with prisoners called the Ska. Any manipulator of the Ska-beat appeared to be as helpless as that wretched, condemned guardsman in *Reading Gaol*— and no less hamstrung. It clearly needed someone to twist those prison bars. Don Drummond, with his slurring, off-beat swing, has obviously done it.

The author of this review alludes to other bands that competed with the Skatalites for recognition, and he or she chooses the word "outclassed" for a reason. There were other bands that received more accolades through political connections, through class connections to the elite or upper echelon, and through their image of not being associated with Rastafarian ganja smoking. One of these artists was Kes Chin and his band which performed at the most elite hotels, like the Flamingo. But the one band that truly had an impact on the Skatalites, and perhaps Don Drummond's sense of worth, was Byron Lee and the Dragonaires, the band that was selected over the Skatalites to represent the country of Jamaica at the 1964 World's Fair in Queens, New York. Those selected to travel to the fair included Jimmy Cliff, Eric Morris, Millie Small, Prince Buster, Ken Khouri, and dancers Ronnie Nasrala and Jannette Phillips. Nasrala was also Byron Lee's manager at that time. One listen of Byron Lee's music compared to any one of the Skatalites tunes will show even the untrained ear that the latter is the better band. It was during this trip that Prince Buster took Jimmy Cliff and his friends to a nightclub in Harlem to meet his comrade Muhammad Ali. Prince Buster had previously met Ali during a visit to London and he was transformed by his faith in the Nation of Islam, thus Prince Buster changed his name to Yusef Muhammad Ali.

The choice to send Byron Lee to the World's Fair to represent ska may have been a sure bet for the well-connected musician, but few others agreed with the decision, although hindsight sheds some light. Ken Stewart says, "Byron Lee was the uptown band who played ska but not with the soul and vigor that Skatalites had. Certainly the Skatalites was the more popular band but the downtown band and they were known for ganja smoking and all kinds of debauchery. It also happened with the James Bond film as it was again Byron Lee chosen to play that scene at Doctor's Cave Beach Hotel." That film was *Dr. No*, which featured a scene with Byron Lee & The Dragonaires playing the song "Jump Up" at Pussfeller's club. As Lloyd Bradley writes, Byron Lee "was not a ghetto man."

Prior to Ronnie Nasrala, Byron Lee & the Dragonaires was managed by Edward Seaga, who had then become Jamaica's minister of culture, long before he became prime minister. Seaga had been interested in Jamaican music ever since he studied indigenous music as a college student, producing a recorded collection called *Folk Music of Jamaica* for the Ethnic Folkways Library shortly after his studies concluded. In 1958, Seaga formed his own recording studio, West Indies Records Limited (W.I.R.L.), which was sold to Byron Lee in 1968. Seaga selected his own band to attend the fair and show the world how to dance to a "monotonic grassroots rhythm that has taken Jamaica by storm," that is "original and indigenous," as they marketed it to fairgoers. Lee was mixed race and played at the uptown clubs to the uptown clientele and was certainly not dreadlocked, like Johnny "Dizzy" Moore, nor a ganja smoker who associated with and identified with Rastafarians, like many of the members of the band.

In newspaper articles for the World's Fair, dignitaries and the noble class were photographed "doing the ska" with the Jamaican dancers flown in for the occasion. In one article from the *New York Amsterdam News* on May 2, 1964, one such dignitary is shown kicking up his heels in his suit and tie while seated onlookers smile. The photo caption reads: "When Arthur Murray takes a dancing lesson, that's news! Here the famed dance instructor catches on fast as he learned the 'Jamaica SKA,' newest dance sensation to hit New York." It was also noted that the dancers introduced the craze to the "jet set" during an event at Shepheard's at the Hotel Drake on Park Avenue in Manhattan.

Another article at the end of that month found in Cathy White's posh "Personally and Socially" column notes,

> Oom ... ska oom ... ska! Oom ... ska! That's the sound of the "up" beat on the bass guitar where the latest dance craze, the Jamaica Ska, gets its name. We headed for Shepheard's and to L'Interdit [a private club, subterranean in what was then the Gotham Hotel at 55th and Fifth Ave.] t'other evening and found Park Avenue gyrating all over the place. Leaving our inhibitions in the "tent" we joined the fun. Believe me, if you can Twist, you can Ska!

The World's Fair Singer Bowl also played host to a "Jamaica ska party" in August 1964, when Byron Lee and his 12-piece orchestra, Millie Small, Jimmy Cliff, and others performed for "youths from an assortment of nations" who "twisted, bounced, wiggled, and shook to the rhythmic beats of the Caribbean dance craze known as the Jamaica Ska."

Even after the World's Fair ended, Seaga continued to send his well-connected musicians to the United States to promote tourism to his country. By October 1965, the *Pittsburgh Courier* claimed that Ronnie Nasrala had "made four promotion trips to the U.S. spreading ska," not only at the World's Fair but subsequently at clubs in New York like the Peppermint Lounge, on TV shows, and at night spots in Miami Beach. They described Nasrala, not as a dark-skinned Jamaican with dreadlocks, as the Jamaican government tried to hide and squelch, since Nasrala certainly was not, but as "a long, lean chap, currently in training as a fencer for the Eighth British Empire and Commonwealth Game scheduled for Kingston next August. An all-around athlete, Ronnie has had quite a career in his 35 years as an actor, dancer, school teacher, and salesman. He is now a partner in McMillan Advertising and an account executive for Red Stripe, the island's famous beer. Ska anyone?"

In July 1966, Byron Lee and His Dragonaires entertained "the huge throng" which watched a ceremony on the Avenues of the Americas to unveil Jamaica's coat of arms. The formal procedure involved ministers from Jamaica, New York City's Mayor John Lindsay, and business dignitaries from the United States. In August 1966, Byron Lee returned to promote ska with his band and the Blues Busters at an event in Manhattan's Riverside Plaza in recognition of Jamaican's anniversary of independence. In October 1966, Ronnie Nasralla, "Jamaica's leading Ska dancer," traveled to the States with the Caribs to promote the country via "the ska — the big sound and dance in Jamaica that rivals the Frug, Wobble, Jerk and other discotheque dances," courtesy of the Jamaica Tourist Board. Karl "Cannonball" Bryan comments, "Byron Lee is not a musician. He is a businessman."

Ska had to be presented a certain way by Seaga and his cronies. Ska was certainly a music of the people back home in Jamaica, but because of its popularity, it could be capitalized upon and exploited to attract money. Years later, Patricia Ann Spence would opine in her article, "The roots of Reggae" for the *New York Amsterdam News*, "Ska was essentially a people's music, 'roots' music — conceived, played, and listened to by the poor. The middle and upper classed Jamaicans avoided it like a plague. And after labeling its 'gutbucket quality as vulgar, they banned it from the island's only radio station, RJR." They may have avoided it like the plague, but some enterprising individuals knew how to put the proverbial lipstick on the pig and use it for their own purposes.

Ken Stewart says it's understandable how the Skatalites weren't chosen during those times to represent the country: "I can see why the government was concerned. Having seen various members of Skatalites act out in public over the years, these were valid concerns. Nobody knew what some of these guys would pull next, especially the drinkers like Tanamo and Jackie. The problem is that their music was so much better and really the best representative of ska at the time. It was a tough call, I am sure, but in the end the Skatalites lost those battles but went on to spread their music worldwide anyway."

But that success came long after Drummond's time, so it was emotionally hard on him not to have the recognition that he felt he deserved. Drummond never, despite his acclaim and talent, was well-connected or light-skinned enough to travel to the U.S. on a promotional tour. He never played in a Peppermint Lounge or on Fifth Avenue. He was never able to find fare to leave for brighter shores. He was not able to fully develop the music in the direction he wanted it go to. Says Winston Smith, "He told me one night that he thought he was better than people like Kai Winding and the people who were on the front pages at that time, J.J. Johnson. I said, 'Donald, you cannot say anything like that because you've not seen the exposure that these men have.' I used to be an ardent reader and got my *Downbeat* magazine every month. I showed him one and said, 'These people judged number one, number two, and number three musicians go all over the place, they got recognized.' Them guys every year they were at the top. I told him he had to travel but he never got to the idea of leaving."

Drummond's songs were lining the pockets of producers and labels in the U.K. as well, further exploiting his talents and alienating him from the success and compensation he

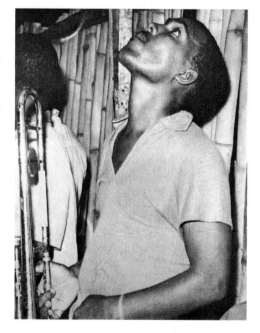

Don Drummond waits to solo, circa 1964–1965 (courtesy EMP Museum, Seattle, WA, and Clive Chin).

109

deserved. "Eastern Standard Time" was released on the Island Record label in the U.K., where it was a hit, and others tunes like "Festival" and "Royal Flush" on the R & B label, "Looking Through the Window" and "I Should Have Known Better (Anniversary Ska)" on Island, and "Roll On Sweet Don (Heaven & Hell)" on the Port-O-Jam label, were released in the U.K. during Drummond's lifetime, for which he received no compensation of any kind. As Timothy White writes in *Catch a Fire*, "Don Drummond's soul has been eaten away a little bit each day, each month and year; one of the best trombone instrumentalists in the entire world, he had steadily been ignored, year after year, and that had slowly sapped his heart and broke his spirit." The great saxophonist Roland Alphonso, speaking from a concert in Chicago just two years before his death, said, "Coxsone is a producer and I record for him. Six days a week I make records for him. Up till now I am a poor guy, babes. I am a poor guy."

Even today, Coxsone Dodd's children, who have fought legal battles with each other over their late father's estate, reap the rewards of Don Drummond's creative genius. In exchange for a few pounds given to Drummond, JAMREC, the publishing arm of Studio One, Dodd's estate receives royalties for Drummond's tunes, including "Cuban Blockade," "Addis Ababa," "Alley Pang," "Cool Shade," "Don Cosmic," "Down Beat Alley," "Eastern Standard Time," "Elevator Rock," "Far East," "Further East," "Freedom Sounds," "Green Island," "Heaven and Earth," "Jet Stream," "Johnny Dark (Ska Town)," "Keep On Coming A the Dance," "Knock Out Punch," "Last Call," "Lawless Street," "Looking Through the Window," "Melancholy Baby," "Mr. & Mrs. TV," "Mr. Prop Man," "Occupation," "Rain or Shine," "Reload," "Roll On Sweet Don," "Roots Undying," "Royal Flush," "Russian Ska Fever," "Scandal," "Scandal Ska," "Scrap Iron," "Sit Back (Just Cool)," "Silver Dollar," and "Valley Princess." According to Skatalites manager Ken Stewart, royalties from Don Drummond's republished tunes also go to the members of the Skatalites and their estates through Patrick Bailey, an attorney in Kingston who collects the monies on their behalf, an arrangement that was made in 1983.

The exploitation broke Drummond's fragile mental state. It is not known exactly how many times Drummond committed himself or was committed by others to Bellevue Mental Hospital (administrators at Bellevue, as well as government officials, say that his records have been destroyed). Vinnese Dias, responsible officer of the Ministry of Health, in a letter dated July 20, 2011, explained that her department no longer has

Drummond's records because "medical records are disposed of after a period of 10 years." Additionally, in a letter dated March 19, 2011, from Dwayne Francis, hospital administrator at Bellevue Mental Hospital, "We regret to inform you that some of our records were destroyed from past hurricanes. Consequently, we are unable to locate any information pertaining to this matter." Bellevue was significantly damaged during Hurricane Dean in August 2007; however it is not known if this storm destroyed any of Drummond's actual records. Repeated requests for more information have been met with vague responses or not answered at all.

During Drummond's tenure with the Skatalites, the 16 months the group was together, he did spend more time in Bellevue, which accounts for a minimum total of three stays — his first in 1960, a second stay during the period of the Skatalites, and his final committal in 1966. There may have been more, but certainly no less. During one of these stays, says Lloyd Bradley, Drummond destroyed his trombone. Headley Bennett, O.D., visited Drummond while he was a patient at Bellevue: "I remember when I leave, I went to Montego Bay and I took a job down here, and when I came back to town, I heard that he was in a mental home, Bellevue. And I went to look for him and we were talkin' and he said to me that he don't like it down there. It's terrible. It's terrible. And we were talkin' good and he told me he soon be back workin'. He said he soon be back and hold on a little and he'll be fine down the road and went back in the institution. And the last words he said to me was, 'Hold on a little, I'll be back.'"

And Drummond did come back. He returned to his musical career just as strong as before, yet he was still struggling with his mental illness. Drummond's great friend Winston Smith says that one day when the Skatalites were supposed to be performing, Drummond was late, yet again. But this time Smith found him and brought him to the show. Smith says, "The Sunday evening he was supposed to be on the bandstand at Bournemouth Club and Tommy McCook said to me, 'Go up into the hills and see if you can find him.' I took somebody's bicycle and rode all over Wareika Hills but I couldn't find him, so I am riding back down the road and when I got to Ocean View, which is the road that led to Bournemouth, where they used to play, I saw him walking down the street with a box in his hand. So I pulled up behind him, 'cause he knew I was looking for him because he saw me coming down, and I took him down to the club and at the back of the club is where the musicians enter from and go up on stage. And I said, 'Well I'm going to put my bicycle up front and then

The Bournemouth Club in Kingston, Jamaica, where the Skatalites had their residency, performing on Wednesday, Friday, and Saturday nights. Postcard.

go through the front door,' and he said, 'No, come on because I got something I want to show you.' I went backstage with him and he took out his trombone and started blowing some songs and said, 'This is something I'm writing.' I said, 'Are you going to play it tonight?' He said, 'I don't know, I want you to hear it first so you can tell me what it sounds like.' He played a few bars of this thing and I said, 'Well that sounds good to me, but if you go up there, how are these guys going to play?' He had sheets of music of the song. So I said, 'What you going to call it?' 'This Man Is Back,' he said. That tune was eventually recorded and became one of his top hits. He went upstairs and that song lasted the better part of one hour."

Charley Organaire recalls Drummond's dedication to his music: "I remember a time when the Skatalites formed and they play at a place called Bournemouth, he sometimes never made it on stage. He's got a mental problem. They call him mad man. He eat and sleeps this music, day in and day out. He would practice in the morning, then he would go to work, come back at lunch and he would practice, and he'd go back to work and he'd come again and he would practice for the rest of the day. That's how committed he was."

But Don Drummond continued his path of self-medication, unable to find relief in Bellevue. Clancy Eccles recounts one time he witnessed this self-medication, as told to David Katz in his book, *Solid Foundation*.

> He did a song named "This Man Is Back," and I worked eight months with Don Drummond on stage after that. While we were recording down by Khouri, they was digging out that piece of land, and Don used to go over and pick up this pretty piece of clay and put it in his Ovaltine. Don Drummond never eat anything hot — everything cold, lot of fruits and so on. One day Roland and Johnny looked in the bottle, it was clay and all those things mixed together, and Drummond said, "People are supposed to live in an atomic energy, you are supposed to build atoms inside of you" — that's why he ate the clay.

Clive Chin says that he witnessed Drummond's unusual behavior as a young boy at Federal, the recording studio his father used. Sometimes the behavior was just absurd, such as stopping their Morris Mini on the way to the recording studio to get a length of sugar cane, then demanding the higgler only peel it but not cut it, so they were forced to drive with the cane extending out two of the car's windows. Other times the behavior was much more disturbing. Chin says, "He would have things like ripe bananas and he would peel it and the yard around Federal at that time had sand around where the almond trees were. And he would peel the banana and then dip it in the sand and eat it. And it was not like it drop out of his hand by mistake or accident, but he literally peeled half of it, dipped it in the sand and was eating it. And I told my dad, 'This guy doesn't seem to be right in his mind,' and my father said, 'Do not stare at him, just act as if everything is okay.'"

Winston Smith also witnessed Drummond eating clay: "This man did things that all of us did, but also did things other folks did not do. He was good. He was crazy too. He was eating dirt. He was just sitting under this small tree and I'm going across the common and I said, 'Hey, what are you going there?' He said, 'I'm reasoning. I'm sitting here reasoning.' I was talking to him for a little while and every so often he would flip something in his mouth. I said, 'Whatcha eatin', corn?' because we used to roast corn and then take it off and eat it singular. I thought he was doing that. He just opened his hand and it was dirt. I said, 'Doggone it!' I took him home. I told him to follow me because I knew he was not feeling so good. His mom said every time he gets that way he eats dirt."

Ken Stewart, too, has vivid memories of Drummond's unusual behavior: "There was a story that Lloyd [Knibb] used to have about the green chicken. As Lloyd would say, 'Don was slightly kinky.' He was taking meds from way back. He had some kind of chemical imbalance. I think it was lithium or whatever they were giving him. So apparently Lloyd was in Don's apartment one day and Lloyd was looking for something to eat or drink and he opened the refrigerator door and saw some chicken that was going bad and it was actually green. And Lloyd threw it in the wastebasket and Don got vexed because he said, 'What are you doing? You threw away my dinner.'"

Eating dirt and clay or anything non-edible or even toxic is a condition known as pica, a disorder that may be caused by a number of different things, including nutritional deficiencies, lack of parental nurturing, or ethnic custom. It seems, from Winston Smith's account, that Don Drummond's mother was aware of his pica and had witnessed it herself, so it is evident that the condition had existed for some time. It is likely that Drummond's pica had another cause — the association to mental conditions such as schizophrenia, bipolar disorder, or autism, although we will never know for certain which was Drummond's diagnosis. Most agree that it was schizophrenia that troubled Drummond mentally, although there are reasons to believe that his actual condition may have been something different.

Herman "Woody" King knew Drummond as well as anyone could and says that he feels Drummond's mental illness was caused from his continued struggle to be fully appreciated for his talent. "To be truthful," says King, "I don't think he was really born with this type of sickness. I think it was brought on by the economic conditions that made him suffer, having to live in the yard in a shed, and suffer some of the indignities of guys who were not really sensitive, his mind go off. He couldn't find money to buy food so sometimes he would go out on the road where the ladies are selling, we call them higglers, selling food by the side of the road and he would steal some to take it back to cook. Little by little you could see his mind was starting to stray. It's just now that if band music hadn't failed him, so to speak, and he was able to get steady employment or migrate or whatever, I don't think he would've ended up mad. The social and economic conditions sort of drove him over the edge. He could've been alright if things weren't that bad for him, but things got real bad and he started walking in the road and walking far out, he ended up in the hills, out in St. Thomas, and people would be so insensitive to him. The police and people would see him on the road, walking in the street with his rain cloak. In Jamaica they treat mad people really bad. Nobody has any love or any kindness for mad people. Sometimes they stone them, spit on them. They're not stars anymore. People would recognize him on the road and say, 'Oh, this is the great Don Drummond.'"

Helene Lee reports that Don "was seen walking in his socks up on Mountain View Avenue, throwing handfuls of coins to children in the streets and talking in tongues." Dr. Gordon Rohlehr relates an "appalling story" about Drummond during one of his bouts of madness. He is said to have stood up for a long time at Cross Roads, his arms extended in a cruciform, staring at nothing, while the traffic swirled around him." These kinds of public displays of madness certainly did not help Drummond's acceptance as a musician. "When we played, people used to laugh because they knew of his problems," Dizzy Moore told journalist Howard Campbell.

Clive Chin remembers another incident, this one at the Ward Theatre: "I was backstage with [Drummond] and he ask me to sit beside him, so I went up and I sat beside him and he always carry a chamois, like that thing you clean, shine and he used it to really clean his mouthpiece because he always carry his mouthpiece separate when it in the case. In the trombone case you would have a little section that the mouthpiece fit, but he used to carry his mouthpiece in his pocket. I notice he never leaves his horn anywhere, curiously. He's very particular with his instrument. He walks with it and he doesn't leave it anywhere for anyone to tamper with it. My memories of him were that he'd hold a conversation with you but sometime in the middle of the conversation he'd stop. It was like he didn't stop to think about what he was going to say or he didn't remember what he was going to say. He was not too sociable. He wasn't like the rest of the musicians.

"Another thing I notice about him is that he was not a photogenic person. If you have to get a snap of him it had to be a candid snap. He would not pose for any picture taken. If you notice on the Skatalites lineup, when you see the full band, you notice you don't see him in the lineup. Either he is not there or he finds an excuse to either go to the toilet or something and then the picture was taken without his presence. A lot of his pictures that you see is all candid snaps. He never posed for any picture taking."

Musicologist Herbie Miller writes that during the Skatalites' recording of Don Drummond's song "The Burial," which they did for Prince Buster,

Drummond showed up late and did not perform his solos. Lloyd Brevett and Lloyd Knibb encouraged Prince Buster to get rid of "this mad man" since recording time equaled money and he was stalling the process. That only made Drummond more irritated, so he purposely blew away from the microphone each time he took his solo so the recording didn't take. Brevett swore while Drummond took his knife from his bag and stood calmly by the only door out of the studio, cleaning his fingernails with the tip of the blade. He plainly and coolly said, "Who want to play, play. Who don't want to play, don't play," and the session resumed with Brevett's and Knibb's compliance.

Tensions were always high in the band, ultimately causing its existence to be short lived. P.J. Patterson became involved in some of the disputes members had with club owners and producers. They were difficult times, as he recalls: "My chambers as a lawyer were at thirty-nine-and-a-half Johns Lane and we represented the Jamaican Musician Federation as a body and in the course of that I came to serve as the manager for the Skatalites. When I came to serve as the manager of the Skatalites it was largely the result of Margarita, Anita, coming to me at my chambers at the end of every week saying that they had no house money because what would happen is when the group played and they got the proceeds from the event, various people made claims on portions of it, and Don, who was never interested in material things, made no claims and nobody gave him or Margarita any money. So, as a consequence of Margarita turning up most Fridays, despite the dances and concerts at which Don had played, to claim money, I decided that the best thing to do was to, I had no choice but to take over the management of the band, and from there we saw that Don's interests were properly reflected."

According to Lloyd Bradley, Drummond was "virtually destitute" and would frequently forget to pick up his money at the end of the night. Patterson says the Skatalites were a tough group to contain, in many ways: "All the while, all the while, I've said that the band is the greatest aggregation of musicians Jamaica has ever seen and will ever see. The band only lasted for eighteen months. Why did it break up? It was too much a clash of personalities, yeah. Lloyd Knibb was the only person who could manage to keep everybody in order, both as a person and as a drummer. When Don was ready to play, it was Knibb who want to let him through and when he came through, everyone knew, just leave him alone. You couldn't touch him."

Drummond had already become a regular at the Wareika Hills, where he could get away to play the music he truly wanted to perform. Even during the years performing with Coxsone and prior to his studio days, he ventured into the hills at night to play with fellow musicians. He didn't have to worry about what the producers demanded, what the crowds demanded, what the government demanded, and, instead, he could be free-spirited and vibe off of the other artists in a musical communion. Drummond brought his fellow musicians into the hills, introducing Rico Rodriguez and others to the music and lifestyle. It was also here that Drummond continued to overlap lives with Anita Mahfood, Margarita, and so they, too, began a communion all their own.

9

The Wareika Hills

On the corner of Rusden and Adastra, the rudies were hanging out, some throwing pebbles at rusted tin cans crushed on the curb, others playing dice in their darkers. Don stood watching the game of pick-a-pow as the sun sank lower in the sky, burning its last minutes of energy red and large over the squelching earth. The sweat turned to sticky honey on Don's skin, salty and sandy. The dice clinked as they bounced off the cinder-block wall onto the foot-worn dirt, pounded flat from generations of street dwellers and their carts. Two crumpled dollars sat still in the center of the game of chance. Don sliced off a piece of mango with his ratchet knife and slipped it into his mouth, dripping with juice. He walked up the road to Wareika.

Ask a cab driver today to take you into the Wareika Hills and you are likely to get strange looks, followed by a comment like, "Why would you want to go there?" and then a negative response. The Wareika Hills is a locale riddled with "flare-ups," or shootings, violence, and gang activity. But the area at the southeast foot of Long Mountain was once a peaceful retreat for those looking to escape violence, a lush and secluded site where Rastas came to congregate, reason, spiritualize, and share music, not unlike other camps at Greenwich Farm, Poker Flat, Ackee Walk, Mountain View, Tower Street, Back-O-Wall, and Dungle. Many Rastas came to Wareika after Leonard Howell's Pinnacle Camp was raided by police and the government in 1954, and so they came to the Wareika Hills at Adastra Road to establish a new camp with their brother and friend Count Ossie.

Count Ossie was born Oswald Williams in March 1926. He is considered to be the originator of Rasta music, which began in the late 1940s at his first camp on Salt Lane in the Dungle, an area that was a refuse dumping ground for the government and tenement yards. Count Ossie was living at the bottom of Slip Dock Road at the time, but he started a camp in the Dungle since he frequently traveled to the area to reason with local brethren about such subjects as Rastafarianism, Garveyism (the teachings of Marcus Garvey, who advocated for repatriation to Africa and who prophesied the birth of a king in Africa), and black awareness. They discussed their belief that Haile Selassie, who was crowned king of Ethiopia in 1930 and was a descendant of King Solomon, fulfilled the Biblical prophecy as noted by Garvey. Selassie was given the title Ras, an Amharic title of royalty, Tafari, the king's family name. He is called King of Kings, Lord of Lords, as proclaimed in the book of Revelations. He is considered by followers to be the incarnation of God and a savior for black people in times of great oppression.

Oswald Williams, better known as Count Ossie, performs on the repeater drum (© The Gleaner Company Limited).

During these conversations with fellow Rastafarians, Count Ossie, who always had a love for music, particularly drums and percussion, met a master Burru drummer named Brother Job. Brother Job played drums in the Dungle and at a camp held by a Rastafarian who went by the name Skipper.

The Burru was a group of men who emerged during the days of slavery on the island. Bands of Burru, African drummers, were permitted by slave owners to play drums and sing for the workers in the Jamaican fields to raise the slaves' spirits — not for emotional reasons, but to impose more productivity. The first Burru drums were heard on the island of Jamaica in 1903 in the parish of Clarendon. Their drum beat was the heartbeat of Africa. After slavery was abolished, the Burru could not find work and so they congregated in the impoverished areas of Kingston. They continued their drumming and music, which was not religious in nature, but still had a ritual component grounded in the Jonkonnu, a West African musical

119

festival and parade. Each Christmas season, the Burru men gathered to compose their own music with words about local events or about people in the community who had committed an act of wrongdoing. They worked on these songs starting in September and then on the holiday they traveled throughout the community, going from home to home, playing their bamboo scraper, shakka, and rhumba box for percussion, singing songs which were intended to purge the evil of the previous year before the new one began. Although the music was composed during the months previous to the event, they also were known to improvise on the spot.

Because the Burru were mischievous in this manner, and because they lived in the slum areas of the city, they were mistakenly considered by many to be criminals or undesirables. They were not unlike the Rastas in their early days. Both groups were persecuted by society and the government, both were anti-establishment, and both were firmly rooted in their African origins. So, in the 1940s, the two groups merged. The Burru acquired a religion (or spirituality) from the Rastas, and the Rastas acquired music.

Although Count Ossie learned his drumming from Burru men like Brother Job, he also developed his own individual style. In the early days, Count Ossie didn't own a drum, so he had Brother Job's teacher, Watto King, make a custom set for him. Count Ossie then traveled to meet with other groups of Rastas and share his drumming with his brethren, spreading the musical form in areas like Brother Issie Boat's camp, which was located in the Wareika Hills. Soon, other brethren learned to drum, and because the communal camps were transient in nature, the music spread quickly. In 1951, Count Ossie's camp at Salt Lane was destroyed by Hurricane Charlie. He then spent some time at the Rastafarian camp at Rennock Lodge before establishing his famous camp in the Wareika Hills off Adastra Road, near the area known as Rockfort. Herman "Woody" King claims that Count Ossie taught them all how to play. He says, "Count Ossie was a magnificent drummer. He not only played in the Rastafarian style, but he was able to play with the musicians, like jazz musicians, so he was very versatile. He could adapt his style. And me being such a lover of music and the Rastafarian doctrine, I was right there when he was coming along and playing."

Count Ossie's camp became a place for groundations or Nyahbinghis or Issembles, a spiritual communion of music composition, herb smoking from the chalice, and reasoning. Nyahbinghi originally meant "death to the whites, or death to the Europeans" in the 1930s, but then evolved to mean "death to the white oppressors and their black allies." During these musical sessions, it wasn't uncommon to borrow from melodies of other songs, such as hymns, a practice that also took place by other musicians in the studios and on stage. The groundations were a time of spiritual bonding meant to heighten one's spiritual consciousness. They were gatherings that took place anywhere from three to seven days in length when brethren and dawtas engaged in communal activities, such as music, chanting, dancing, and smoking herb. A purpose of the Nyahbinghi was to restore the natural order of creation through purging the evil from the world. The music had an emotional purpose, a healing purpose, and a religious or spiritual purpose. Numerous visiting musicians came to participate in the groundations, including Roland Alphonso, Cedric Brooks, Little G McNair, Bra Gaynair, Rico Rodriguez, Tommy McCook, Johnny Moore, Vivian Hall, Ernest Ranglin, and Don Drummond. This group of musicians, sometimes called Count Ossie's Band, performed until dawn throughout Jamaica at dance sessions and at Coney Island, an amusement park in Kingston.

Carlos Malcolm recalls the days when music was created in the Wareika Hills: "We used to practice against the hills. Oliver Road used to come down from Wareika Hills and that is where the Eastern musicians mostly used to congregate. This was, when we started, a little before Count Ossie started recording. He grew up in the hills. Don Drummond used to hang out at Oliver Road with Vivian Hall [the trumpeter]. Everybody used to go up to the hills."

Clive Chin remembers the times he, too, went into the hills, not as a participant, but as a spectator: "They used to go up there and my dad would take me up there and at times he would leave me out in the car and sometimes I could get upset because he would leave me out there for hours, although he had someone watching me, but I ask him permission on a number of occasions to come out and look and see what they are doing, and I think one of the things my dad didn't like was the atmosphere of the ceremonial things that they had to do, the smoking and stuff, he didn't want me around it. Ossie would be playing a full setup of drums and it was mostly just rehearsals where Don would come in and solo and then back out and Tommy come in and do a solo and Johnny Moore come in and it give them a little way to introduce themselves and flow in. They were improvising. Herman King was there a lot, too. He'd always be there. There were quite a few men, mostly men."

Drumming was always the foundation of the music in the hills. The drums used involved three drums: a repeater, or akete, which is the melody line; the fundeh, or funde which plays the steady rhythm or life line in addition to syncopation; and the bass drum, a two- or three-foot drum hit many times with a paddle, which keeps the same basic beat of the fundeh but varies it in rhythm and tone. Count Ossie's bass drum featured a phrase written in large letters on it — "Behold how good and how pleasant it is for brethren to dwell together in unity," a passage from Psalm 133. Percussionist Larry McDonald recalls that the camp was a popular place for musicians in the 1950s and 1960s: "I used to go up to Wareika on Sunday evening because on Sunday evening the Mystic Revelation of Rastafari would play up there, Count Ossie. Ossie is a friend of mine, so I go up and carry my drums up and every Sunday they'd set up and we'd play a big set. And me and the little kids would hang out. It was just about going up and getting a chance to play the music." The Mystic Revelation of Rastafari was a group consisting of Count Ossie and some of his drumming brethren. They later recorded music and performed on stage, even for the visit of Ethiopian emperor Haile Selassie to Jamaica on April 21, 1966. This date is marked each year still today with celebratory groundations.

The musicians came to Count Ossie's camp because it was a chance to be free with their music and they could truly expand their skills in a way no studio or stage would allow. But they also came because of the spiritual and emotional connections to their fellow brethren, led by Count Ossie, although there was no leader in a strict hierarchical sense. Rico Rodriguez, who spent time actually living at the camp, respectfully says, "Count Ossie was like a chief. He was like a chief in the hills. Everyone look up to him. Once he told me he wanted to learn trumpet but he was more into the drums, so he played the drums instead of the trumpet. A lot of Rastas around and I used to go home. I used to go home. We go away and play and I don't go back to my mother's house no more until I'm ready to come to England. I was leaving from Wareika Hills to come to England. Some of us stay in Wareika Hills. It was safe there. We cook and eat and they had Wareika school for the children to teach them about history. Communication everyday was about prayers, psalms and we chant psalms and play instruments. No really bed, just makeshift, yeah. Rough living, you know? No house, shelter, sheltered place. Everybody lived in stiffs, a variety of stiffs, you know? But it was a community. We play music all day, all day, all day and night."

He says that he was brought to the camp originally by Don Drummond. Rico says, "When we go, he used to tell me, 'Don't play, man, just listen. Don't play, just listen to me.' Sometimes I get to play with him, sometimes. Listening to Drummond gave me a much deeper opportunity to hear it. Not being in a band, just free playing. I am happy to have heard him playing the trombone with the drums around him, more than anything else. He was a Rasta in the Wareika Hills, so I went. I used to go up there and look for them, you know, if Drummond was one of the trombone players, so I just go and look for him and he could give me a good ting or two. When we go to Wareika Hills we used to play together. Sometimes he was so busy I don't wait for him. Sometimes he call me to go play with him. And when I go up to Wareika then I used to go home, you know? And he said to me, 'Rico mon, you see this area? Come up.' And when he used to tell me that, I stay at Wareika and I don't leave until I leave for England. I never leave that year until I was coming to England." King claims that Drummond lived at the camp from time to time out of necessity: "At a point when band music was going out and electronic music was coming in, they started having sound systems playing at the dances and Drummond had difficulty getting jobs. He even came and live at Count Ossie's camp. Things got really bad financially."

Trombonist Calvin "Bubbles" Cameron says that Drummond didn't live at the camp for a long period of time, just for a few days, like many of the others: "There was a little place on Adastra Road where Count Ossie live that they would go learn how to play music, and Don would play along with the drums on a Sunday night mostly with other horn musicians, locally and some who come from abroad and come by and play music with Count Ossie. Count Ossie was the leader of that group. Don didn't live in the hills, but he would stay in the camp because before he live on Rusden Road he was staying at the camp and he would stay there for days. There was a house there in which they congregate and get together. You could come through the fence and go in. This was the back of the hill before houses were built there. There weren't any houses, just bush. Houses are built there now. You would find a track which would lead straight down to the base house. Count Ossie used to live there with a lady." The house had several rooms where musicians frequently stayed for extended periods of time.

Ken Stewart says Drummond introduced some of the members of the Skatalites to the camp and the influence is felt in their songs: "He was one of the only ones, at the beginning anyway, one of the only ones who really cared about the whole Rastafari thing. That's reflected in some of the names, like 'Reburial of Marcus Garvey,' 'Marcus Garvey Jr.' He definitely was an attendant up there. He was probably one of the few people that brought the other members of the Skatalites. Because some of the other Skatalites, like Tommy, was more of a refined gentlemanly type, although Tommy was a big ganja lover, so that was one of the other attractions up there was the big pipe full of ganja going around."

Clive Chin insists there was another reason Drummond went to the hills: "He was just going there for the music. He was never Rastafarian faith. Definitely not Don." King concurs and says that even though Drummond's song titles and sound may reflect the beliefs of the Rastafarians at the time, the reason why Drummond went to the Wareika Hills was for the music, not the religion. "He came up in the hills to play," King says. "Most of the musicians came up there to play when they finish working in the clubs at two, three o'clock in the morning. They would head up in the hills to get a smoke. And then jam. At the time I would be able to drive my dad's car. When I used to go to train to be a pilot, in between shifts, I would have use of my dad's car and would use it to carry men sometimes and Drummond to play at different locations, so we were very, very close. The drum style of the Rastas is very nice and they can adapt to any kind of music almost, so that was his primary interest. He was more into music. I never really heard him talk about Rastafarianism." (One of the only known recordings of this time in the Wareika Hills, a reel-to-reel made in the 1960s, deteriorated before it could be digitized, according to Roger N. Williams, director of the School of Music at Edna Manley College of the Visual and Performing Arts.)

In the 1970s, music scholar Verena Reckord wrote of Don Drummond's affiliation with Rastafarianism and his connection to the music and themes discussed by brethren:

> The late Don Drummond is regarded as the jazz composer and instrumentalist most influenced by Rasta music. Indeed his fame as a composer ahead of his time came about after his plunge into Rastafarianism. Drummond's "Schooling the Duke" and "Addis Ababa" during the ska period are among his works influenced by Rasta music.

Herbie Miller writes that Drummond's music had another quality rooted in the African tradition.

Drummond's compositions, written mostly in minor keys, consisted of simple melodic lines, often repetitious, stated in a sing-song almost ring game-like theme. It was a call and response device derived both from the Anglo-plantation influences and the African song styling.

This style, introduced by Drummond, is what is known as the "Far East Sound" that later reggae bands continued.

The music Drummond learned to play in the Wareika Hills brought a new element of schooling to his repertoire. Here, free flowing with the other musicians, elements of the Rasta and Burru styles became part of his being, part of his song. So, too, did the Rastafarian beliefs, whether or not Drummond followed the doctrine. Dr. Gordon Rohlehr wrote in a 1970 review of Drummond's life,

> He imposed Rastafarian rhythms in his compositions and with the Skatalites, the most articulate folk-jazz band in Jamaica, he helped transform Ska from the imitation be-bop that it was, to the peculiarly Jamaican sound that has swept the entire Caribbean and abroad. He gave his tunes names directly pertinent to the man on the street — names like "Addis Ababa," the Ethiopian heaven of the Rasta man; "Beardman Ska"; "Ghost Town" and "China Town," two depressed areas in Kingston; "The Reburial," which is a Pocomania ritual of West African origin; "Marcus Junior," which refers to Garvey's son and the growing Black Power movement in Jamaica.

Miller goes so far as to credit Drummond with creating this new aspect of music.

> He was father to what is called the Far East sound, a sound carried forward by the Wailers (Bob, Peter, and Bunny), Burning Spear, Big Youth, the Abyssinians, Congos, Augustus Pablo, Jackie Mittoo, Pablove Black, and Earl "China" Smith to name a few. These represent a group of artistes who continue the ethic of resistance.

In May 1969, Bongo Jerry, an historian, social activist, and poet whose real name is Robin Small, wrote an article entitled "Roll On Sweet Don" for the publication *Abeng*. Bongo Jerry, in addition to penning a beautiful poem, "Don De Lion," noted Drummond's connection to Rastafarianism and black awareness inspired by Marcus Garvey. Bongo Jerry writes: "Don Drummond is a natal Black Artist, always selecting performances in a historical light and is the centre of modern musical history."

Keep in mind that at the same time the conversations at Wareika centered around black awareness, events in the United States also revolved around similar issues on a much grander scale. The Civil Rights Movement had been on the covers of newspapers and on radio broadcasts all over the States, and so Jamaicans would have been fully aware of the actions taken by black Americans in their fight for equality. Rosa Parks refused to give up her bus seat in December 1955, beginning the Montgomery Bus Boycott. A Supreme Court decision in November of the following year struck down Jim Crow laws in buses. In September 1957, National Guard Troops ensured that integration was brought to Little Rock Central High School. In 1963, John F. Kennedy gave a speech asking for "the kind of equality of treatment which we would want for ourselves." Throughout the 1960s, Martin Luther King organized sit-ins, protests, and peaceful demonstrations that were met with violence and arrests, resulting in his literary work on civil disobedience, "Letter from a Birmingham Jail." In 1964, King was awarded the Nobel Peace Prize. And all throughout this decade there were firsts for African Americans making landmark history — the first to enter the National Hockey League, the first to attend an all-white elementary school, the first to enroll at this university or that college. And it was also a time of violence and injustice and horror when the KKK beat and hanged black boys from trees, when NAACP worker Medgar Evers was murdered in the South, when peaceful civil rights marchers were beaten and killed in Selma, Alabama, on what is now known as Bloody Sunday. All of these actions were known to the Jamaicans as the world's eye was on America.

The sound of these struggles, the sound of the black identity, the sound of Africa could be heard in the music of the Wareika Hills. The heart of that music was the drum. Even though drummer Lloyd Knibb may not have been a frequent participant in the Wareika Hills, this fellow member of the Skatalites certainly did visit the camp and learned from the Burru drummers, combining these techniques with Latin styles and styles all his own. Self-taught as a child, Knibb's drumming for the Skatalites heightened Drummond's solos and brought an inventive quality to the music. "I am the originator of the ska beat," says Knibb. "In the studio, me and Coxsone Downbeat try out a beat. My beat sound different, heavier, so my drumming is distinct. So all the drummers try to play like me. They like the beat but then can't get it to sound like me. So that's how it started."

Drummond could frequently be found in the Wareika Hills with the drums, even when he was supposed to be recording in the studio or at a show. So producers often sent fellow musicians or friends up to the hills to look for Drummond when he was late. Winston Smith says, "I had to go up there because when Don couldn't be found, Tommy would send me. The only reason I knew of the Wareika Hills there is I would go up there and most of the time I didn't find him. There were so many camps because of the weed. They smoke weed up there like it was goin' out of style. If you don't have the capacity to hold that stuff, it's not going to help you, and I guess that's what happened to him. I know some people like that too. I grew up amongst those people, the whole of them, and I would see them smoking. I've never touched the stuff. Never, ever. It never fascinated me, plus the fact that when I was growing up I heard it was against the law and I was afraid of the police. I knew quite a few guys who did it. Well all of these guys who played music did it. All they did was play music and smoke. They would cook, drink lemonade, smoke, and play music. There wasn't much else to do up there 'cause it was in the bushes. It wasn't like any neighborhood where all the people lived at. There were camps here, camps there. I didn't do much traveling up there. I didn't want to be seen amongst those people at the time because I was afraid of the police, although they never bothered them because these guys weren't very boisterous people. They just did what they were doing and took it quietly."

Smoking marijuana likely only exacerbated whatever mental condition Drummond had. Studies have shown a link between cannabis use and schizophrenia and other like conditions, particularly later in the afflicted person's life. Dr. Frederick Hickling, executive director of the University of West Indies Caribbean Institute of Mental Health and Substance Abuse, says, "All the evidence that is available in the world is that there are some people who have significant psychosis when they use marijuana that it exacerbates the illness. That is the general opinion in the world at this time." Researchers at the Institute of Psychiatry at King's College in London contend that "cannabis use is associated with later schizophrenia outcomes." They further state that "based on the best evidence currently available, cannabis use is likely to play a causal role in regard to schizophrenia." Other causes, they say, include genetics, urban birth and adverse life events, infectious disease in utero, obstetric complications, poor nutrition, and pollution. Researchers note that cannabis use is but one "part of a complex constellation including other component causes." Certainly no one is claiming that use of marijuana causes schizophrenia. However, there are studies which indicate that those who are already prone to having schizophrenia may be apt to set off that condition. In the words of researcher

Robin Murray, "One possibility is that cannabis on its own is insufficient to cause psychosis but it can trigger psychosis in predisposed individuals."

Derrick Morgan says that he noticed the detrimental effect ganja had on Drummond: "He would take the weed and smoke. That's when he got freak. Every time he took the weed in his hand, that's when him get freak. If he don't smoke, he would be calmer, yeah."

Even if Drummond was drawn to the hills for the music, the message, and the self-medication, he was also drawn to Margarita, who was a regular at the camp. Many artists, including dancers, went to the camp to take part in the groundations. Margarita was a fixture at Wareika, where she not only brought her dance to the hills, but she brought the hills to her dance, spreading the culture of the Rastafari.

According to Herbie Miller, "Margarita became a regular on Count Ossie's camp at Rennock Lodge, joining a group of sisters already there." Other women included those with names like Sissy Maybel, Big Cynthia, Baby Lov, Panzie, Topsie, and Shuggus. Margarita participated in the sessions of reasoning, chanting songs, reading passages from the Bible, drumming, dancing, and smoking herb. Miller writes, "By the late 1950s Margarita was captivated by the Rastafari way of life. She was particularly drawn to their chanting and drumming, and participated in Groundations, where, like Rasta sister, Shuggus and Mauthe, she danced to the drumbeat of Niabinghi rhythms and jazzy horns performed by Count Ossie and the African drums." He contends that Margarita's involvement with the Rastafari culture would have only alienated her further from the social classes of her family.

Margarita's dancing during the groundations was integral to the total air of creation, the spiritual communion that allowed for free-flowing expression. Miller writes, "Her movements were a demonstration of diverse Caribbean influences animated by staccato movements, sanguine attitude, subtle Mediterranean nuances, and a muse informed by Rastafarian ethos." Her dance transformed in the hills, from the rhumba and Latin-based dances she grew up performing at a young age, to a dance full of jumps and breaks, a dance to the drums of Africa.

Her relationship with the brothers and sisters in the hills was strong, and so when she performed one time on stage, she refused to dance without the accompaniment of Count Ossie and his group, which were once known as the Rastafarian Repatriation Association of Adastra Road in Eastern

Kingston and later became known as The Mystic Revelation of Rastafari. Reckord writes,

> The group got its first legitimate stage break in the late fifties. It was an occasion when the late, famous rhumba queen Marguerita (Mahfood) insisted that she would not appear on a Vere Johns variety show (*Opportunity Knocks*) at the Ward Theatre on Christmas morning unless Ossie's group was on the bill. Johns was wary then about using Rastas on his show, but Marguerita was his star attraction. He had no choice. Count Ossie and his drummers were hired. They were a hit. They soon became regulars on Vere Johns' show and other functions.

Margarita was the one who introduced Rasta music into mainstream culture, as well as the jazz musicians who accompanied them which is why Miller calls her a "seminal figure in the island's musical and cultural growth."

In Helene Lee's work *The First Rasta*, Brother Royer, a member of Count Ossie's camp, credits Margarita with helping Rasta music come to the mainstream through her tenacity. Despite Norman Manley's demand that "anywhere you see Rastaman, you have to lock them up," Margarita refused to perform unless Count Ossie and his drummers performed, and it was only after the "people got crazy about the new sound," says Royer, that Rastas were from then on welcomed onto stages. "Great girl! Our Helen of Troy!" said Royer of Margarita. She was more like the Josephine Baker of Jamaica.

It was after this introduction that Prince Buster, looking to capitalize on the new sound, sought Count Ossie and his drummers to record for him in 1960 on the song "Oh, Carolina" by the Folkes Brothers. Because competition in the studios was so rough, when Duke Reid caught wind of this session, fearing a success, he bribed the studio booker at JBC Studios, taking Prince Buster's time slot. But that didn't deter the ruthless Prince Buster, who utilized a tiny closet with a microphone set-up at JBC. The musicians knocked out "Oh, Carolina," as well as two other tunes, "Chubby" and "I Make a Man" after eight hours of frustrating toil. "Oh, Carolina" became an instant hit in the dancehalls. The tune was composed off of a Stax Records R&B hit called "'Cause I Love You" by Carla and Rufus Thomas, according to Prince Buster, although a British high court sided with John Folkes in November 1994 in his claim that *he* was the songwriter.

Don Drummond and Margarita were key figures in the Wareika Hills in the 1950s and 1960s. They were incredibly powerful in spreading the seeds of jazz, ska, Rasta music, African rhythms, Jamaican rhythms, artistic creation, improvisation, collaboration. Like Count Ossie, they were part of the backbone of the Wareika Hills, drawing others to communicate their expressions. Don and Margarita were the storytellers, the teachers, the prophets.

Count Ossie died in a car crash on October 18, 1976, at the age of 50.

10

Love in the Afternoon

Ayata, Jah dawta, from Venturian border, a come
Aya, Ayata woman a come
Ayata Jah dawta woman a come
Jah dawta Ayata a come to sound
Ungu Malungu man
Ungu Malungu man
Ungu Malungu man
Ayata Jah dawta from Venturian border woman a come
If you see him before I do
Please give him my heart message so true
Tell him I just don't want to be without him
For I'd be lost and lonely and blue
He is my love, my life, my all
Ungu Malungu man
Ungu Malungu man
The king of ace from outer space
Ungu Malungu man
He speaks the language of the breeze
And harmonizes it with the symphony of the trees
And when I'm in my solitude
I can hear, I can hear the breeze singing to me
Not imaginary sounds but true melody of my beautiful
Ungu Malungu man
So if you see him before I do
Please give him my message so true
Tell him Ayata Jah dawta from Venturian border woman a come
— from "Woman A Come" by Margarita and
the Baba Brooks Band

In 1964, Margarita recorded the song "Woman A Come" for Treasure Isle. Baba Brooks performed on trumpet, Tommy McCook was on tenor saxophone, and Lloyd Knibb provided the Burru drums. The song was originally called "Ungu Malungu Man" but Duke Reid changed the title because he thought the name sounded too "obeah" or folksy, even though

Knibb contends that Drummond was opposed to the suggestive name "Woman A Come." Keyboardist Glen Adams says he helped Margarita to rehearse the song at Duke Reid's studio and helped to form the song. He says Reid sent Margarita to him so he could help her with the tune; he even comments that had he been a little older, he would have liked to have had her as his girl. Despite Adams's and Reid's fingerprints on the production, the creativity, the words, the meaning, the tune is all Margarita's invention, and the song is a testament to her connection to Rastafarianism. Malungu is an exiled godlike character in East African folklore, so these lyrics reflect Margarita's involvement with the Rastararianism she acquired in the Wareika Hills, as well as a tribute to the African roots of her Jamaican brethren and dawtas. The song reached number seven on the Jamaican charts.

It is also important to note that this was one of the very few songs written and sung by a solo female artist. Most songs that featured female vocalists, up to that point, were duos with other prominent male artists such as Derrick and Patsy (Derrick Morgan and Millicent Todd), Stranger and Patsy (Stranger Cole and Millicent Todd), Roy & Millie (Roy Panton and Millie Small), Roy & Yvonne (Roy Panton and Yvonne Harrison), Derrick & Yvonne (Derrick Morgan and Yvonne Harrison) and Alton & Phyllis (Alton Ellis and Phyllis Dillon). Even though Millie Small had an international hit in 1964 and paved the way for ska in other countries, especially the U.K., her song was not an original and was written a decade earlier by Robert Spencer and recorded in 1956 by Barbie Gaye. Anita Mahfood, schooled by years of performing with musicians, composers, and producers, wrote and sang her own song, a true feat in those male-dominated times. Marcia Griffiths re-recorded Margarita's song in 1981, which is also evidence of its worth.

The lyrics of the song are a sweet but painful love poem to Don Drummond, her Ungu Malungu Man. Herbie Miller says, "It was a song considered by many [as] an ode to Drummond." Margarita's best friend, Norma Faye Chin, remembers this song well and remembers Margarita writing it: "I think it was at the camp she made a song called 'Ungu Malungu Man.' She sit down and wrote part of it at my house. If I can remember the words, 'Ungu Malungu Man, Ungu Malungu Man, if you see him before I do, please tell him I'll be faithful and true, I don't want to lose you,' something like that. Those are the words [*sobbing*]."

The words of the song are painful today when you hear Margarita's longing and devotion to her spiritual man, Don Drummond. Herbie Miller writes, "Margarita's song is both a work of art or art song and an incredibly moving love song. Her vocal tone describes completely a woman deeply in love talking about her man." Their relationship was a natural progression of being close professionally for a decade, spiritually in the Wareika Hills for many years, and then living together in the same home. Chin says, "When you're in show business you meet all the people that play music, in a band, singers, dancers, you know? You always end up on a show together or you go out on assignment and different companies hire you and you meet somebody there and you exchange phone numbers, you keep in touch, things like that. Don Drummond now, I didn't know him like to sit and talk to. I know him if I go to the shows and he's there and we have a drink or we sit and chat after the show. And then when Anita got involved with him, and start having the children, he would come by my house because a lot of times I had her children and he would come by to see the kids."

It is evident that Drummond and Margarita had known each other on the entertainment circuit for many years, but according to Paul Jad Mahfood, it was Drummond who first approached Margarita with romantic interests. "He came up to her," Paul asserts. "He had been interested in her. And she reciprocated the interest because she felt he was a guy who had popular recognition. It was said he was ranked number one in the Caribbean and number three in the world at the time. Males dominated the music world and so, to be a female, you'd have to be a dancer and you'd have to be a seductive dancer because the lecherous interests of males were at these clubs. You'd have these wealthy men who would leave their wives and go off to these clubs and they'd see these women dancing and it would turn them on and they would do what they would do later that night with whomever, so she would generate a certain amount of income and so on, and being exposed to other musicians, Don Drummond introduced himself in some fashion and that's how that started." Conchita claims that Anita's devotion for Don became so fervent that she even turned down a contract to go to the United States to dance.

Chin says that Anita was fascinated with Drummond because of his musical talent. In fact, she says that Drummond was teaching Anita to play the saxophone so that she could share in their musical intimacy. "He's a fantastic trombone player, he was," says Chin. "Worldwide he is known. He's very, very good. And that was the thing that draw Anita to that man.

Margarita shows off her own saxophone which Don Drummond was teaching her to play (courtesy Suzanne Bent).

That was the thing that drew her to him because she always wanted to play instrument like the saxophone and he would teach her. He would tell her how to do it and things." Conchita adds that Anita was also taking piano lessons; she even started wearing Rasta colors when she was with Don.

But Chin contends that Anita and Don Drummond were a platonic couple — a perception that virtually everyone else who knew the two negates. "They were friends, they weren't lovers," insists Chin. "Everybody think they were lovers. They weren't lovers, they were friends. They didn't become lovers. What happened was she was married to a no-good, Bent, and he used to beat her a lot. When he used to hit her, she would take the kids, when he was gone and she would bring them up to my house, in Harbor View, where I was living at the time. And she would leave the kids with me and she would come back days later or weeks later or months later because she was moving from place to place where he couldn't find her. Don played at some place that she dance and they were talking and she tell him she have nowhere and he said, 'You could come stay by me.' So she went to live with him. I'm just picturing the room as I'm speaking. They had two small beds, one on the left-hand side of the room. One was his bed, one was her bed. So they share it like roommates. But she also like to smoke and he likes to smoke, you know? So she was okay for a while being there, I think, but she wasn't happy because I had the kids at that time and she wanted to get her own place, but she did not have a permanent job. She only depend on the gigs, so months later she got this job where she danced and the owner of the club decide to have her as a featured dancer every week."

Sergi believes that the reason others watched Anita's children is not just because she was getting away from Bent after the divorce, but because the relationship with Drummond was developing. "She met Don Drummond and she would leave, say she'd be back in a few hours and not come back for days," says Sergi. "My mom had three kids by then and with Anita's two more, it was very hard, very difficult. She and Don Drummond would break up and she'd come back home. Then they'd get back together and she'd leave again."

Conchita remembers that her sister told her that she loved Don. They moved in together at 9 Rusden Road, in the Rockfort area, in August 1964. Drummond was already living at this address prior to Margarita moving in. In fact, it is likely that this was Drummond's first place away from his mother's home or Alpha, unless one considers the times he spent living in the Wareika Hills. According to genealogical records from the Jamaican Registrar General's Department, Doris Munroe, Don's mother, married on February 4, 1962. Perhaps this is when Don began living in the hills or on Rusden Road. Munroe, whose marital status was listed as a "spinster," and her occupation was that of "domestic." She married 54-year-old "laborer" Claudius Smith, a "bachelor." The wedding was held at the Salvation Army Hall in Savanna-La-Mar, in the parish of Westmoreland, an area on the other side of the island and the same parish where she was born. Drummond was left to live on his own as a result. It is not known what kind of impact this marriage had on Don's fragile psyche.

Drummond's solitary nature likely was suited to solo living, but he simply couldn't resist Margarita's magnetic appeal. Tommy McCook has said that Don and Anita were inseparable, a description echoed by others who saw them together. Marcia Griffiths, for example, says, "I knew Don Drummond and Margarita as man and woman living together. Sometimes you would see them together, herself and Don Drummond. They would both be together waiting on the bus." Rico, too, recalls that the relationship flourished in the Wareika Hills, even though Anita was still married legally, but not spiritually, to Rudolph Bent. "Margarita now, she used to come up to the Wareika Hills, you know?" Rico says. "And Drummond made friends with her, and so forth, but I don't know much about that.... She was really into him." Referring to Anita, Owen Grey says, "Don Drummond had one of the prettiest girls in Jamaica." Sparrow Martin says, "She loved Don Drummond dearly because of his music. Whenever he play, she would dance. She was a beautiful woman, she had long hair down her back. And when she danced, people look at her. And Don hold his head, he don't like that. When he came to play she come up to him when he play his trombone and she danced all over him just like a snake dancer, and he would play his serenade and she'd dance. And she never love anyone but Don."

But this relationship was disconcerting among those who knew the couple. Herbie Miller writes,

> The relationship of the couple created concerns for the "brethren" in the community and in particular among the musicians who worried that the trombonist fragile mental state would be unable to withstand the dancer's free spirited nature and enticing persona. Impervious to the opinions of skeptics, the dancer set up domestic residence in the vicinity of the Wareika Hills with Don Drummond.

The love affair between Don Drummond and Anita was difficult from the start, for many reasons. As Miller points out,

He was from the black lower class, a representation of the enslaved plantation family, further stymied by circumstances which made it difficult for his parents to care for him and that led to his institutionalization at Alpha School for Boys. She was the product of a family with name recognition in the business community, perceived as middle class, and was considered Jamaican white. Yet they represented the "art couple" of the marginalized Afro-Jamaican community they were a part of. He was her mystic man, she his cosmic love light.

Anita may have felt herself a protector, a caretaker for her love. She refused to allow Don to spend time away from his higher calling, performing on stage, performing in the studio, realizing his potential. Calvin "Bubbles" Cameron recalls, "When I went to Rusden Road to get lesson from Don Drummond, she says to me, 'Well he is not teaching you today. Don Drummond don't have the time to do that now.' She says that in such a tone, and I am a younger person, so I never want to go back. The tone was not really in line with what I want. He told me yes, he would teach me. He told me. She was a strong lady. She was a strong one."

"It was a relationship that cut across the traditional class relationships at the time," says P.J. Patterson. "It was a strange relationship. They were two very very talented people and while Anita was a sort of jovial and fun-loving person, I think, I have often said that he is one of the most melancholic people that I've ever known. He really rarely smiled, and watching him on the bandstand, anytime he was really into it, he would express himself simply by jumping on the stand. But hardly would you ever see him like the other members of the band. The chamois, you never saw him with a kerchief. He would take the chamois and wipe his face when he got excited and was carried away. The person hardly spoke. He hardly spoke."

It is important to realize that, in Jamaica, social classes are the defining structure in the culture, more so than race. Heather Royes comments, "We are sort of a class society, so it's a very stratified situation. It's not even race because we're all so bloody mixed up. You can choose your race in Jamaica, but it's more class, so I would imagine that in the 'fifties and 'sixties that had a lot to do with it."

But the relationship was also troubled because Don Drummond had not been socialized in the ways of female interaction. His Catholic upbringing in an all-male school like Alpha Boys School only further isolated him from the romantic world. In her dissertation on Alpha Boys School, Dr. Sandra Mayo writes, "The ability to forge relationships with women and enter into a marriage relationship is difficult when those types of bonds were not fostered in the adolescent and early years."

Herman "Woody" King claims that Don had little experience with women: "Even though he was a good-looking guy, he never had a lot of girls like most of the guys, you understand? When he finally met Margarita and got together I think she overwhelmed him. He couldn't handle it. He got jealous very easily. You could tell he wasn't accustomed to having the ladies around. He would do things like tell her not to dance when the band was playing. He wanted her to sit there. At this time with the Skatal-ites, they were so powerful as a group that it's like putting butter by a cat's mouth and telling him not to lick it. It's almost impossible. She always get up and dance, and he would stop playing and get in a fit of jealousy and when he had a break he would hold her by the throat and pull out his knife and act as if she was doing something bad. You could tell he wasn't used to the ladies and eventually that destroyed him."

Derrick Morgan also witnessed these violent interactions: "Once I was in a club with him and Margarita, the girl that he was along with, and she was sittin' with me around the table and he just come up, pull a pen out that she have in her hand, put it down and give her a stab with it. He stab her with that pen because she was sittin' with me. He pulled the pen away from her and stab her with it. I remember that of Don. I always say to Margarita, 'What you doing with Don? Like it's two mad people together, because he is mad and you are with him so you must be mad, too.' She and I used to talk very good."

Karl "Cannonball" Bryan saw warning signs as well: "Their love life was weird because every time she perform at a club, Don was there, watch-ing her and he make a little sign and she have to come to him. Sometimes they have a fight."

Chin recalls, "She used to tell me, 'I think this man is crazy.' So I used to tell her, 'Anita, you know, Don *is* crazy.' She used to say, 'But he plays such good music, how can he be crazy?' To her she was looking at the pureness of his music. That's what attracted her to him. Everybody tell her he's crazy, he might kill you one day. She was the only one who was with him every day and they smoke together, them play the music. She would do anything, I guess."

Brian Keyo in the liner notes to Foundation Ska writes of Lloyd

Knibb's account of one of Don and Margarita's violent arguments that took place in the back of one of the recording studios.

> Marguerita bothered Don with an argument and he just stick her with the pen [a steel fountain pen]. He was writing out a next tune, to get it ready and she rush in. I have to go and carry her to a doctor nearby. It was on top of her right hand, I think. It needed to be dressed and plastered. The doctor was at Three Mile, near the roundabout. It was a pharmacy place and he just pressed it and put a bandage on and she can come back to the session. When we get back her and Don just a hug up like nothing happen. Apparently, Margarita was writing the song "Ungu Malungu Man" and asked Drummond for input on the song, interrupting him, because he was writing a song at the same time.

Sergi says, "When Don Drummond stabbed her in the leg once and came to my mom [Conchita], she kept Anita's dress for years with blood all over it. My mom told her to stay away from him, he'll kill you, but she went back." Conchita adds that Don had even cracked a bottle over Anita's head, requiring her to go to the hospital for stitches.

The pattern of abuse that Anita used to shape her life had taken her from the home of her father, to the home of Rudolph Bent, and now to the home of Don Drummond. And even though Don may have thought he, as a Jamaican man, could call the shots and forbid her to dance, just as she had told her own father, dancing was her calling, her passion, and her spirit. And so, one New Year's Day, just like any other performance night, Margarita and Don had gigs at different locations. Only this night was different. This night would not end with an hour-long solo to cheering crowds. This night would not end with a final quiver of voluptuous ruffles. This night would not end with a post-performance smoke and jam in the Wareika Hills. On this night, Margarita stepped out of their shared home at 9 Rusden Road, closed the door quietly as Don Drummond lay inside napping on his single bed, walked down the dusty road and onto the bus. She sat, still, calm, peaceful, as the Rockfort bus rode up to Club Havana, where she would give the performance of her life.

11

Rusden Road

When rat like fi romp 'roun' puss jaw, one diay 'im gwine en up inna puss craw.
—Jamaican proverb meaning, "When one flirts too much with danger, soon he or she will get hurt."

Soft wax, vinyl, a record, with a crack, throws the needle from its groove. Looping, repeatedly, the sound, not music, but a skip. The needle jumps. The refrain jumps. Static punctuates the mesh of the speakers. The rotating spiral, one continuous furrow of vibrations, is broken. The record is ruined. The song is destroyed. The music is shattered.

On January 1, 1965, Don Drummond was scheduled to perform at a gig with the Skatalites at the La Parisienne Club in Harbour View, a club near the Palisadoes Airport in east Kingston. He never made it to that performance. It was not the first time he missed a gig. He frequently missed performances or was late for a gig. Tommy McCook has said that he sent Lloyd Knibb to pick up Don at eight P.M., prior to the gig, and found him asleep so he left without him and returned after their first set during intermission to try again. Still, Don was asleep, a side effect of the medicine he took, said McCook.

But many have thought over the years that Drummond became upset when he finally awoke to find not only that he had slept through the show, but that Margarita was gone. His defenders claim that Margarita manipu - lated his medication dosage or gave it to him late so she could go dance at the Baby Grand on Crossroads for her first show, and at Club Havana in Rockfort where she had her residency to dance the rhumba for wealthy, gawking men. There is no way to prove such a claim. Zola Buckland Sergi, Margarita's niece, feels that many fans, band mates, or Rastafarians are skeptical of the events and merely looking for an explanation, looking to put the onus on Margarita for Drummond's actions. She dispels this myth: "People say she must have given him his medication improperly and so he slept through it. She didn't give him his medication! He took his own medication! My mom said it was impossible and people are looking for a reason why he killed her. The reason is, he was nuts!" Such accusations defy logic.

Who knows what visions ran through Don's mind while he sat there in his small room at 9 Rusden Road, images of his young lover, dancing, barefoot, bare legs, long arms gliding like serpents toward the crowd of ogling men and their submissive dates. Long locks swaying to the drumbeats, the Latin rhythms, ruffles shaking, waving, stealing the attention of everyone, all eyes upon her, the solo dancer.

Margarita knew Don did not want her to dance that night, or any night, but she was her own woman. She made her own decisions. Her dance was for the crowd, but her love belonged only to Don, and so she thought he could see her "heart message so true" as she sang in her song, the only song she ever wrote, one for her lover. No one stopped her from dancing, not that night, not ever.

"We were playing sound system music right behind Sabina Park," says Winston Smith, Drummond's close friend, remembering that night when he went out with a few of his friends and ran into Margarita after her dance. "We didn't stay too long. At one o'clock we went up to this club up on Crossroads. Just as we sat down to start drinking, because what we did at night was nobody's business. We'd drink until daylight and then go to work late. And she ran in there and said, 'One of you guys are going to have to take me home because Junie doesn't know where I am. He told me not to go.'" Junie was Margarita's nickname for Don. Smith continues, "She didn't have a way to go home. She didn't even change her regalia yet. She was still in her dancing clothes. And Lennie [Hibbert] decided that since we were living next door to each other, I'd drive with him. I didn't have a motor vehicle and we were coming from what was known as the Glass Bucket Club. And what happened was we took her home, got to the gate and went in and we just saw her go in. The door open and we drove off. If I had known that the man was in there, cause I'd expected that he would've been working at the Bournemouth Club or wherever and he probably wouldn't have gotten out yet. But I didn't know there was a rift or anything like that going on. 'Cause we could've gone in with her and things would've been different. Apparently he thought whoever she was out with brought her home, not knowing it was us, because he knew me very well. We knew each other very well, not to mention Lennie, a musician he used to play with sometimes."

141

Anita's best friend, Norma Faye Chin, says that the argument that took place inside their room at 9 Rusden Road was not over her dancing, but about her plans for the future. Chin says, "She was talking to some woman in the yard earlier in the day because Don was going to play out that night and she was going to dance that night, but she told this woman that she was so happy that she had gotten this permanent job and now she can find a room for herself and get her kids, and talking and talking like that. Apparently the woman must have mentioned to Don, 'Oh, Miss Anita going to move, she find a place.' She was smoking that day, he didn't go out to work, she went to work. She came home after show business that night."

Most who knew the couple say that the argument they had that night (one they had frequently) was over Margarita's dancing. Smith says, "There is no question as to whether he was seriously in love with her, but he warned her not to go out and do any more of this rhumba dancing because

Margarita performs at Club Havana only hours before her murder (© The Gleaner Company Limited).

his woman is not supposed to be exposing her body to other men. She was half naked most of the time while dancing and that's what she did on that fateful night. It is hardly likely that anyone could fathom the feelings that run through a mind such as his. He could be a pussycat this minute and raging tiger the next, and what he did mostly was exuded his rage into music or peacefulness." Ken Stewart says, "He didn't want her to be out dancing. He liked it when she came to the show with him and danced at the Skatalites show." Derrick Morgan also says the fight was over her dancing. "He was jealous. He took her life, yeah."

Paul Jad Mahfood, Margarita's half-brother, says that neighbors had observed strange behavior at the home in the weeks prior to that night. "I learned from neighbors that they observed Mr. Drummond in the backyard of their house, sharpening a knife," Paul claims. "He would sharpen the knife around the same time every day for about two weeks. And they never knew why he was doing it. It didn't seem to be important to them but the fence that separated houses back then was basically shrubbery. And back then with their laundry, they would wash it and hang it up on the line, so they could see him back there. And he was seen back there on many occasions. He would sharpen the knife and then he would put the knife in a certain spot in the back yard and then he would go in."

Margarita arrived home at 9 Rusden Road in the early hours of January 2, 1965. The events that followed could clearly be heard through the house's thin walls. Faye Chin says, "Now this place was like a house and you rent a room and another person rent a room and another person rent a room. So this woman that her room was behind their room, she said she heard when Anita came in and she laid down on her bed, she heard a scream and said, 'Oh God, Don, what are you doing?' She's screaming, 'Don, what are you doing?' And he stabbed her so badly. There was no blood. The knife stabbed her in the chest. I got a call early in the morning and I phoned Conchita, her sister, I tell her, 'Okay, I'm coming to pick you up,' and I drove over to Conchita's house, pick her up and we went down to identify the body. She had on her skirt [*sobbing*] and she had on a shirt with a stain in the front at her waist and she was just laying on her bed on her back [*sobbing uncontrollably*]." The clothes she wore, the last clothes she would ever wear, were ones made by her own hand, the ones that Conchita herself witnessed being cut off of her the next day at the morgue as a team collected evidence and prepared her body for burial.

Sergi remembers vividly that dreadful phone call early that morning:

"Aunt Faye — we all [call] her Aunt Faye because she is like family — called the people across the street, the Hemmings, who had a phone. We didn't have a phone. They got my mom and told my mom. They took her to ID the body and took her into the murder scene. When they went to the murder scene there were a group of Rastafarians lined up on the street, all dressed in black. She was on the bed, a single bed, laying across it and the knife was stuck in her chest. It was embedded. They couldn't get it out. That's the image my mom has in her mind. And then my mom had to go to court as a witness. It was very difficult." The Rastas all called Anita by their nickname for her as they brought her body from the house in a metal box covered with a red blanket. "All right Maggie. All right Maggie," they said with sorrow. Her half-eaten ackee and salt fish still lay on her bed, her wedding ring was still on her finger. Anita's oldest sister, Monira, destroyed, brokenhearted, took from her collection of records all that contained the sounds of Don Drummond's wailing trombone and broke them.

Heather Royes, whose father was administrator at Bellevue at that time, recalls the moments after the murder: "I remember the morning he stabbed Margarita because the porter and the doctor came running over to our house, not far away, and they had him in the police station nearby. I was there that morning, will never forget it. They said it was a 'fuss.' I think some jealousy was involved. Dr. Shoucair was my father's protégé. He was a general practitioner. His family was a well-known Lebanese family. He would work with my father and that was part of his internship. He was the first person called that morning. I remember Dr. Shoucair and one of the porters, or male nurses, rushing in. I can't remember what time of the morning, waking us up saying, 'Doctor! Don Drummond has murdered his girlfriend and he's in the police station now,' which was just around the corner, and they were describing the whole thing. Apparently it was a pretty brutal thing. It was clearly a very brutal murder."

Indeed it was. There were four deep stab wounds in Anita's body. Dr. Frederick Hickling, who was present at the post-mortem, recalls, "It was clear that the stab wound that would have killed her severed the intercostals artery and very likely she would have died by exsanguinations, bleeding into her chest cavity. The wounds were deep enough to get into the chest cavity." When asked if the wound could have been self-inflicted as Drummond would claim at the Rockfort Police Station moments after the murder, Hickling replied, "It certainly didn't seem so."

Musicologist Herbie Miller says what many recognize as the truth,

"It may even have been a clinical state of madness, an attack of the schizophrenia that he had to live with that caused Drummond to commit this nefarious deed." And even though everyone knew that Don Drummond suffered from mental illness, it still came as a shock to many close to him that he could be capable of such a violent, brutal attack. Some are still in disbelief even today. Close friend Eddie "Tan Tan" Thornton says, "I was supposed to send for Don Drummond. I came to England to perform in 1954. I was supposed to send for him in England, but it wasn't possible. When I leave, everything just happen to him. He was a good boy. He used to live with his mother. He was a very good boy, I don't know what happen because he was a decent good boy." Headley Bennett, O.D., has a similar reaction: "It was a surprise for me because when I leave him, he was okay. I got the job with Eric Deans Orchestra, and when I came to Kingston I heard he was in Bellevue."

Perhaps no one was more stunned though than Winston Smith who, along with Lennie Hibbert, had given Margarita a ride on the evening of her demise. "I was at work and somebody said they heard it on the radio between the nine-thirty A.M. and ten-thirty A.M. news or something like that," Smith recalls. "What they used to do in those days was they used to bring over the news on the half hour, the important headings. So a girl came and told me, she said, 'Mr. Smith, you know what? Don killed Margarita last night.' I said, 'No, he couldn't have killed her last night because I took her home this morning, unless it was somebody else I took home.' So I waited until the newscast came back again and I heard it. I didn't believe it. Everybody loved this guy. They went up there and just took him and I never saw him after that. I came to the U.S. shortly after."

For others, though, the murder came as no surprise. Graeme Goodall says, "The thing is, when he got into violent troubles with killing, nobody was shocked by it or surprised by it. I certainly wasn't. None of us were shocked, we just said, 'Well Don Drummond's finally lost it, yeah, right, we'll go on to something else.' It wasn't one of these, 'Really?! He did *what*?!' All of the musicians were very upset when Ernest Ranglin's son drowned tragically and Ernest went to pieces, completely. Now, there we were, all surprised because Ernest was completely the opposite to Don, very talented and a good musician who got on well with everybody and when he went through his tragedy, everyone was surprised, but with Don, eh, it was going to happen one day. Not quite as bad as it turned out, but we all thought something huge would."

Helene Lee recounts the memory of Sister Shuggas, a fellow dancer at Count Ossie's camp. Sister Shuggas says that Don Drummond actually came to the hills after the murder to visit Lloyd Knibb, who was living at Wareika. She says that Lloyd Knibb knew that Margarita would die that night, although it is not known how he knew, perhaps simply because of Drummond's deteriorated mental state, or perhaps because he knew that Margarita had found knives hidden under Don's mattress on many occasions. But when Drummond came to the camp that night, before he went to the Rockfort Police Station, he told Knibb, "She's up there."

Ken Stewart recalls that Knibb was quick to arrive at the crime scene: "Lloyd was on the scene shortly after [it happened] and he was somehow allowed access into the apartment that Don lived in and he grabbed all of the music. Because Don had a bunch of unfinished music in his dresser and this is the music you hear on the *Return of the Big Guns* album as well as some of what's on *Rolling Steady*. That music that Lloyd found in the dresser drawer of Margarita's desk was the music that Lloyd got, passed it to Tommy [McCook] and Tommy did his best to finish it because some of the tunes weren't finished and that's what they recorded on the two albums."

Trombonist Calvin "Bubbles" Cameron says, "I was fortunate to record five songs out of Don Drummond's book because Tommy gave me his book and said, 'Take any songs you want to do out of this book,' and I took five and I recorded them on *Return of the Big Guns*. It was Don Drummond's book, I saw his own writing. A guy name Arnold Brackenridge [the trumpeter] and myself went to Tommy McCook's home and Tommy had more confidence in me because he taught me certain things, and I had the opportunity to have the book in my possession a time, took songs out of it, wrote and played, and I return it to Tommy McCook. They were ska songs. They were finished but they weren't recorded. I was the first person to record out of that manuscript and everyone is asking me, where is the manuscript. I don't know. I gave it back to Tommy. If it was right now I would probably photocopy it and keep a copy for myself, but it wasn't that modern for me to have a photocopy machine around. They were recorded at Dynamic Studio." Janet Roper, Tommy McCook's daughter who some say had her father's belongings after he immigrated to the U.S., says she doesn't know what happened to Drummond's notebooks, nor does she remember ever having them. There are reports that they may have ended up tossed in the trash after Roper joined a religious group whose members lived in tents and denounced material possessions.

The pallbearers at Anita's funeral included her ex-husband, Rudolph Bent; her ex-brother-in-law, Louis Bent; her best friend's husband, Carl Chin; and her brother-in-law, Keith Buckland, Conchita's husband. According to the *Daily Gleaner*, mourners for Anita included Murad Mahfood (Anita's uncle), Paul Mahfood (Anita's half brother), Norma Faye Chin, Michael Laughton, Ben Johnston, Vera Scott, W. Robinson, W. Mahfood (likely Wadeeha, Anita's aunt), Fay Bennet, and A. Rodriguez (perhaps Amy Rodriguez, Rico's mother). There are some family members who are so traumatized by the murder that they cannot bear to relive the memory of losing their deeply cherished Anita. Daughter Suzanne says, "I know my mom, she was rebellious, but for anybody to kill a woman like that...." The words are not easy, even today.

Sergi says, "People spoke negatively about my aunt Anita, and it's always the same thing. They never have anything good to say. They speak highly of Don and make it look like she asked for it because she was dancing and he didn't like her dancing." Sergi's father, Keith Buckland, took his sister-in-law's death especially hard. "My dad was on the road [at the time of the murder]" Sergi remembers. "He traveled with work. He came back and he didn't know she had been killed. My mom told him and he went out onto the veranda and went to the floor. He started to bawl. It was the only time I've ever seen my dad cry. He paid for her whole funeral." Also deeply affected is Norma Faye Chin, who continues to mourn the loss of her best friend and fellow dancer. "She goes to the cemetery where my aunt is buried," Sergi says. "There was no marker, but she found it."

Paul Jad Mahfood remembers the life-altering effect Anita's death had on his father: "I went to her funeral. I could see in my father's face, something happened. My father's face was changed. There was a black curtain that was drawn. He began to smoke more, he drank more, he would have more women over. The activities, in hindsight, and with my knowledge and interest in science and psychology, he was trying to drown out the pain he was experiencing."

The following year, 1966, Anita's father, Jad, died, the official cause of death being pneumonia. Another death occurred as well. According to an article in the *Jamaica Gleaner*, on June 7, 1983, Drummond's fate "seemed to sound the death knell for the band whose career was intertwined with his own." The Skatalites, despite having a few remaining pieces of Don Drummond's music smuggled out by Knibb, were unable to continue on for long without their famed trombonist. And without the Skatalites, ska would not be able to sustain. The music was forever changed. Tommy McCook later said, "And that was the end of that era. 'Cause they put him away indefinitely, so he couldn't come out again as before. We went on a few months after he got himself in trouble, but every time the band play, people keep lookin', hopin' that he would show up and now they know that he won't show up, so we may as well call it a day." Klive Walker writes, "Drummond's departure from Jamaica's popular music scene in 1965, as a result of his incarceration, left a huge void in the Skatalites and in the continued expression of ska."

By 1966, a brutal heat wave came to the island and slowed the music down. The era of rocksteady was ushered in. This music was marked by more vocals, fewer brass instruments, and a rhythm that was less frenzied and slower for dancers in the stagnant temperatures. "In rocksteady it is the bass and the drum that changes and make it slower and we call it rocksteady," says guitarist Lyn Taitt. It was only a matter of time before the music slowed down even more, the rhythm altered yet again, and reggae emerged to bring in an entirely new period for the island.

Today, the home at 9 Rusden Road — if one could even call it a home anymore — is a weathered heap of rubbled cement blocks and wooden planks hidden from the remote street by a tall zinc wall along the broken sidewalk. The foundation is gone, suspended on a few remaining pillars of concrete with completely exposed guts, plastic crates and 45s strewn underneath in the dirt, broken glass, wires, and trash left there by a tenant decades ago, one assumes. The current tenant, Carmen, a large woman with a toothless smile, lives in the house, alone.

12

Tear Up

The music may have gone on without Don Drummond, and the dance may have continued without Margarita, but nothing was the same. Certainly life for Margarita's two children was changed forever. At the time of their mother's death, Suzanne, aged four, and Christopher, aged two, were living with their grandmother in Belize. "It was something, the night when she got killed," Suzanne recounts. "She had just come in from a New Year's dance, and I heard it was one of her best performances ever. Her last performance. And she died January second, not January first, because it was after four o'clock. And at that particular time, both my brother and I, we got up. We went to the window, because it was spooky in Belize, and we looked at the moon and I was hugging my little brother, and we just started screaming. We were just crying, and my grandma and my aunt, they came, and they were like, 'What's wrong with these kids? What's wrong with them?' And we were just bawling. The next day my grandmother got a telegram that said our mother just had got killed that same time."

Her grandmother never told her about the murder, but a few years later, Suzanne found out on her own. She says, "I could never see what was in the newspaper. My grandma never wanted us to read it. But I learned to read real good. At about eight years old I learned how to read and I grabbed the paper when she went out to the store and I called my little brother because he was inquisitive, too. I grabbed a newspaper and read it to my little brother because my mom's face was on it. It was just me and him all the time, me and my brother, so I read it and it said my mom had a knife in her left breast, and that's most of what I remember, that he left a knife in her left breast. But Conchita told me she took the knife out of her. The bed my mother died in, she was laying across the bed, 'cause he turned her over and put the knife there. She kept my mom's bed. My aunt Conchita wanted to raise me, take me first, 'cause she was already struggling, she said. She wanted to take me but they [my father's parents] wouldn't allow me to come to Jamaica."

Life was hard for little Suzanne and Christopher. "Poverty in Belize," Suzanne recalls. "It was poor. But my grandma, she made ends meet. She worked hard. You know how them black women were back in them days, way back when, she'd call on Jesus." Does Suzanne have any personal memories of her mother? "I have absolutely none, absolutely none," she says sadly. "I had a dream and I seen a lady with real light skin and some pretty hair. I'm like, 'Was that my mother in that dream?' Sometimes I wonder because I actually don't know." She does have a few photos of her mother given to her over the years by family and friends. "How I got any pictures of my mom is through her [Norma Faye Chin] or through the Internet. She sent me my baby picture and she sent one where my mom is holding me as a baby. I have absolutely no memory and she tells me about my mom, because my father actually took my brother and me from her yard, is what I was told. The Mahfoods had no idea what had happened to us. We were stolen. Stolen. Stolen and deprived are my words for it."

Suzanne says she is not certain if Don Drummond is the one who killed her mother. Suzanne says, "My mom never even got a chance to say anything. This lady was not sick. She was twenty-four years old. I feel like due to the fact that my father stole me and my brother, 'cause she died the next year, not even a year I believe [since we were taken], my father really had a lot to do with it, I truly believe. She didn't tell him to take her kids. I feel like if you take my kids, then what do I have to live for? I couldn't go on. This is what I feel my mom was going through and then she just chose a crazy man."

As Anita suffered abuse, so, too, did Suzanne: "Abuse and everything for a motherless child, mind you. My father's family never even knew my mom or anything but the lies my father spread, bad rumors about my mom, too. Like they used to tell me I was Don Drummond's daughter when I was growin' up. The worst part of my life was what my father's side had to say about my mom. Mind you, these mother-freakers ain't knew nothing about her, never met her, or her family. Today I'm still going through situations, letting them know, 'Listen, you never knew my mom so please leave my mom's name out of your mouth.' When I was getting beaten, it was like, 'Oh, you're not a Bent.' They were saying Don Drummond was my father. When my mom went with Rudolph, she was a virgin. They didn't play that stuff, understand? He didn't even marry my mom until I was born. My father told me he wasn't my father. He told me I was going to die like my mother, with a knife in my heart. I never forgot that. And I forgive him so I can move on. I forgot it, but it just came back. It's like that little child in you still."

There was physical abuse as well, especially at the hands of their grandmother. "She was whipping my ass like I was a little slave girl," Suzanne says. "Even though I love my grandmother, the brutal beatings I got, let it be known. I'm not going to sugar coat anything. Here's a child that don't have a mother, mother was murdered, you're supposed to love that child. Guess where I got love from? People came from the United States, they were nuns and Christians, and they hold me dear to their heart, they give me the Bible. When I would go home I would get a straight beating, and I mean brutal. Maybe it did help me in my life, because I wouldn't do that to anybody, not even if I didn't like somebody. I'm non-violent. How could you do that to a child? It makes no sense to say I'm not your grandchild because I have a round face. I love my grandmother and all that, she raised me, but she told me I wasn't even her grandchild.... For me, all I could do was pray to my mom and Jesus."

How did Suzanne's abusive childhood impact her life? "I'm not past the worst yet but I'm way better now than I would've expected me to be," she says candidly. "When I inquire about my mom and I hear good things and I know the person I am, I know she was a good person. The majority of people tell me she was very nice. I am a part of her."

Suzanne is still conflicted about her mother's life, her death, and the ties to her own existence: "When your parents want you to grow up a certain way and so does society, and what happened to her was truly a tragedy, but if she would've went the way her parents really wanted her to go and how they were living, she wouldn't have wound up with him. Maybe that was her destiny, I don't know, but I don't believe that. I feel like my mom was rebellious due to the fact that she married a black man. My father is so black. By her doing that it was already a rebellion against the Arabic culture. But her father was the same way, only he chose a white woman from Jamaican descent. My grandfather, Jad Mahfood, used to hold me up and say, 'Oh, poor little Susie,' so what do you make of that? The only think I could think is, well, 'cause I'm black and I have black features. I'm half black and I'm half I don't know what I am."

Suzanne, Christopher, and their grandmother immigrated to the United States, specifically the borough of New York known as the Bronx, in the early 1970s. Suzanne was ten years old at the time; she moved out on her own when she was 15. "My grandma, I still love her because she did show me some good ways," Suzanne says, revealing her conflicted feelings. "She couldn't help herself, back in them days that's how they were. I got it the worst. I was the only girl with six boys, so I was washing other kids' clothes, bathing kids, I was taking care of kids and maybe that's why I have so much. My grandma, she passed away at ninety-three." Suzanne's brother, Christopher, is currently incarcerated.

Over the years, Suzanne has tried to honor her mother's memory by displaying the few photographs she has of her in the family home, but that has proven difficult: "My father had a picture of my mom and he charged me a hundred and fifty dollars for that picture one day. He kept this picture in his wallet. Then I met my uncle Paul Jad Mahfood. He had a whole shrine of nothing but my mom. That was his favorite sister. And he gave me one picture off of his bureau in his bedroom and he told me not to let my dad see it, and I did, and I never did get that picture back."

13

Her Majesty's Pleasure

To determine if Drummond should be committed on a charge of murder, a preliminary inquiry took place on January 19, 1965. The court filled with spectators early in the morning and the crowds overflowed onto the steps and street inside the number No. 3 Court at Sutton Street. People came from miles away to catch a glimpse of the action. They blocked the doors and windows in the hallways inside the white stone building. They craned their necks around the corners of the hall each time a door slammed. They mumbled to each other about what they had read, what they had heard from a friend who knows a friend who knows a friend. The case was front-page news and the talk of the city. Suddenly the "su-su" in the yards about who was pregnant or who was a "chi-chi man" had changed to the events of the murder.

Drummond entered the courtroom, heavily bearded. He wore a light green Guernsey (a sweater popular in Jamaica) and cocoa-brown trousers. He took his place at the front of the room next to his attorneys, P.J. Patterson and Anthony Spaulding. Although Drummond sat quietly for most of the questioning, reports say that he frequently interrupted Anthony Spaulding's cross-examination of witnesses; Spaulding handed him a pen and a "foolscap," or a pad of paper.

The first person to be questioned during the January 19 inquiry was Mrs. Alvinel Stoddard, a housewife living in the same building as Drummond and Margarita at 9 Rusden Road. Stoddard's mother owned the entire five-room building and Stoddard served as a caretaker while living there. During her questioning by Errol Hall, clerk of the court, she testified that during the short time that Drummond and Margarita lived at that residence, that she had heard many incidents of discord. She testified that the two quarreled and that "sometimes I have to bawl at them about their conduct." Stoddard said she had a talk with them only one month prior to the murder and that the commotion seemed to subside.

Don Drummond and Margarita's home at 9 Rusden Road (photograph by the author).

But at 4:30 A.M. on January 2, 1965, Stoddard said the fracas started again, and this time it turned violent. She heard every word through the thin wooden walls of the structure. She testified that she heard Margarita yelling, "No, Don! No, Don! No, Don! Help! Murder!" and then there was complete silence. Stoddard's response was to pound on the wooden wall, which was essentially just a board, and she hollered at them to stop. She testified that she next heard the gate slam out front and about a half hour later she heard policemen arrive on the scene. When she went to the door of their room it was then she saw Margarita lying on her back with a knife in her chest.

During cross-examination, Spaulding asked Stoddard about the words she had heard screamed that night. Stoddard said that even though Margarita frequently called Drummond by her nickname for him, "Junie," on the night in question she called out "Don" instead. (Nicknames are common in Jamaica, and Junie is a popular choice.) The cross-examination abruptly ended, and Constable Aston Pennycooke took the stand. Pennycooke testified that when he was on duty that night at Rockfort Police Station, Drummond came into the station and stated, "Ah woman in de yard stab herself with a knife and ah would like de police to come and see her." Pennycooke said that he asked the man to identify himself and he said his name, "Donald Drummond." Pennycooke said he asked the name of the woman in question, and Drummond replied, "Anita Mahfood." Pennycooke testified that he asked Drummond what his relationship was with Mahfood, and Drummond stated that she was his friend. Pennycooke then asked Drummond why he didn't try to get Mahfood to the station. Drummond replied that he wanted the police to go there to see her.

Pennycooke testified that he continued to ask Drummond questions, including, "What caused the woman to stab herself?" to which Drummond replied that "she went to a dance and came back." He said he locked the door and opened it and when both of them were inside they "had a fuss," according to Pennycooke's testimony. He continued that Drummond said Mahfood questioned whether it was a knife he had in his hand and he replied, "No," that the knife was in his pocket. But when he felt his pocket, he told Pennycooke, the knife was not there.

According to the journalist's account of the testimony, Drummond then yelled out in the courtroom, "Would you excuse me, your Honour? There was no fuss." Magistrate Lascelles Lister Robotham, who oversaw the proceedings, advised Spaulding to talk to Drummond and warn him that such behavior was not appropriate. Pennycooke then continued his testimony and stated that Drummond said he looked, saw the knife in Mahfood's hand, and she then stabbed herself with it.

Pennycooke said that he then dispatched Constable Horace Reid to the scene and asked Drummond to accompany Reid there. Pennycooke said that only ten minutes later the two returned to the station and Reid reported to Pennycooke that Mahfood was indeed dead and that Drummond had no response. Drummond was then detained and arrested by Det. Cpl. Stanford Bernard, Pennycooke testified. He said that Drummond asked to make a statement to police and Pennycooke said, "He was cautioned," which is likely similar to Miranda rights in the U.S., that statements made can be used against the accused in a court of law. Drummond then provided a written statement which he signed with Constable Reid as witness, before making one correction in the last paragraph of his declaration. Magistrate Robotham said the statement would not be read in open court.

Spaulding then cross-examined Pennycooke, who said he did not write down the questions he asked of Drummond that early morning. Pennycooke said that two statements were, in fact, taken from Drummond and that no one witnessed Drummond actually signing the statements. The defense's cross-examination ended. Reid then took the stand and gave the same testimony as did Pennycooke, but he told how he went into the front room of the building which was located just off the veranda. He described the scene as being lit, that there were two single beds, and "on one of them a woman was laying on her back with her head hanging over the head of the bed and her right hand hanging downwards." Reid said that Drummond noted a chamois that was placed over Mahfood's left breast and Drummond commented to him, "This is de cloth which she held the knife with and stabbed herself." Under the cloth, said Reid, he discovered the knife "protruding from the woman's left breast. She appeared to be dead." Reid said he then replaced the chamois over the knife and left the room. He and Drummond returned to the station and Reid sent a constable to guard the home. However, when Reid returned to the scene a short time later he said he found the room in disarray. Drummond's trombone was in its case and Mahfood's hand, which had previously dangled from the bedside, was now positioned in the bell of the horn.

Someone had apparently been at the murder scene and tampered with the evidence. (As this was prior to strict codes of conduct for such events, and given the history of those involved and the apparent domestic altercation, no one made notice of the breach, except for a statement at the questioning and a sentence in the newspaper.)

At 7:40 A.M., a police photographer, Constable Joseph Little, was sent to the scene, where he took six photographs, each from a different angle. Little took the stand and described each of his photographs.

Next to take the witness stand was Conchita Buckland, Anita's older sister. She testified that the victim had lived with her until one year ago. She said that she went to the crime scene at nine o'clock on the morning of the murder, and that on the following day she attended the postmortem, which was performed by Dr. Harrihar Pershadsingh, the medical examiner for the city of Kingston. Buckland said that she had last seen her sister alive on Boxing Day, which would have been December 26, just five days prior. When asked if Mahfood was depressed, she responded no, that she was in "good spirits, because she brought a piece of cake for me." She said that Mahfood visited her every week and that "she would have never killed herself at any time." Buckland testified she only knew Drummond to say "hello." She said Mahfood brought Drummond to Buckland's home three months prior and that Mahfood said she had taken a job in Ocho Rios and had a room there. Buckland testified that she knew Mahfood was married to Rudolph Bent, although she didn't attend the wedding because "she got married behind my back." She said she knew that her sister and Drummond had recently begun living together.

Buckland was questioned about whether or not Mahfood was easily angered, whether or not she smoked ganja, and whether or not she got into fights at clubs. To each question Buckland answered that she did not know. She said that Mahfood always confided in her, so she would have known if her sister was suicidal. Conchita says that she told the jury that Don had stabbed Anita before, but Spalding told her, "I didn't ask you that."

Det. Cpl. Aquilla Elliott next took the stand, saying he received a report at five A.M. to come to the Rockfort Police Station. When he arrived, he saw Drummond and accompanied Reid to the residence at 9 Rusden Road. Elliott reported that, on the premises, he saw Mahfood lying on the bed, on her back, a knife in her left breast, chamois on the knife, so he returned to the police station and there arrested Drummond. Again, Elliott "cautioned" Drummond, who said, "Mek me tell you how it go, seh." Elliott returned to the scene where the photographer and medical examiner were working, after which, Elliott said, the examiner ordered the body to be removed. He said he saw Pershadsingh remove the knife from Mahfood's chest. Elliott was cross-examined by Spaulding without any note and the inquiry was adjourned.

On February 2, 1965, the pre-trial examinations continued at the No. 3 Court at Sutton Street. First to take the stand was Enid Hibbert, a dressmaker who lived in one of the rooms at 9 Rusden Road. Hibbert testified that at 3:30 A.M. she was still awake in her room, which adjoined Drummond's and Mahfood's room. Hibbert was reading scripture from the Gospel of John when she heard Margarita shouting, "Help! Murder!" Hibbert said earlier in the day, at two o'clock in the afternoon, she and Mahfood had a friendly conversation in their yard. She didn't see Mahfood for the rest of the day, nor did she see Drummond. But at 3:30 A.M. she was alerted by a car door slamming twice in front of their home. She heard footsteps coming up the stairs. She heard Mahfood's voice say, "Junie, please open the door for me," and she knocked on the door. Hibbert said she heard Drummond respond from inside the room, "No, it is not locked."

Mahfood replied, "Junie, open the door for me nuh man," as she knocked again. Drummond responded the same, "It is not locked." Again, Mahfood knocked and Drummond asked her, "It is locked?" "Mahfood then opened the door and went inside," said Hibbert.

Hibbert testified that she heard the couple speaking to each other, although she could not specify exactly what they said; she did, however, hear a laugh and then the expression, "Eh! Eh!" After five minutes of silence, she heard Mahfood exclaim, "Imagine I taking a five-minute nap and when I wake up I see you sitting beside me, very serious. Wha happen, man?" Hibbert said that Drummond responded, "You don't want to sleep nuh man. Ain't you just come in?" Mahfood replied, "Ah can't sleep under these conditions, for you have a knife wrap in a chamois between you feet." Hibbert said that Drummond responded that the knife was not there, that it was in his pants, behind the door. Next, Hibbert said she heard footsteps in their room and heard Mahfood say to Drummond, "No, the knife is not in your pants pocket, it is wrapped in a chamois between your feet." Drummond replied, "No," but then Hibbert said she heard Mahfood yell, "No, Junie! No, Junie! No, Junie! Help! Murder!" Hibbert said the last word she heard Mahfood say was "Miss..." and then no more sound issued from the room. (The detail of this testimony may seem incredible to those who have never seen the home at 9 Rusden Road, but each room was only sectioned off with thin wooden boards, so all conversation could easily be heard by each resident.)

But with such a commotion, it was curious that Hibbert didn't report the crime in some way. She said it was because she had heard such episodes from their room before. It was only when she saw police arrive about 30 minutes after the occurrence that she realized the situation was dire. She went into their room and saw Margarita, dead. P.J. Patterson cross-examined Hibbert, asking her why she was awake, and she responded that she was reading Scripture because they "say you must watch and pray." Patterson questioned exactly which passages of the Bible she was reading, asking her to cite what the third verse read, but she could not remember. She said she was interrupted by the commotion. The cross-examination ended.

Dr. Pershadsingh took the stand and testified that he performed the post-mortem on Mahfood. He said that she had been stabbed four times, all penetrating the chest wall. He said that any one of the wounds could have caused her death. He then testified as to the exact location and direction of each stab wound. The last wound, said Pershadsingh, appeared to have been twisted, causing a hole and all wounds caused massive hemorrhaging and clots in the left chest cavity. When asked if Pershadsingh thought the wounds could have been self-inflicted, he replied, "No, they could not have been."

According to the reporter, Drummond then interrupted the proceedings and asked if he could say something, but his counsel silenced him, as did one of the police guards in the courtroom. During cross-examination, Spaulding questioned Pershadsingh, who said he examined Drummond at the police station the morning of the murder and found "fresh scratches on his wrist-joints, which could have been inflicted by a finger nail," a statement which likely bolstered the Crown's case.

Det. Cpl. Stanford Bernard took the stand to say that at six A.M., when he reported to work at the Rockfort Police Station, he found Drummond sitting on a bench. Drummond greeted Bernard with "Good morning," and then told Bernard why he was there by stating, "Anita took a knife and stabbed herself." He told Bernard he wanted to make a statement, which he wrote down and signed, after being "cautioned," and then had more to say, so he wrote another statement and signed it as well.

Another witness who was summoned for inquiry, David Bowen, a tailor who lived in the building at the time of the murder, did not report for the court date. Therefore, Robotham issued a bench warrant for his arrest.

On February 5, 1965, the inquiries continued and began with Errol Hall's examination of David Bowen who had "turned up," according to the reporter. He told the court that he had gone to Caymanas, which is a very popular horse race track about 25 minutes away from Kingston; and he had intended, he said, to return in time for the questioning, but he "fell ill." He said he came back to Kingston when he heard the warrant for his arrest announced on radio stations. Robotham told him, "Whenever subpoenas are issued I expect the witnesses to attend Court." Bowen apologized, and questioning resumed. He told the court that he was a furniture polish salesman and, at the time of the murder, had occupied a room in the back of 9 Rusden Road. He said he knew both Drummond and Mahfood and, on the day in question, was awakened about four A.M. when he heard the two "stumbling" and then heard Mahfood shout, "Help! Murder!" He said it sounded like they were fighting but he thought nothing of the situation because he had heard them fight and had heard Mahfood yell "Murder!" before. He said, however, that he came out of his room and went into Stoddard's room where, 15 minutes later, they saw the police arrive. Bowen said he never went into Drummond's room.

P.J. Patterson cross-examined Bowen, asking how long the "stumbling" went on, to which Bowen answered, "About a minute." He told Patterson that the couple had fought about three or four times during the month of December and that one time he witnessed Drummond throw Mahfood onto the verandah after hitting her. Cross-examination ended.

With all questioning done, Robotham asked Drummond if he wanted to say anything, a question he was required to ask, according to statutes. Drummond responded, "So far, no." The inquiry was therefore closed, and Drummond was committed on a charge of murder.

P.J. Patterson remembers that Drummond was not able to help his own case: "I want to make it clear that at no time, at no time, did we have any instructions from him as to what happened. He was not in a state and condition to give any account at all. He was nonresponsive for all questions. And, in fact, the question was, was he even fit to stand trial and there was some gap between the time he was apprehended and the time the medical examination said he was fit to stand trial." The gap to which Patterson is referring was, in fact, a year and a half. After Drummond was committed on a charge of murder, it would not be until July 21, 1966, that the trial would commence. During the interim, Drummond was kept at Bellevue Mental Hospital; only when Senior Medical Examiner Dr. K.C. Royes said that Drummond was fit to stand trial would the proceedings take place. Patterson says, "He [Drummond] couldn't give us any instructions and we couldn't call him to give testi-

P.J. Patterson, photographed four years after the trial. Patterson served as Drummond's defense attorney during his murder trial (National Library of Jamaica).

mony. But the medical evidence was that he was capable of standing trial. That evidence had to be given before the trial could commence."

Patterson recalls that Drummond's mental state shaped their case. He says that it was fairly evident that Drummond had murdered Mahfood, even if that evidence was circumstantial, so they had to try a different approach: "I should say, we never got, at any time, any account from anyone who had witnessed the incident. The Crown's case was based on the fact that two people were at home that night, Margarita had stab wounds all over her body, they could establish there had been no breaking into the room, no physical evidence of a third person, and Drummond had turned up at the Rockfort Police Station to make a report. The Crown was mainly relying on essentially circumstantial evidence in that the jurors were being asked to draw the deduction that there were two people in the room and one had stab wounds, which did not appear to be self-inflicted then they could draw the conclusion that the wounds had been inflicted by Drummond."

The testimony during the trial was the same as during preliminary questioning a year and a half prior. The Crown's counsel was Churchill Raymond, who questioned Alvinel Stoddard, Enid Hibbert, Conchita Buckland, and David Bowen. Patterson says, "We made no attempt to challenge the veracity of their testimony. We had no instruction to the contrary."

But there was one person that Patterson did cross-examine: Aston Pennycooke, the final witness to take the stand. Patterson asked him about those statements that Drummond had written and signed at the Rockfort Police Station that morning. Raymond, however, objected, saying the statements were inadmissible. Patterson challenged this objection and the two debated the point. The judge, Justice Fox, donning his colonial peruke, said he would take the arguments into consideration in his chambers and adjourned the case until the following morning.

On July 22, 1966, court reconvened and Fox ruled that the statement Drummond made would indeed be admissible, and he admitted the statement into evidence. But the statement didn't really shed any new light on the case as Drummond only said that Mahfood had stabbed herself and he wanted an ambulance. When Pershadsingh, Dr. Leonard Arnold, and Aquilla Elliott repeated their testimonies, it appeared that Drummond's defense was not credible. Patterson admits, "Having regard to the number of wounds, the nature of them, the location of them, the expert evidence was that they could not have been self-inflicted."

After that, the defense's only available strategy was to argue insanity. Patterson recalls, "I think there were two issues that arose. One, how did Miss Mahfood meet her death.... In our law, and in American law, the prosecution has to prove its case beyond a reasonable doubt. And the onus of proof lies upon the prosecution. What would have been Spaulding's submission is that the Crown had to discharge that onus, and if there was any doubt in the jury's mind that the onus had not been discharged, Drummond was entitled to the benefit of that. Now, the second thing which arose was the defense established, and English case law runs back to the eighteenth century, it is a verdict of not guilty by virtue of insanity. And that was the defense. And we had to call medical evidence for that, including persons who could testify as to [Drummond's] medical history."

The defense, therefore, called Dr. K.C. Royes on the third day of the trial. Royes was the senior medical officer at Bellevue at the time and he told Judge Fox and the jury that Drummond "did not fully understand the nature of what he was doing" when he stabbed Margarita. He said that, when he examined Drummond in March 1965, he found that he had "an abnormality of mind in January of that year." He added that Drummond "was suffering from lack of control as a result of lack of understanding" and that his state of mind could have been "triggered by some annoyance, by the use of drugs or any disappointment."

Next to take the stand was Lennie Hibbert, Drummond's musical colleague, great friend, and by this time, bandmaster at Alpha Boys School. He was also one of the two friends who drove Anita home that fateful night. Hibbert told the court that he first met Drummond at Alpha when he came to help tutor the band. It was 1954, and he recognized that Drummond was "a young genius" and that he was "quiet, most studious, willing to help other musicians, but definitely a very withdrawn person." He added that Drummond was a great young musician, the number-one trombonist in Jamaica, and in the top five in the world, according to the renowned American pianist George Shearing. Hibbert said that he had worked with Drummond over the years and had visited him three times while he was in Bellevue prior to the murder.

Matthew Beaubrun, a registered medical practitioner, testified that he would find it difficult to determine if wounds were self-inflicted or a homicide, even after an autopsy was conducted. Noel Clinton March, also a registered medical practitioner, said that, after examining the wounds, he felt it could have either been a suicide or a homicide. Certainly the defense was trying to establish a spark of doubt in the minds of the jury.

The fourth day of the trial, Judge Fox began summing up. The Crown's case was that Drummond stabbed Margarita to death, and the defense's case was that Drummond should be set free because, said Spaulding, "The evidence is that there is reasonable doubt. The evidence says that you cannot trust the witnesses for the prosecution. The evidence says that he is not guilty of murder or of manslaughter." He pleaded with the all-male jury to "send Drummond back to the dance-halls to make the contribution that he has made already in Jamaica and live to develop our culture to carry on the work he has started. Give him a chance. He needs it. He deserves it." The Crown's Churchill Raymond simply responded, "It's not a question of giving anybody any chance. You are here to pronounce guilt or innocence." He said that the evidence proved the wounds could not have been self-inflicted and that the defense did not prove that Drummond was insane, therefore a guilty verdict should be returned.

The jury only took one hour to deliberate. Of the 12 jurors, 11 agreed that the death of Anita Mahfood was a homicide, not a suicide. Judge Fox advised the jury that there were three courses open to them in light of this finding. One, they could find Drummond guilty of murder. Two, they could find Drummond guilty but insane. Or three, they could find Drummond guilty of manslaughter. After ten minutes they returned and the unanimous verdict was read: guilty but insane. A journalist described Drummond's "puzzled look on his face" and said he was led out of the packed courtroom "barefooted and with a heavy moustache." If the verdict hadn't declared him insane, surely the reporter's description did.

Patterson says that the defense team had anticipated Drummond would be found guilty and had prepared the medical evidence on his mental state so that the judge would sentence Drummond accordingly. "I had to do submissions to the judge so that he couldn't be subject to incarceration in a prison," Patterson avers. "At that time the sentence would have been for him to be detained in a medical institution at 'Her Majesty's pleasure.' That sentencing provision has now been altered by changes in the law. In other words, it can't be an indefinite detention at the hands of the executive; it has to be a judicial review. But this was the law at that time."

Drummond was committed to Bellevue Mental Hospital, "To be kept in strict custody," according to the court order. No one was surprised at

JULY 27, 1966.

Killing of 'Margarita' . . .

Drummond found guilty but insane

Trombonist Donald Drummond was yesterday ordered by Mr. Justice Fox to be kept in strict custody as a criminal lunatic in the Bellevue Hospital until the Governor-General's pleasure is known.

The order came after a special verdict delivered by an all-male jury in the Home Circuit Court, that Drummond was guilty of murder but insane.

The Crown had alleged that Drummond, on the early morning of January 2, 1965 fatally stabbed 23-year-old rhumba dancer, Anita Mahfood otherwise called 'Margarita' in a room the couple shared at 9 Rusden Road, Kingston 2.

With a puzzled look on his face, Drummond, barefooted and with a heavy moustache, was led from the packed courtroom after the judge's order.

Divided 11-1

Yesterday, the fourth day of the trial, the judge summed up to the jurors. They retired for a little over an hour and on their return, the foreman told the court they were 11-1 in favour of a guilty-but-insane verdict.

Questioned by the judge the jury foreman said the jury had agreed, all twelve of them, that it was homicide and not suicide but in considering other matters, they were divided 11-1.

Mr. Justice Fox then explained to the jury that three courses were open to them in the situation with which they were faced: 1) guilty of murder; 2) guilty but insane and 3) guilty of manslaughter. In each case he explained how they could arrive at their conclusion.

The jury retired a second time and returned after ten minutes with the guilty-but-insane verdict.

Mr. Justice Fox: The special verdict which the jury has returned namely, that the accused was guilty of the act charged against him but was insane at the time when he did the act, I direct that this special verdict be recorded.

"I further direct that the accused be kept in custody as a criminal lunatic in such a place

and in such a manner as the Court shall direct and I direct that he shall be confined to the Bellevue Hospital until the Governor-General's pleasure shall be known."

Then, not now

Mr. Churchill Raymond Crown Counsel, said that the effect of the verdict was that Drummond was insane at the time of the act on January 2 last year but not insane now.

The judge said he would direct that the prisoner be kept in strict custody at the General Penitentiary until the Governor-General's pleasure be known, this having regard to his mental condition on July 19 last.

But the defence counsel, Mr. Anthony Spaulding, drew the Court's attention to Section 18 of Chapter 242— The Mental Hospital Law—and stated that it seemed no order could be made to send the prisoner to the General Penitentiary for the law, seemed to indicate that the prisoner has to be sent to the mental institution.

Crown Counsel agreed that it seemed the prisoner ought to be committed to the mental hospital at this stage.

Mr. Justice Fox then directed that Drummond be kept in strict custody as a criminal lunatic in the mental hospital until the Governor-General's pleasure be known.

World court's ruling shocks ICFTU

NEW YORK, July 26
(Reuters):

The International Confederation of Free Trade Unions (I.C.F.T.U.) — a big non-communist labour group — expressed dismay over the World Court rejection of a suit brought by Liberia and Ethiopia against South West Africa's white administration.

A statement by Omer Becu, the general secretary, said responsibility for the South West African people, whose human rights were "shamefully flouted by the South African regime", thus had shifted to the international community, including the trade unions.

He asked that the U.N. take urgent action to ensure that human rights were respected in the territory.

Lake back as JHTA head

Mr. Robert Lake, Kingston hotelier, was re-elected president of the Jamaica Hotel and Tourist Association at its annual general meeting held at the Runaway Bay Hotel on Sunday.

Elected to the position of vice-president, in succession to Mr Sam Levy, was Mr. Heinz Simonitsch of Montego Bay.

These two top officers of the association were chosen by the councillors, who were themselves elected by the general body of the meeting representing the island hoteliers.

Those elected to the council for the 1966-67 term of office were:

KINGSTON AREA — Messrs. Lake, Russell Schmidt, and Sir Anthony Jenkinson.

MONTEGO BAY AREA — Messrs. Simonitsch, Dick DeLisser and James Hooke.

OCHO RIOS AREA — Messrs. Levy, Nick Brimo, and Franz Irving.

Other councillors for the new year are Messrs. Ferdie Martin, Murlin Arner and Guillermo Machado (representing Allied members); J. F. Lord and John Issa (representing Associate members).

House when they called on His Excellency the Governor-General, Sir Clifford Campbell.

Headline of the July 27, 1966, *Daily Gleaner*.

the outcome. As Patterson explains, "He had had mental problems before. There were periods where he was out of the musical field because he had health problems. Don Drummond was a person well loved, greatly admired for his musical talent, but I think most people knew that he wasn't all there."

14

Bellevue

In the mid–1800s, Kingston had only a single public hospital located on North Street and West Street. This hospital served the city's 30,000 people and contained the Jamaica Lunatic Asylum, as it was called at the time. Accommodations were so awful that one former senior medical officer claimed they were "little better than stables for animals." Treatment for patients during these early years was primitive at best and included such procedures as "tanking," or submerging patients into a shallow tank of water many times to reduce their aggressiveness, or rather forcing compliance, not unlike today's torturous water boarding.

When a private medical practitioner named Dr. Lewis Bowerbank moved to Kingston from nearby Spanish Town, he noticed this neglect and abuse in the hospital's facilities and treatments, and so he traveled to London to appeal to the Colonial Office to make investigations into the mistreatment of patients. In 1845, the legislature agreed to move the asylum and set aside money to construct a new facility. Delayed initially by an outbreak of cholera in 1850, which led to the deaths of an estimated 40,000 people on the island, the new building was not constructed until 1861. This structure is still in use today.

Over the years, improvements were made in the areas of nutrition, uniforms and sleeping conditions, recreation, occupational opportunities, and skilled treatment. Prior to these years, the main medication for patients in the asylum was alcohol — brandy, wine, rum, and gin were given to patients. This was greatly reduced and replaced by drugs and castor oil.

In the 1860s, a brass band was even organized to help provide recreational and therapeutic opportunities for patients. By 1871, population at the Jamaica Lunatic Asylum was 220 patients and overcrowding became a concern. Newer wards were constructed over the next 50 years and the hospital began to spread across 35 acres. By 1928, the resident population was 1,600, equal parts men and women, and in 1938 the hospital's name officially changed to the Jamaica Mental Hospital.

In 1945, even though the maximum the hospital could accommodate was 1,819 patients, the resident population was actually 2,550 which had a deleterious impact on the patients' mental progress. As a result, the staff went on strike to oppose these conditions and the fact that they were over-worked. Consequentially, many changes came to the hospital, including relief of overcrowding through expansion, additional training for staff, improvement of working conditions, and recreational opportunities for patients. But conditions were still terrible during Drummond's tenure. In fact, during a study of nurses conducted in 1967 by a committee appointed by the government, nurses reported "primitive" conditions at Bellevue, citing understaffing, overcrowding, and unsanitary rooms and plumbing. Even though the hospital changed its name to Bellevue, as there was a stigma attached to mental illness in Jamaica, more than a mere facelift was required.

This stigma on mental illness continues today and, certainly, it had an impact on Don Drummond's life. Sparrow Martin says, "When you have a mental problem, you are a problem in society. If someone start to say you are a mental, society will start to treat you differently." And it was hard to recover from such a stigma when the illness persisted for Drum-mond. He was unable to receive the kind of treatment that today would have likely helped to remedy or abate his condition because such treatments in the 1950s and 1960s simply did not exist, and certainly not in the middle of urban Jamaica in an unwilling culture.

Heather Royes, daughter of Dr. K.C. Royes, who was senior medical officer during Drummond's various stays at Bellevue, remembers the days when she was young and lived on the property: "At that particular time, my father was the acting SMO, senior medical officer. We lived there for 16 years, it was 300 acres, and it was a beautiful plantation. There were these old huge colonial houses and the doctors all had houses. They were very big and we had a wonderful life. But of course we wondered why some families didn't wish to come and visit us! But my father was very progressive because he taught us never to fear. He said there's no such thing as insanity. Everyone who worked in our house was a patient—the cook, the cleaner, the gardener, so we were just brought up that way."

Royes surmises that Don Drummond was likely kept in one of the wards for those who were found criminally insane, but he was able to participate in the activities of the hospital that would have contributed to his rehabilitation. "My father tried to introduce open wards, rehabilitation therapy, outpatient therapy, group sessions," Royes asserts. "There was a ward, it was known, whether it was G Ward or D Ward, it was for those who could not be rehabilitated because medications were non-existent. There was a particular ward for those who were uncontrollable. I'm not sure if Don Drummond was uncontrollable but it's possible that he had to stay somewhere where he wouldn't murder anybody else. And there was a ward and once a person was there it's like, that's it, they just have to be kept. I suspect that he was in one of those wards, but probably treated okay."

Dr. Frederick Hickling confirms that Drummond was kept in a different area from other patients: "It was really never a penal facility. It was always a treatment facility, although a number of patients who came under what was called 'the governor general's pleasure,' were kept in a special ward at that institution." Devon Williams, director of nursing at Bellevue, also says that Don Drummond was kept in a ward for the criminally insane, but it wasn't a prison. "I wouldn't call it a cell," he says. "What we had back then were individual rooms and cubicles, so you had a room where a person could be. It was small, just a bed. For recreation, patients played dominoes, went on walking parties where staff took a number of patients and walked on the compound; [they played] board games, card games, but not anything much to speak about." Institutionalized men, like Drummond, wore short white pants and white T-shirts.

Dr. Aggrey Irons, senior medical officer at Bellevue in the years following Drummond's tenure, says that he remembers the building where Drummond was kept: "He would have been in D Ward, but my memory tells me he was also in Western N Ward. It was an intermediate ward. He started off on the ward for the criminally insane and was transferred to N Ward. He would not have had a roommate because there were dormitories with several roommates in the dormitories, but there were also individual rooms built almost like cells. You have to remember that Bellevue was built in 1864. They got a colonial grant and they built both the prison and the mental institution around the same time, under the direction of the same colonial governor. And in those days the emphasis was on detention and retention rather than rehabilitation." Bellevue staff confirms that the building where Drummond stayed is still in use today.

Although medical records have either since been destroyed or are classified by the government, Don Drummond's mental diagnosis was likely schizophrenia during his days at Bellevue. Devon Williams agrees with this diagnosis, based upon the stories he has heard over the years: "From my own experience, Mr. Drummond seemed to suffer from schizophrenia because of his activities. He was mental long ago. He exhibited ritualistic behavior, blowing his trombone even when no sound was played, eating dirt, he was paranoid because he wouldn't let anyone dance with Margarita, so my own feeling was he had a split personality, schizophrenia."

However, during the 1960s and even before, diagnosis of urban males as schizophrenic was common. Whether this was because the condition was more prevalent among this population, or if it was because this population elicited the diagnosis from those who were racist or discriminatory, the true situation may forever be debated. Nevertheless, Dr. Irons feels that Don Drummond's diagnosis as a schizophrenic may have been in error because his condition may have in actuality been something similar but different due to the social class disparity that filtered into every aspect of Jamaican life. Irons says, "If they diagnosed Don as schizophrenic, they may have misdiagnosed him. In those days, people were not diagnosing bipolar disorder sufficiently and effectively. If you were fair, you were more likely depressed or bipolar. If you were dark, you were schizophrenic. And we know in retrospect that Don Drummond would likely have been bipolar. Marijuana-modified mania looks to the uninitiated like schizophrenia. But if you think about his mood swings and his music and his lifestyle, one would understand that he probably would have been bipolar. If he had been schizophrenic he would not have been such a social person. He would not have been so easily incorporated into a band. Schizophrenics don't do bands very well and they tend to manifest themselves a little earlier than Don did. So in retrospect, he was probably bipolar and manifested some marijuana-modified mania."

Whatever the exact diagnosis of Don's mental condition, it is evident from biographical and anecdotal information about the behavior of Don Drummond that he suffered from mental illness. The incidence of mental illness in creative musicians, specifically in jazz musicians in the era in which Drummond lived, is a studied phenomenon. Geoffrey I. Willis, Ph.D., in his study, "Forty lives in the bebop business: mental health in a group of eminent jazz musicians," published in the *British Journal of Psychiatry*, found a link between outstanding jazz musicians, such as J.J. Johnson, Frank Rosolino, Bud Powell, Charlie Parker, Miles Davis, Thelonious Monk, and Charles Mingus, and "above average levels of psychopathology." The study, by looking at the lives of 40 jazz musicians who were considered "innovators on their instrument" or were composers or arrangers in their field, found more mental illness in this profession than any other.

The stories of jazz musicians who suffered from mental illness are well known and inspired Willis's study. Charlie Parker, who suffered from heroin addiction, was committed to a mental institution for six months after an alcohol-fueled episode in which he appeared nude in a hotel lobby numerous times before being locked in his room by the hotel manager. He subsequently set his room on fire. Thelonious Monk was known to pace back and forth for days, forsaking sleep and recognizing no one. Art Pepper was terrified of telephones. Bud Powell suffered from paranoid delusions and hallucinations and was committed to mental institutions numerous times for schizophrenia. Frank Rosolino committed suicide after shooting his two sons, killing one and wounding the other. Miles Davis endured auditory hallucinations and paranoid delusions and searched his house repeatedly for people he thought he heard. Charles Mingus experienced paranoia and mood disorders.

The list goes on and on, and, like Drummond, many of these artists, in an attempt to manage their mental difficulties or emotional or even physical pain, turned to self-medicating for relief, further complicating their ailments. Keep in mind that many of these cases, like Drummond's, are based upon biographical information during a time when clinical information on mental conditions was not as advanced as today. However, the study does provide food for thought and continues discussion of a belief held by many, that there is a fine line between genius and madness.

The treatment that Don Drummond would have received at Bellevue was not much better than those used at the onset of the hospital's inception. Williams says, "We used strait jackets to restrain different patients. We also had chemical restraints, sodium barbital. The patient would be tranquilized to the extent that they would sleep for a few days and given glucose. They would come out and be in a different state. We also used chlorpromazine, or CPs for short." Royes confirms that these are the treatments used by her father, as well as other methods: "EST was definitely the thing, electroshock. The medication would have been basically heavy sedatives. There were basically things to kind of conk you out. Drummond was pretty zonked out from early on."

169

Many who were close to Don Drummond during the time he was committed to Bellevue after the murder say that he was not allowed any visitors, although they tried to see him. Eddie "Tan Tan" Thornton says, "When I went back to Jamaica, he was in the asylum. You can't go. They claimed he killed somebody and he was a murderer in the asylum. I wanted to go but they said no, he's a murderer, sorry. They wouldn't let you in." Vin Gordon says that one time when he came to perform at Bellevue for the patients' recreation, they were able to see Drummond, but it was no use anyway since Drummond was no longer the person he used to be. Gordon says, "When I left school, Don Drummond was mad. And I remember my band master by the name of Lennie Hibbert, who taught me music in Alpha School, we went to Bellevue to play, but Don Drummond, he was mad. And we ask him to play, to illustrate us something. We used to play classic and we wanted him to play something with us and he said no, he didn't want to, and he walked off. He was mad, he was totally out of his head." Former Alpharian and saxophonist Winston Harris concurs, "Don did not perform at Bellevue, although Lennie tried." Royes says, "I cannot remember anyone getting visitors. Maybe he was so knocked out and not able to function. I do not remember any large amount of visitors or many people wishing to admit that their friends or family were mentally ill."

Before the murder, Don Drummond was able to leave Bellevue to perform. But afterward, he was essentially imprisoned. Chuck Foster in his book, *Roots Rock Reggae*, quotes Tommy McCook on Drummond's time spent in Bellevue. "We were playing without Don on a number of occasions when he was in Bellevue, but he was always able to come out periodically and join the group for recordings and play with the band." Herman "Woody" King says that he was able to see Drummond only during the times he was in Bellevue before the murder, not after. He remembers, "I did visit him a couple of times. A schoolmate of mine was working there in the office so I always ask him to look out for him. He knew Don because he had a piano at his home and sometimes when I'm riding with Don he would want to stop and play the piano at this friend's home. And then when he escape from Bellevue once he came straight to my friend's home who lives not far away and I brought some clothes, a change of clothes, so he could melt away because he escape wearing Bellevue clothes. So I would sometimes chat my friend up and get to see Don. After the Margarita incident he was in the section for the criminally insane so I wouldn't get to see him. He was locked away in a more secure area. Bellevue was not a nice place. It was very cruel. In those days, the medicines were really old-fashioned. If you were acting up they would either give you one type of medicine that turned you into almost like a zombie. You would be sleeping for three days and wake up all spaced out and it was more easy for them to control you, or they would shock you with electrical shock treatment that didn't really work. The staff, I don't know if the staff was that well trained."

But there was another kind of medication going around at Bellevue during these times, and given Drummond's mental condition, it is not likely that this form of treatment helped his condition either. In fact, it likely only made it worse. Royes says, "I do know Drummond probably continued his use of ganja. I know that the warders used to take ganja into the wards because my father, on many occasions, would find it and he even planted it upstairs and a policeman said, 'Doc! Is that ganja growing in your room?!' So I suspect Drummond was still on ganja. I am convinced, because not that you could get everything, but I knew they were still smoking and in fact there were one or two psychiatrists who said that sometimes it really helps. I know he was smoking and I know in Bellevue he could get it."

Ganja was likely used in Bellevue because there were a number of Rastafarians in the hospital during these days, even though they didn't suffer from any mental disorders. Certainly, this was not the case with Drummond because his situation involved a murder, but for others, Bellevue was a place for the government to try to control what they saw as a social disease. Royes says, "It has to do with how they treated Rastas and ganja in those days. My father, being more progressive, told the government that they could not lock up Rastas for smoking herbs. But I think the English administration just wanted to put them away. Don Drummond's schizophrenic state was probably aggravated by the drugs. The English administration wanted all of the Rastafarians and ganja smokers in Bellevue. They would either put them in jail, and that wouldn't be worth it, so they had it unwritten to put them in Bellevue. And I remember my father saying if someone smokes ganja that does not mean they are mentally ill. This was the way the administration wanted it. It was clear that because of Drummond's state and ganja use, he was a patient of Bellevue and also I heard that they did not want to commit him to jail, so basically they just shoved him into Bellevue. I don't remember much of a trial, but we all knew he was coming to Bellevue. Basically that's where he was going to be. After thirty years I heard my father verbally say that in the end, ganja should not be used by certain people and in fact it can be something that can accelerate or chemically imbalance someone."

While in Bellevue, Don Drummond was said to be just a ghost of his former self. Johnny "Dizzy" Moore told *Jamaica Observer* reporter Howard Campbell that Drummond had become "even more reclusive, never talked." He also said that Drummond lost his passion for music: "It was never in him anymore." Not so, says Dr. Aggrey Irons: "Don sat about teaching other inmates how to play the trombone. By the time I got there, his trombone had been left for an inmate, a young inmate. They knew him as Trommie for short. He was taught by Don and learned how to play and was a part of our Bellevue Band which was formed in the seventies," says Irons. This patient's birth name was Eleazor Beckford, but he has since died, confirms the hospital. In 1979, Beckford, identified by the *Jamaica Gleaner* as "one of Drummond's students," performed a saxophone solo in a theatrical presentation at the hospital as part of mental illness therapy, a technique called "sociodrama."

Royes says that she remembers a few times Drummond's immediate doctor, Dr. Frederick Shoucair, came to visit their home and told a few stories of Drummond. Shoucair was part of a musical family who performed together on stage. According to newspaper records, Frederick Shoucair performed as a child in a "Musical Evening at Ormsby Memorial Hall" on September 30, 1935. His brother Albert was a musician who gave regular piano recitals at Ormsby Hall in the mid- to late '30s. People who knew Frederick Shoucair, or "Shoucs," as they called him, describe him as warm, caring, and a friend. Tony Shoucair, Frederick's nephew, says, "All of the family had a love for music because a lot of them played instruments and one of his sisters was a very good singer, an opera singer almost. He lived with me up through my teen years and then he left to live in Gainesville in Florida. He was very very compassionate, a soft, quiet person."

Heather Royes says that Shoucair was honored to have Drummond for a patient. She says, "Dr. Shoucair never married but was part of our family since he came from a large Lebanese family and they turned him over to my parents, whom he adored. Every evening he would bring over lots of patties and take us for drives in his big U.S. car. Dr. Shoucair was a bit of an excited person and would say, 'Oh, Don Drummond was playing the trombone in the ward this morning.'" Heather's sister, Gillian Royes, also remembers these visits: "Dr. Shoucs used to come and visit us almost every evening and he would talk about Don. He said that he would ask him, 'Why?' and Don would be very, very repentant about what he had done. He apparently loved her very much."

Perhaps because it was a crime of passion, as many deemed it, there was still widespread support for Drummond, even from the nuns at Alpha. Sparrow Martin says, "When he was incarcerated, the people rally around him. There was the former prime minister, P.J. Patterson, who try to help him. There was a musician who died now, Lennie Hibbert, he tried to help him. There was a gentleman by the name of Major Williams, Joe Williams from the military band, he and myself, we went to visit him at Bellevue. When we went to visit him, they didn't want us to see him. We couldn't see him because where he was there was just a little hole inside and he was incarcerated, locked up in there. They didn't treat him well."

Despite not being able to reach Drummond physically on the inside of Bellevue, some of his comrades tried to express their support the one way they knew how — through the expression of music. Martin says, "There is a theater, it's now a church that they call Peace Theater, and it was right in front of Bellevue Hospital on Windward Road and they decided to keep a concert there, for Don. And they had two bands. They had two groups playing. They had Carlos Malcolm and the Afro-Jamaicans and they had the Skatalites. Carlos Malcolm played first. I was a drummer with the band at that time. And we were playing. We play the first half of the show, and the Skatalites would play the second half of the show. While we were playing, the people got impatient because they wanted to hear the Skatalites. So while we were playing, a young man came to the stage and said, 'Drummie, Sparrow, come off of the drums and go behind the stage.' So I stopped playing and I went around in the back of the stage. When I was around there, a stone went into my bass drum, the foot drum, and it went, BOOM! and it burst the drum, and then a lot of people started throwing things on the stage so the band had to come off the stage and they wanted to bring on the Skatalites. They started yelling, 'Don Drummond! Don Drummond!' The place was doing it for Don. So the Skatalites went on, they cleaned off the stage, took off the bottles and the stones, and took on the instruments and started playing. They didn't go off until late the next morning. The Skatalites just keep on playing. We assumed that in the room they put him in, the cell, he was listening to the music playing because it was pretty near his cell and he was inside there listening to the music, but he didn't get the chance to play. We thought they would let him come and play and go back in, but no, they wouldn't let him go out. I don't remember who was the officer in charge at that time, but he didn't give Don a fair time. It didn't work for him and it is sad really to know some are like that."

While Don's physical environment and his physical treatment can be determined based on recollections from the past, what cannot be known, and what we cannot accurately imagine, is how Don was treated emotionally at Bellevue — how he was made to feel, how he was belittled, removed of his dignity, ridiculed. How he turned into a shell of his former self by being surrounded day after day by the insane and their catatonic stares or caterwauling. How did it feel to be the madman? How did it feel to be the criminally insane and viewed by and treated by others as such? Did they even look him in the eye when they talked to him? What was the tone of their voices and what did that say to him? Did they treat him as a child, or as a villain? What did he feel in his hours alone at night in the dark when Anita came to visit him in his mind?

On May 6, 1969, at age 35, Don Drummond died at Bellevue Hospital. According to his death certificate issued by H.M. Dixon, the coroner for the Parish of Kingston, the official cause of death was "due to congestive cardiac failure and anaemia and no one was criminally responsible." According to the Registrar General's Office in Kingston, if a person dies of natural causes in a hospital, such as medical conditions or illnesses, no post-mortem is required by law. Only if a person dies by "sudden" or "violent" causes is one required; however, according to the *Jamaica Gleaner*, issue of May 15, 1969,

> A spokesman for the Bellevue Hospital said last night that the law required that a post mortem examination be performed on all patients who died in the hospital before a certificate of burial could be issued. He said a post mortem examination was held on Drummond. He also said that, from all information he had received on Drummond's death, he died from natural causes as he had been ailing for several weeks prior to his death.

That post-mortem record, despite the author's multiple attempts to obtain it, either no longer exists or is no longer accessible. According to Professor Carlos T. Escoffery, head of the Department of Pathology, UWI, Mona, Jamaica, if an autopsy did exist (and he is of the mind that one did

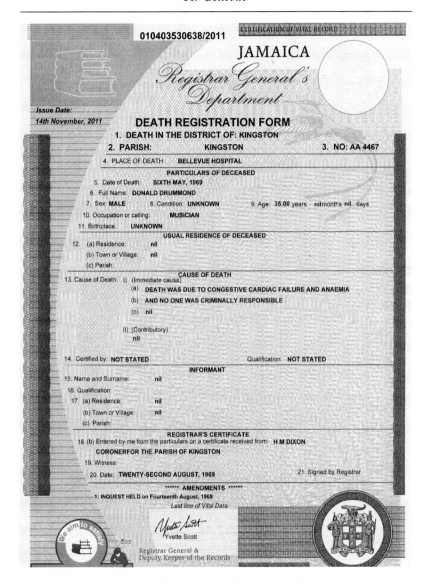

Donald Willis Drummond's death certificate.

not for Drummond) then it was most likely destroyed during a devastating fire at the Government Laboratory in 1989.

Heart disease and cardiac failure were the leading causes of fatality at the time of Drummond's death. In 1969 there were 4,518 deaths from heart disease, which accounts for 32 percent of all deaths, according to Registrar General's figures. That figure was three times the second leading cause of death in Jamaica that year, 1,505, or 10 percent, from cancer. At the time, some 40 percent of all hospital beds in the country were occupied by patients suffering from some form of cardiovascular disease, and the greatest mortality from heart disease was in males aged 39 to 50 years old.

In their obituary for Don Drummond, the *Daily Gleaner* said that he was "rated Jamaica's top trombonist and up to 1965 reputed to be among the five best trombonists in the world." It went on to read that he was "the leading figure in the Skatalites, a band which emerged during the early days of the Ska and took popularity among music lovers. The band is now defunct.... He was ... both an exponent of jazz and all-around music. He was also a competent music writer."

Drummond's funeral was held at Madden's Funeral Chapel in downtown Kingston on North Street, not far from Jubilee Hospital where he was born. He was buried at 9:25 A.M. on May 18, 1969, in the May Pen Cemetery, in grave number A346. He is listed in burial records as a Roman Catholic. Entombment was private, for only family. Musicians such as Sonny Bradshaw took up funds to pay for Drummond's funeral as his mother was unable to afford the cost. And according to Eddie "Tan Tan" Thornton, Alpha paid for the burial: "Sister Ignatius, she's the one that buried Don Drummond. When Don Drummond died, Sister Ignatius is the one that bury him. He died in Jamaica and the nuns, they're the ones that bury him because there was no one else to bury him. And Alpha is the one that bury him, Sister Ignatius and Sister Margaret, those two bury him."

Musicologist Vaughn "Bunny" Goodison, O.D., recalls Drummond's cheap coffin: "It was a wooden box covered with Formica. Nothing to look at. Nobody knows the exact spot where he was buried because he was not treated like a normal person, so the spot was not marked. You have to understand Jamaica to understand that. To be charged with murder of a Mahfood, that caste, they just threw him away. He couldn't defend himself and there was no respect for him. He was buried in a pauper's grave, an unmarked grave."

John Cornwall, the superintendent at May Pen Cemetery, has been unable to locate Drummond's grave and says that although he has a grave number, that system of numbering is long gone and he has no knowledge of its former use. He says nothing has been transferred digitally and all records are in stray boxes. "It is hard for us now to find this grave," Cornwall says, which is not surprising considering the condition of the cemetery today. Over the course of history, May Pen has had thousands interred on its unsecured acres, many piled into mass graves without any documentation. May Pen was also the final resting place for those who died from a cholera epidemic in the 1850s; their bodies were all buried in a mass grave on the western side of the cemetery. Over the years the cemetery has been home to unclaimed dead and paupers who could not afford a burial. There were assertions that many who died in rioting and military assaults at Tivoli Gardens in 2010 were buried here without notification to their families. Bodies have been buried on top of bodies, others have lain exposed, decomposing in the tropical sun. The graves of former heads of state and military officials have been ransacked and robbed for scrap metal, from gold jewelry entombed with the corpse to metal handles on coffins. It is no wonder then that Don Drummond, labeled at the time of his death by the island's newspaper as a "criminal lunatic," was buried in a pauper's grave, not unlike Wolfgang Amadeus Mozart, another musical genius. According to Vin Gordon, Drummond was buried in an area of the cemetery that was used for the remains of criminals, near some railroad tracks. "Bush up, nobody knows that part, down in the back, that's where they bury criminals," he says. "So nobody can ever find where he's buried. Nobody will ever find it. They didn't even put up a sign because he was a criminal lunatic, these are the exact words that are in the newspaper."

The burial included a few attendants other than just family. Present at the cemetery were "a few CID men [security] from Denham Town and Central Station ... in case of any incident," according to the *Daily Gleaner*. This was done in order to keep a sense of decorum for the family in a time when emotions were still raw, and is a likely reason the exact location of Drummond's grave remains unknown. Just four days earlier, on May 14, 1969, pandemonium broke out at Drummond's funeral when drummer Hugh Malcolm moved past an enormous crowd of those paying their last respects to Drummond. He burst into the packed funeral home just as the priest was about to officiate the services. Reports that Malcolm tore up the death certificate are merely rumor or embellishment, unless it was a prop certificate, since the death certificate was not issued until August 22, 1969. But Malcolm did demand the service be stopped and that there should be no burial until the results of the post-mortem were known.

According to the *Daily Gleaner*, a "relative of Drummond said that the protestor declared that he had been informed that Drummond had not died from natural causes but that before his death he was beaten by four men in the institution." The service was then called off because the family did not want anyone to get hurt or for a riot to break out. No one from Drummond's family protested the cause of death. A classified ad in the May 22, 1969, issue of the *Daily Gleaner* reads,

> PERSONAL: The Relatives Of Don Drummond take this medium of thanking all his close friends and a acquaintances for their sympathy and floral tributes in their recent bereavement. Sgd. D. Monroe. [D. Munroe was Don Drummond's mother, Doris.]

For Drummond's death certificate to include the disclaimer "No one was criminally responsible" in the section for Cause of Death seems unusual. The certificate was not entered into record by Coroner H.M. Dixon until August 22, 1969, some three and a half months after Don Drummond's death, long after the contentious funeral. Perhaps Mr. Dixon added this statement to the death record in an attempt to stave off any future skepticism over Drummond's cause of death, knowing it had been called into question by Hugh Malcolm. It is not possible to know why Malcolm made this claim: the drummer has since died and his surviving sister, Marjorie, says her brother never discussed the subject with her.

"I have never seen or heard of such a notation on a death certificate before," says Dr. Carlos Escoffery of the cause of death comment, "no one was criminally responsible." Escoffery tried to obtain the post-mortem document but was unsuccessful. "I don't know if this was the practice in the old days but I've not met this since I became a doctor in 1979. When we do coroners [forensic] autopsies we often make a comment at the end of the report as to the manner of death, whether natural, homicide, accidental, et cetera, but manner of death is not usually stated on the death certificate. It would appear to me that the doctor went out of his/her way to emphasize that there was no foul play. One wonders why?! Perhaps it was because of the stature of Don D. and the rumors about the cause of his death circulating at the time." The certificate also notes in a section titled "Amendments" that an inquest was held on August 14, 1969. This was likely the coroner's legal inquiry into Drummond's cause of death before judging it to be without criminal involvement, knowing the background of the case. A follow up to obtain that inquest proved fruitless. "The inquest seems to be buried in the same unknown grave as Don!" says

Escoffery. "I get the feeling that most people I've contacted or tried to contact are either not particularly interested in Don D. (those who even know who he is!), or don't want to dig up anything that might prove to be controversial. In his day, he would have been regarded by the status quo as a ganja-smoking, mad layabout rather than as a musical hero, and though he's paid a lot of lip service nowadays, I don't think that 'certain people' want to throw any new light on his death or be a part of a possible apotheosis."

But many today corroborate the cause of death stated on the certificate. A spokesperson at Bellevue during the time of Drummond's death said that Drummond had been "ailing for several weeks prior to his death," a claim confirmed by Sparrow Martin: "Don was killed with his kidney. Apparently he got sickness in his kidney and he wasn't treated. His two feet were so swollen. You have people who could get a chance to visit him so when they go to visit him he would tell what kind of condition he was in." Drummond's own attorney, P.J. Patterson, says that although he never was able to visit Drummond he did feel that his death was from natural causes, it was "just that he never recovered."

Devon Williams says that it is possible that Drummond's condition contributed to his death: "Based on his history, I feel Mr. Drummond wasn't being treated regularly. When you become delusional you become aggressive. But if he'd been receiving treatment I don't think he would have been a problem. There is a lot of conjecture as to how he died. I have no record he was killed by gangsters or murdered. He was young. But one of the reasons we stopped using sodium barbital is it can lead to death if not administered properly. We do not know [enough] about his physiological makeup to know how things may have impacted him." Studies have concluded that people with schizophrenia have much higher incidence of coronary heart disease. Additionally, the overexposure to sodium barbital has been implicated through lab studies to the development of aplastic anemia. It is the same class of drugs that killed Marilyn Monroe and Jimi Hendrix.

"Lloyd [Knibb] used to tell me, 'Oh, he died of leukemia. He drank too much white rum,'" Ken Stewart says. "Like the white rum took out your red blood cells or some weird conception that they gathered. But I know there was serious suspicion that the Mahfood family had [hired] some kind of a hit man or whatever."

It is evident that Jad Eid Mahfood was a violent man when it came to his guns and his opinion. His son Paul recalls, "He was the kind of man who would actually go up to you with his gun. He did that with my mom's first marriage she had with Mr. Chin, who was somewhat abusive, so he learned about it and he went up to him one day and said, 'I understand that you have done so-in-so, is that true?' and I don't know what the response was but he said, 'If you lay another hand on her, I'll blow your brains out.'"

The idea of Mahfood's family ordering a hit on Drummond is prevalent among those who were stunned to see their friend die in a mental institution after a horrific murder. Vin Gordon still contends that Mahfood's father was responsible, that he paid a nurse inside Bellevue to give Don Drummond a lethal overdose. It is not possible that Anita Mahfood's father, Jad Mahfood, murdered Drummond or ordered Drummond to be murdered as Jad died the same year as Anita, three years earlier than Don. It is possible that another member of the family ordered a hit, but it is a fantastical idea without any foundation in fact.

Sergi contends that there is no way anyone from her family was involved with Drummond's death, although she has heard the rumors promulgated mostly by Jamaican men: "When it comes to Jamaicans, they believe a lot of strange things. I know, I was born and raised there until I was seventeen. My family had nothing to do with Don Drummond's death."

Some have indicated that they think that Rudolph Bent may have been the one who murdered Drummond, but his daughter, Suzanne, doubts this: "I don't think my dad had anything to do with that, but I do think he had something to do with my mom's death." It's likely that Rudolph Bent wasn't even in Jamaica during the time of Drummond's death. At the end of April 1969, Bent was still in the United States, according to boxing records, and he frequently stayed there for long periods of time; he hadn't even fought in Jamaica since 1965. Conchita confirms that Bent was in the U.S. during the time of her sister's death.

Those who believe Don Drummond was murdered may be suffering more from disbelief about the death of their brethren. Eddie "Tan Tan" Thornton says, "It's a big, big story because he die in the asylum. It's a big, big story. I hear them kill him inside. That's what I heard. The girl that he was going out with, a rich family. You know in Jamaica you have the rich people and what I heard, when he was in the asylum, they kill him. I was very depressed and sad. I couldn't believe it because he's a good guy. He's a decent guy, very decent. I couldn't believe it would come to this, I know him, I know that person. Even now I'm shocked, I can't believe it. I can't believe it because the guy is a quiet, decent guy. He's a mother's boy, may God rest his soul. When you grow with somebody and you live with somebody and something like that happen, it just shock you. I don't know if he kill a girl or not but I know that he wouldn't take his life, I personally know that. So it must be bigger things than that, you know what I mean? And the girl's family is one of the richest families in Jamaica, so maybe it got set up, you know what I mean? That is my thinking. If you know Don Drummond you love him."

Heather Royes claims she never heard anything unusual about Drummond's death while she lived at Bellevue: "Dr. Shoucair loved to bring all the gossip to my mother, so if anything happened to Don D. I think we would have been the first to know. Murdered? I don't think so. Maybe if there was a fight among the inmates. But nobody would trouble Don Drummond. I remember him as being very placid, very placid. If there had been trouble, I would have heard and I never heard anything. I personally feel it was probably a mixture of the schizophrenia and smoking. I would have heard if it was a suicide."

Dr. Aggrey Irons, who joined Bellevue's staff on July 1, 1975, says that there were rumors about Drummond killing himself, but no proof, and that murder would be unlikely. "His story was legend by the time I got there," Dr. Irons attests. "Some people say it was suicide. But I am not sure. It [the facility] was extremely secure. Extremely secure. It was run in those days on the pattern of a prison and you really had to go through the ropes to get into that part of the yard and I'm not saying that murder was impossible, but highly unlikely." Conchita contends that the "madmen" in the institution beat Don to death because of their love and respect for her sister, Anita.

Had Don Drummond not died that May in 1969, Dr. Aggrey Irons feels it is likely he would ultimately have been released, given the nature of his sentence: "I think he would have benefited from 'her majesty's pleasure' because there would have been a lot of lobbying for his release, especially from people like Patterson and others like him. The entire country viewed that it was a crime of passion and although we all knew he was guilty, the circumstances were such that I think even a strict colonial society would have understood."

15

Burning Torch

When the four teenage boys sat down on a wooden bench across from me in the Lennie Hibbert Music Hall at Alpha Boys School in the summer of 2011, all they wanted to know was, "Miss, what musical artists are popular in America?" Some say Kingston looks nothing like it once did, during Don Drummond's lifetime, but in many ways it is still the same. Jamaican music is still influenced by the innovations of the U.S., only now young musicians are blending electronic, rap and hip hop forms to create their sounds. Jamaican musicians have always been influenced by America's musical output, and certainly Don Drummond is no exception.

But my response to those four barefoot boys, just before they picked up their instruments to demonstrate their knowledge and skill under the tutelage of Bandmaster Winston "Sparrow" Martin, was to call on what made Don Drummond different from all of those other musicians who took the American music and envisioned it through the lens of Jamaica: "Make your music your own. Put yourself into your music. America may love Beyonce or Jay-Z today, but the world looks to you for the future because you have the past in your bones. You stand on the shoulders of giants. You have greatness inside of you."

Ten minutes later, I walked over to one of the boys, his flute in his hands, sheet music in front of him on his music stand. The top of the page, above the staffs of notes, divulged two words: "Addis Ababa." I asked the boy, "Did you know that Don Drummond wrote this?" Wide-eyed and incredulous, he turned to me. He had no idea. On his face I saw the realization, the recognition. Don Drummond was just like him.

Don Drummond was so well loved because he was a man who was all too human. He was the Man in the Street. His friends, his colleagues, his fans, the nuns at Alpha, still speak of him with great respect, despite his horrific crime and struggles. "Mr. Drummond is up there with the rest of the original line up from 'sixty-five, blowing up a storm and hopefully making peace with some of the other angels," says Lee "Kix" Thompson of Madness. Vocalist Owen Grey says, "He respected people. He respected you because he didn't visit a lot of talkin' and arguin', but his music has traveled throughout the world. He was a good man. He was like a teacher, too. Very uplifting, lively. He always smilin'. He's always givin' you encouragement. He was more like a professor. That's the word. Not a genius, a professor."

Drummond taught the boys at Alpha when he returned, fostering the growth of numerous young students, as well as fellow patients during his time in Bellevue. Perhaps no one knows Don Drummond's teachings better than his closest friend and protégé, Rico Rodriguez. Drummond helped to shape Rico's education in music, taking him into the Wareika Hills, tutoring him at Alpha Boys School, standing together with him as a fellow musician. "He was a good man," Rodriguez says with pride. "He was so excellent, he was so good that I want to be as good as him so I work real hard, reading and so forth, writing. When he write the music, he get you to come and sit with you and play the music with you. Drummond was a quiet person, but he was my very good friend, you know? I held his music stand [for] him. Whenever he wrote any music he always call me to come play it with him, you know? He was a very good person. He was a very good person. He always come and pick me up to go and practice with him, you know? And sometimes I didn't have a trombone and I used to go and borrow his trombone. But sometime he don't want to lend me. Before he give me he always shine it up. 'Look after this and bring it back.' I didn't have one, he used to lend me his." Through Rico, Don Drummond's legacy lives on in a way that only Rico can express.

Any trombonist from Jamaica is likely to be compared to Don Drummond, no matter how much time passes, simply because Don Drummond was the first and the best. Rico says this happened to him since day one, and he never really minded. Trombonist and Alpharian Basil Hylton says, "I had never met Don although for a while I felt I was in his shadows, for not only did I also learn to play the trombone in Alpha Boys School, but anyone of us who subsequently played the trombone was immediately likened to Don. For example, when I played in the 1962 Independence musical road shows with the Mapletoft Poule Orchestra, people got really excited when one got up to play a solo because, to them, he who plays the trombone well must be like Don. I know both Vin Gordon and Felix Taylor had the very same experience."

Vin Gordon says that his playing was compared to Don Drummond's playing so often that producers even mistook it for Don's, which Gordon considered the ultimate compliment. "Don Drummond was better than me but he send a message to somebody and tell me that I am good," Gordon recalls. "He send somebody with a message and said, 'Tell him that he is good, very good, keep it up.' That was when I am young, when I was young in Studio One. Then there was a big mistake made in Studio One. I played a song called 'Heavenless,' and Coxsone put it on Don Drummond's album because he thought it was Don Drummond because I sound so close to Don Drummond that he put it on Don Drummond's album. He eventually told me it was a mistake. He swear he thought it was Don Drummond." Other songs, like Rico's "Let George Do It," were attributed to Don Drummond by unscrupulous producers who wanted to capitalize on his clout.

It is undeniable that Don Drummond's immense talent wasn't fully recognized during his lifetime. That fact killed Drummond and inspires journalists and musicians today to give him his due. Writer Andrew Clunis in the *Jamaica Star* newspaper writes,

> Don Drummond deserves more homage than is currently paid to him. He mastered one of the most difficult musical instruments in the world, and with such brilliance that hardly anyone has been able to better his recorded work. The trombone is a large brass instrument with a sliding tube, which gives a brash sound. Don Drummond was able to get a refined sound from the instrument, a sound which has made the Skatalites famous for decades.

Bunny Goodison, O.D., says that he feels that the full appreciation of Drummond's music is yet to come: "Time alone will make him more important because the younger generation will realize his talent. Dancehall is our music today and more and more people are getting sick of it. It's uncouth, undisciplined and they will turn away from it. It's bad news. Some bands have started to spring up now and the instrumentalists will creep back in to the people. Don will come and live again. When you call Drummond's name, there is awe. There is silence."

During his short time on earth, Don Drummond produced massive amounts of brilliant music and shaped the music of countless others. "He was a great inventor," says Karl "Cannonball" Bryan. "'Man in the Street,' 'Schoolin' the Duke,' 'Confucius,' 'This Man Is Back,' oh my God, all those great songs." Don Drummond was a virtuoso. He helped to establish ska as the foundation of Jamaican music. "It's not going anywhere anytime soon," says percussionist Larry McDonald. "That stuff is like a fixture." Ska's strength is unbreakable, and Drummond is a pillar that will only grow more powerful as future generations dig deep into the roots of the music. Plus, his ten years spent in jazz prior to the ska era yielded a wealth of live music that can never again be heard. He was incredibly productive, writing anywhere between 300 and 500 songs, say many of his fellow musicians, although much of his repertoire was never recorded. Ken Stewart says, "Don Drummond was by far the most prolific composer and soloist in the Skatalites. Although Tommy McCook was the leader and Don was more of an introvert, he was also the driving musical force in the group as the others would play and feed off of his riffs, moods, and energies. It can be heard in the recordings, especially from Lloyd Knibb and Dizzy. Their energy changes as Don plays differently and they answer in their own way. He could make a sad melody happy with his solo, or vice versa. He could write a tune with one chord and get multiple moods from it just by what he played for a solo or added a bridge. His absence was felt instantly and caused the demise of the group. He is still missed by the remaining members, compatriots, and fans, even to this day. Unfortunately, he crossed that fine line between genius and insanity. His story is a true tragedy but some would argue that he was most influential trombonist of the 20th century, myself included."

Robin "Bongo Jerry" Small discussed this phenomenon of how Drummond was able to take a very independent form of music and turn it into interplay. From Dermot Hussey's radio program *Requiem to Don Drummond*, which aired on RJR in 1969, Robin "Bongo Jerry" Small says,

Music like "The Reburial of Marcus Garvey," it insisted on our being attentive and it also made the man maintain a folklore by being emotional. Listen to that tune again. And listen to him in "Don D Lion" when he comes to agreement with the trumpet of Johnny Moore. The unity that reveal in that music is something civil, like sweet. They maintain attention with their horns that made the drummer alert. Listen again. Listen to "Treasure Isle" and you will hear how man can make his instrument suggest like traveling and motion and floating. Listen to the tune "Scandal" and you will hear a man suggest a certain amount of shocking happening just by the way of the emotion of the tune. You listen and you listen and you hear Lester Sterling take over the music and introduce the improvisation and by the time Don Drummond is ready to speak again he is like a man telling of the said scandal. We can go back to one of his earliest recordings, "Blue Moon," you hear Drummond painting not only the name of that tune, but also the blueness of the moon in a different light. You hear a man submitting himself to the will of the vocalist and helping that vocalist express what that tune was trying to say.

As Lloyd Bradley writes, "His real strength lay in his ability to observe the music from the outside and direct it as a feeling or a mood rather than as a technical exercise. Often that mood was intriguingly dark." Dr. Gordon Rohlehr, historian, wrote just one month after Drummond's death that songs such as "Marcus Junior," "The Reburial," "China Town," or "Fidel" express an extreme frenzy, drive and anarchy, especially in the drumming and the use of the cymbals. Yet Drummond's solos in these pieces often bear little relation to this frenzy. He blows a slow and sometimes calm trombone, in a desolate, abstracted minor key, as if he were part of the band only by accident. It is not that he is not in time or in tune with them, but his message is different. Perhaps his best compositions reflect something of his own schizophrenia, the contrast between the disinherited and distracted consciousness."

Trombonist Calvin "Bubbles" Cameron says that split personality is part of Drummond's own repertoire as a musician. Cameron lived a few yards away from Drummond in Rockfort and was so influenced by Drummond's practicing on his verandah and in his home that Cameron took up the instrument himself. Drummond, he says, changed the face of music for trombonists: "You can hear it when it is Don Drummond in a song. You can hear it because he stay in certain keys because the keys have certain mood. In my writing now and as a musician, I absorb some of that because I was visiting him since I'm around seven years of age, and watching Rasta man play music and watching Don Drummond playing. If I stay too late out my mother beat me, but I'm going to school, I have to pass there, so I hear them playing. And then he lives by me now at a certain age and in the morning I would hear him playing sometime. And at lunchtime he'd go down the road and buy his ice and come back to make his limeade. Yeah. We still speak about him today because he was one of the first person that take trombone to a next level, like J.J. Johnson and Kai Winding. The trombone is an instrument that play in the bass line. The trombone was never a lead instrument, until J.J. Johnson and Kai Winding and Don Drummond come along and start to do that. People have to give him more credit."

In countries all over the world, Don Drummond's music has been heard in the years since his death, engendering respect and popularity. Eddie "Tan Tan" Thornton says, "There's Don Drummond's music all over the world. I was in Tokyo, Japan, and [I heard] Don Drummond's music.

I was in Australia, New Zealand, everywhere I go, 'Eastern Standard Time.' Away from Bob Marley, Don Drummond is the most popular guy we have. I pray for him every day, every day." His songs have been covered by countless ska and jazz bands over the years, perhaps none more so than the 2 Tone bands who gave Drummond's music and ska music a whole a new interpretation for a new audience. The 2 Tone bands that then performed these tunes through their punk, pop, and uniquely British filters re-disseminated the music to the youth of America, who then interpreted the music yet again with their own vision.

Just one example of the evolution of Drummond's music can be seen in the song "Guns of Navarone." Seizing on the popularity of American movies in Jamaica during the '50s and '60s, Drummond penned a cover of the theme song for the movie *Guns of Navarone*, originally written by Dimitri Tiomkin, which was then popularly covered by The Special AKA. This song was also covered by the Upsetters in 1970 and, in later decades, by such bands as the trendy No Doubt and Lee "Kix" Thompson of Madness, who performs it with his Lee Thompson Ska Orchestra; German band, the Busters; the Uplifters and the Mighty Offbeats of England; Dancing Mood from Buenos Aires, Argentina; the Horns of Babylon of Denmark; Rocksteady Times from Mexico; the Ska Flames of Japan; R Slide from Surakarta, Indonesia; and countless others.

Some more surprising covers of Don Drummond's tunes come from such bands as the Hooters, whose songs "And We Danced," "All You Zombies," and "Day by Day" hit the charts in the 1980s. Their demo tape, which got into the hands of a Philadelphia DJ who was a fan of ska bands and thus helped to launch their careers and land them a spot in the Live Aid concert, featured "Man in the Street"—but not with the soulful melodies of a trombone, nor the Hooters' signature melodica, but two wailing electric guitars which played that catchy riff in harmonic thirds. Almost every ska band has tried their hand at a Don Drummond tune at one time or another because these songs are now part of the ska canon. They are classics, they are standards. In Jamaica, they call them the oldies.

Drummond's tunes with the Skatalites have influenced countless musicians in the decades since his death. Neol Davies of The Selecter has drawn upon Drummond's music for inspiration because it was so expressive. Davies says, "The music Don Drummond created is timeless and beautiful. His flowing choice of notes when he played was unique and easily capable of moving emotions in the way that only music from someone's soul can do." For Marc Wasserman, member of Bigger Thomas, New Jersey's first ska band, his own repertoire was influenced by Drummond's creativity even though, like many American ska fans, his introduction to Drummond came through an indirect route. Wasserman says, "My journey as a ska aficionado and musician started with 2 Tone, but, lucky for me, wound its way backwards from The Specials, The Beat, and The Selecter to the originators of it all, the Skatalites. I was immediately taken with the chugging sound of their traditional ska but more so with the magical trombone melodies played by the band's founder, Don Drummond. Since the band played instrumentals, Drummond's notes took on an other-worldly quality. His inspired playing captured my imagination and convinced me that my fledgling ska band must have a horn section. The opening of 'Man in the Street' still makes the hair on the back on my neck stand up every time I hear it. Though his life ended tragically, he remains a musical hero to many and the Beethoven of ska music to me."

There have been numerous recorded tributes to Don Drummond, namely from Carlos Malcolm and Rico Rodriguez. In 2007, Motion Records released the Skatalites' album, *Rolling Steady*, which featured the song "Big Trombone," a tribute to Don Drummond sung by Lord Tanamo, one of the Skatalites' four original vocalists. Busty Brown recorded "King of the Trombone" in 1969 and mourns the loss of Don D., singing that no one can take his throne. Plays and poems have been written in memoriam and scholars have spoken at conferences about his life and influence. There was even a Don Drummond Symposium that took place at the University of the West Indies for a number of years. The inaugural event began in 2000 and was attended by scholars and musicians, such as Dermot Hussey, Branford Marsalis, and Coxsone, all of whom spoke on various topics about Jamaican musical history. There was also a concert held to commemorate Don Drummond's memory, where such greats as Ernest Ranglin, Vin Gordon, and Deadly Headley Bennett performed, and 13 years after his death, in 1982 a memorial concert was held at Bellevue in his honor.

For Thornton and many others, Don Drummond's popularity today is bittersweet: "He never make no money! The school is the one that bury him! Who gets all the money? I can see him turning in his grave. The guy that own Studio One, Dodd, all of them is criminals, every one of them, criminal, mon. The guy that own Studio One, the recording company called Studio One, owned by a guy named Dodd, he was a thief, he was a thief. Wicked and evil. Evil people, mon, evil. Don Drummond make him rich, and then he die and the nuns have to bury him. That's why I got to leave Jamaica."

Who knows how fast that exploitation sent Drummond to his grave, and fostered the mental decline that led to such tragedy. There are the stories of people (Bob Marley, Johnny Cash, Elvis Presley, Loretta Lynn, and others) whose talent was so great they overcame the poverty and oppression in their lives to achieve the embrace of the world. But Drummond's hurdles were too high and despite his immense creativity, skill, and genius, he was unable to become a household name. "For the pursuit of the dream also destroyed the pursuer," comments Hussey. Dr. Gordon Rohlehr says Drummond's music was "a courageous statement of the daily miracle of survival in that harsh world." He adds that Drummond was a "representative figure, perhaps all the more so for his bouts of lunacy. Few people of sensibility retain pedestrian sanity in Kingston." Rohlehr notes that the true testament to Drummond's genius is that so many trombonists have tried to emulate his sound and his skill.

So the good that has come from Drummond's talent continues, at Alpha Boys School, and every time a person familiar with his work picks up an instrument to play or a set of earphones to listen. Sparrow Martin says he uses Drummond's music, like "Addis Ababa," to teach his boys to play: "I let them listen to Don Drummond and Tommy McCook and let them play what these guys play. I have fourteen boys who play for me in the band, but I have more than twenty-seven in class. I enjoy it. We teach everything here. When they outside, they have to say to the world, 'Here I am! This is what I'm going to do for you!' Everything is out there, good and bad, but you have to choose." Martin clearly recognizes that the streets of Kingston and life in the world can be tough on a fragile genius, or anyone.

Dr. Aggrey Irons says that the boys at Alpha were well served then and are still well served today, following in the footsteps of greatness: "His brethren shared in his creativity and any trombonist who plays the ska or even the reggae is going to style himself off of Drummond. And so all they have to do is put on a hat and they become Drummond, if you know what I mean. Even the nuns, the holy women, think of him with terms of endearment, even though some of them weren't around at that time. That school is really a nursery for our wind instrumentalists and so we all owe a lot to those Sisters of Mercy in that regard."

Don Drummond literally shaped all Jamaican music that came during his time, and all Jamaican music that came afterward. Carlos Malcolm says, "He was, if not the first, among the first composers of original instrumental ska music. He planted the seed of creativity, encouraging local musicians to produce original works. Don's unique, original musical phrasings have been adopted by many composers and, in my estimation, have 'crossed over' into other genres of music." Drummond helped to establish a profitable music business for every major record producer in Kingston — Coxsone Dodd, Duke Reid, Vincent Chin, Justin Yap, Leslie Kong, and Prince Buster. "Don's music, in my view," says Clive Chin, "was very deep, very deep. His execution, how he did it, was unique. He was number one in my view. If you really consider his compositions, they're very haunting. Augustus Pablo said he patterned his sound after Don, the Far East sound and minor chords. What Bob Marley is to reggae, Don is to ska."

Without a successful music industry in the early years, reggae would not have emerged to give the world the sounds of Bob Marley and Jimmy Cliff, whom Don Drummond backed up on their earliest tunes, and the myriad of others since. His music has been able to launch careers and sustain through time because, simply, it was so good. "Every piece of music that Don Drummond ventured into was like a theme for a very great movie or a very great Broadway show," says Tommy McCook. "Every one of them, like 'Street Corner,' was like an announcement of some sort, 'Man in the Street,' every one of these tune sound like a very great theme song and every one of them was."

It is impossible to separate the musician from the music, at least in the case of Don Drummond. Knowing his story, knowing his suffering, his longing, his potential, his body of work, the tragedy of his early death infuses the music with a connotation that cannot be disregarded. In Hussey's radio broadcast in the days following Drummond's death, Robin "Bongo Jerry" Small recalled,

> In my short association with Don Drummond, during the time of the Skatalites, I find him being withdrawn most of the time, but that's always the way of a great musician. Some people would say he is antisocial, but he's always thinking about his work. As a jazzman, he's rated among the best in the world. As a technician, I think he's the best. His ideas are deep. Most of them filled with sadness. I remember once we were listening to a Don Drummond production and my wife always admire his playing, and I say to her, "Why do you like his playing so much? What is it you see in his playing?" Her remark was that everything he does and his instrument is always filled with sadness and her heart goes out to him. And I think that's one of the main reasons for his

achievement. He has been sad most of his life. He has been ignored by society, so to speak, but, in my estimation, he made it. Only a few have made it the way Don did, and I know his name will live on forever, and I must say it has been a pleasure and a real joy working with the man. And to you, Don, I say, keep up the good work, and wherever you are and wherever you may go, we will always remember you as the greatest.

Roll On, Sweet Don.
Roll On, Sweet Anita.

Discography
by Michael Turner

This discography was compiled by Michael Turner (Roots Knotty Roots www. reggaefever.ch/rkr) and comprises a best estimate of Don Drummond's body of work. Due to Don Drummond's repeated internment at Bellevue Mental Hospital, and the lack of producers' documentation on their instrumentalists and session musicians as a result of non-existent royalty payments, it is difficult to determine Drummond's presence on every recording. As a result, there may be a few inadvertent errors, but the following discography reflects a proportion of the recorded work made by Don Drummond.

Song Title	A Side Artist	Label
1959		
On the Beach	Owen Gray	Coxsone
1960		
Don Cosmic	Don Drummond	Sensational
1961		
This Man Is Back	Don Drummond	All Stars
1962		
Dewdrops	Don Drummond	Blue Beat
Dewdrops	Don Drummond	D Darling
Fisherman Sam	Skatalites	Randy's
Fisherman Sam (Sam the Fisherman)	Skatalites	Blue Beat
Four Corners of the World	Roland Alphonso	Blue Beat
Four Corners of the World	Roland Alphonso	D Darling
Musical Communion	Baba Brooks	Dutchess
Ruff & Tuff (Rough & Tough)	Stranger Cole	Dutchess
Schooling the Duke	Don Drummond	D Darling
Schooling the Duke	Don Drummond	Island
Strong Arm	Baba Brooks	Dutchess
Twelve Minutes to Go	Don Drummond	Duke Reid's
When You Call My Name	Stranger Cole & Patsy Todd	Dutchess

Song Title	A Side Artist	Label
1963		
Adam's Apple (Don't Bother Me)	Skatalites	N D Records/All Stars
Adam's Apple (Don't Bother Me)	Skatalites	Island
Air Raid Shelter	Lester Sterling	Rolando & Powie
Air Raid Shelter	Lester Sterling	R&B
Away from It All (Ska Train, Siberia)	Skatalites	Randy's
Back Biter	Delroy Wilson	Rolando & Powie
Back Biter	Delroy Wilson	Island
Bank to Bank	Baba Brooks	Dutchess
Bank to Bank	Baba Brooks	Island
Bank to Bank (Part 2)	Baba Brooks	Dutchess
Bank to Bank (Part 2)	Baba Brooks	Island
Beat Up Your Gum	Stranger Cole	Dutchess
Beautiful Baby	Delroy Wilson	Rolando & Powie
Below Zero (Drifting)	Skatalites	Studio 1
Below Zero (Drifting)	Skatalites	Island
Blackhead Chinaman	Prince Buster Dice	
Blackhead Chinaman	Prince Buster	Prince Buster
Blackhead Chinaman	Prince Buster	Prince Buster Voice of the People
The Blazing Fire	Derrick Morgan	Beverley's
The Blazing Fire	Derrick Morgan	Rio
The Blazing Fire	Derrick Morgan	Island
Blue Dot (Hot Rod)	Roland Alphonso	Island
Bollo Man (Boller Man a Come) (Bullo Man)	Theophilus Beckford	King Pioneer
Bollo Man (Boller Man a Come) (Bullo Man)	Theophilus Beckford	Island
Buster's Welcome	Prince Buster All Stars	Blue Beat
Buster's Welcome	Prince Buster All Stars	Prince Buster
Cally Bud	Skatalites	Randy's
Can't You See	Delroy Wilson & Paulette	Muzik City
Can't You See	Delroy Wilson & Paulette	Island
Cherry Pie (Sweeter Than Cherry Pie)	Cherries	Beverley's
Close of Play	Don Drummond	R&B
Close of Play	Don Drummond	N D Records
Come Down	Lord Tanamo	S E P
Come Down	Lord Tanamo	Island
Coming Home (Emmy Lou)	Delroy Wilson	Supreme
The Conqueror	Stranger Cole	Dutchess
The Conqueror	Stranger Cole	Island
Country Town (The Mood I Am In)	Baba Brooks	Blue Beat

Song Title	A Side Artist	Label
Country Town (The Mood I Am In)	Baba Brooks	Dutchess
Distant Drums (African Blood)	Baba Brooks & Trenton Spence Orch.	Island
Distant Drums (African Blood)	Baba Brooks & Trenton Spence Orchestra	Top Deck
Dog War Bossa Nova	Don Drummond	Black Swan
Dog War Bossa Nova	Don Drummond	S E P
Don's Tune (Machine Shop)	Don Drummond	Randy's
Don't Believe Him	Delroy Wilson	Rolando & Powie
Don't Believe Him	Delroy Wilson	R&B
Eastern Standard Time	Skatalites	Randy's
Exclusively	Beverley's All Stars	Beverley's
Federal Special	Roland Alphonso	R&B
Federal Special	Roland Alphonso	N D Records
Feeling Good (Namely You)	Roland Alphonso	D Darling
5 O'Clock Whistle	Baba Brooks	Island
5 O'Clock Whistle	Baba Brooks	Top Deck
Fowl Thief (Rough & Tough)	Prince Buster	Blue Beat
Fowl Thief (Rough & Tough)	Prince Buster	Prince Buster
Further East (Trolley Song)	Don Drummond	Blue Beat
Further East (Trolley Song)	Don Drummond	D Darling
Further West	Skatalites	Randy's
Gravy Cool	Lester Sterling	R&B
Gravy Cool	Lester Sterling	N D Records
Heaven	Delroy Wilson	Coxsone
High Noon	Beverley's All Stars	Beverley's
Hit & Run (Blockade)	Roland Alphonso	Randy's
Hit & Run (Blockade)	Roland Alphonso	Island
I Shall Not Remove	Delroy Wilson	Rolando & Powie
I Shall Not Remove	Delroy Wilson	Island
I Shall Wear a Crown	Richards Brothers	Dutchess
I Shall Wear a Crown	Richards Brothers	Island
I'm Gonna Tell You My Mind	Joe White	Dutchess
Jelly Bean	Baba Brooks	Dutchess
Jelly Bean	Baba Brooks	Black Swan
Jet Stream	Don Drummond	Rolando & Powie
Jet Stream	Don Drummond	R&B
Joe Liges	Delroy Wilson	Rolando & Powie
Joe Liges	Delroy Wilson	R&B
Junior Jive	Skatalites	Rolando & Powie
Junior Jive	Skatalites	Island

Song Title	A Side Artist	Label
King Pharaoh (Prince Pharaoh)	Delroy Wilson	Rolando & Powie
King Pharaoh (Prince Pharaoh)	Delroy Wilson	R&B
Last Love (Lost Love)	Stranger Cole	Island
Lion of Judah	Delroy Wilson	Rolando & Powie
Lion of Judah	Delroy Wilson	R&B
Little Love	Delroy Wilson & Paulette	D Darling
Little Love	Delroy Wilson & Paulette	Island
Loving Baby	Delroy Wilson & Paulette	D Darling
Loving Baby	Delroy Wilson & Paulette	Island
Make Hay	Cornel Campbell	Randy's
Malcolm X	Skatalites	Randy's
Man To Man	Lord Creator	Randy's
Man To Man	Lord Creator	Island
Mighty Rose (100 Ton Megaton)	Raymond Harper & Torchlighters	Blue Beat
Moon Bird	Roland Alphonso	J B & R A
Morning Star	Stranger Cole	Dutchess
Musical Communion	Baba Brooks	Blue Beat
My Time For Fun	Delroy Wilson	Rolando & Powie
Naughty People	Delroy Wilson	Rolando & Powie
Naughty People	Delroy Wilson	Island
Nothing Tried	Stranger Cole	Dutchess
One More Time	Skatalites	S E P
One Two Three	Delroy Wilson	Island
Open Mind	Roland Alphonso	J B & R A
Out of Many One	Stranger Cole	Dutchess
Outer Space	Prince Buster	All Stars
Over & Over	Roy Panton & Millie Small	Blue Beat
Over & Over	Roy Panton & Millie Small	Prince Buster Voice of the People
Peace & Love	Lester Sterling	Rolando & Powie
Pennies from Heaven	Prince Buster All Stars	Prince Buster
Perhaps	Roland Alphonso	R&B
Perhaps	Roland Alphonso	Rolando & Powie
Pipe Dream (Clean the City)	Lester Sterling	Rolando & Powie
Pipe Dream (Clean the City)	Lester Sterling	Island
Pomps & Pride (Squeeze You Toe)	Delroy Wilson	Coxsone
Reload	Don Drummond	Blue Beat
Reload	Don Drummond	All Stars
Robin Hood	Baba Brooks	Dutchess
Robin Hood	Baba Brooks	Island
Rock Away	Don Drummond	R&B

Song Title	A Side Artist	Label
Rock Away	Don Drummond	N D Records
The Rocket	Don Drummond	Rolando & Powie
The Rocket	Don Drummond	Island
Royal Flush	Don Drummond	Rolando & Powie
Royal Flush	Don Drummond	R&B
Ruff & Tuff (Rough & Tough)	Stranger Cole	Blue Beat
Scandal	Don Drummond	Rolando & Powie
Scandal	Don Drummond	Island
Scrap Iron	Don Drummond	All Stars
Scrap Iron	Don Drummond	Black Swan
Shock Resistance	Baba Brooks	Top Deck
The Shock	Don Drummond	Rolando & Powie
The Shock	Don Drummond	R&B
Ska Ba	Skatalites	Island
Ska Ba	Skatalites	Rolando & Powie
Sly Mongoose	Baba Brooks	Beverley's
Smiling Face	Dotty & Clive Bonnie	Dutchess
Snow Boy	Skatalites	Beverley's
Snow Boy	Skatalites	Island
Spit in the Sky (Remember Your Nest)	Delroy Wilson	Blue Beat
Spit in the Sky (Remember Your Nest)	Delroy Wilson	Black Swan
Spitfire	Don Drummond	Black Swan
Streamline	Roland Alphonso	Rolando & Powie
Streamline	Roland Alphonso	Island
Strong Man Sampson	Eric Monty Morris	Dutchess
Strong Man Sampson	Eric Monty Morris	Black Swan
Summer Day	Dotty & Clive Bonnie	Dutchess
Things Come to Those Who Wait	Stranger Cole	Dutchess
Things Come to Those Who Wait	Stranger Cole	Ska Beat/R&B
Three Blind Mice	Baba Brooks	Island
Til My Dying Days	Stranger Cole	Beverley's
Ti-Pi-Tin (Mellow Trumpet) (Tippin' In)	Skatalites	Top Deck
Toothache	Prince Buster All Stars	Blue Beat
Treasure Isle	Roland Alphonso	Supreme
Voodoo Man	Delroy Wilson	Black Swan
Voodoo Man	Delroy Wilson	Blue Beat
Voodoo Man	Delroy Wilson	Rolando & Powie
Watermelon Man	Baba Brooks	Dutchess
Watermelon Man	Baba Brooks	Ska Beat/ R&B
Way Out West	Roland Alphonso	Supreme

Song Title	A Side Artist	Label
When We Walk Down the Street	Delroy Wilson & Paulette	Coxsone
When You Call My Name	Stranger Cole & Patsy Todd	Blue Beat
Words of Wisdom	Eric Monty Morris	Dutchess
You Bend My Love	Delroy Wilson	Muzik City
You Bend My Love	Delroy Wilson	Island
You're No Good	Jackie Opel	Studio 1

1964

Song Title	A Side Artist	Label
20–75	Roland Alphonso	Studio 1
Adis-Aba-Ba (Addis Ababa)	Skatalites	Coxsone
Alive & Well (Ska Boo)	Don Drummond	Randy's
Alive & Well (Ska Boo)	Don Drummond	Randy's
Always On Sunday	Tommy McCook	R&B
Always On Sunday	Tommy McCook	C&N
Around the World	Skatalites	Treasure Isle
Around the World	Skatalites	Island
Away from It All (Ska Train, Siberia)	Skatalites	Randy's
Baby Elephant Walk	Baba Brooks	Randy's
Baskin Hop	Skatalites	Ska Beat/ R&B
Baskin Hop	Skatalites	Rolando & Powie
Beat Up Your Gum	Stranger Cole	Ska Beat/R&B
Black Orpheus (Black Sunday)	Skatalites	C&N
Boat Ride	Baba Brooks	Treasure Isle
Boat Ride	Baba Brooks	Island
Bollo Man (Boller Man a Come) (Bullo Man)	Theophilus Beckford	Ska Beat/R&B
Boof Ska	Beverley's All Stars	Beverley's
Bridge View	Roland Alphonso	Ska Beat/R&B
Bridge View	Roland Alphonso	Coxsone
Broadway Ska (On Broadway)	Skatalites	Prince Buster Voice of the People
Bus Strike	Baba Brooks	Black Swan
Bus Strike	Baba Brooks	Giant
Carry Go Bring Come	Justin Hinds	Treasure Isle
Carry Go Bring Come	Justin Hinds	Island
Catch a Fire	Baba Brooks	Treasure Isle
Catch a Fire	Baba Brooks	Island
Cherry Pie (Sweeter Than Cherry Pie)	Cherries	Beverley's
Cherry Pie (Sweeter Than Cherry Pie)	Cherries	Black Swan
China Town	Skatalites	Top Deck
Christmas Is Here	Bob Marley & Wailers	Muzik City
City Riot	Prince Buster All Stars	Blue Beat

Song Title	A Side Artist	Label
City Riot	Prince Buster All Stars	Prince Buster
Climb the Ladder	Bob Marley & Wailers	Coxsone
Confucious	Don Drummond	Top Deck
Cool Smoke	Don Drummond	Treasure Isle
Cool Smoke	Don Drummond	Island
Coolie Boy	Don Drummond	Muzik City
Cork Foot	Baba Brooks	S E P
Cork Foot Simpson	Baba Brooks	Black Swan
Corner Stone	Justin Hinds	Treasure Isle
Corner Stone	Justin Hinds	Treasure Isle
Cotton Tree	Skatalites	Treasure Isle
Cotton Tree	Skatalites	Ska Beat
Cuban Blockade (Good Gravy)	Skatalites	Rolando & Powie
Dallas Texas (This Is a Hold-Up)	Prince Buster	Blue Beat
Dallas Texas (This Is a Hold-Up)	Prince Buster	Prince Buster Voice of the People
Darling When	Dotty & Clive Bonnie	Treasure Isle
Darling When	Dotty & Clive Bonnie	Island
Desefinado	Prince Buster All Stars	Prince Buster Voice of the People
Dog War (Broadway Jungle)	Maytals	Blue Beat
Dog War (Broadway Jungle)	Maytals	Wildbells
Dog War (Broadway Jungle)	Maytals	Island
Donkey City	Baba Brooks	Dutchess
Donkey City Pt. 2	Baba Brooks	Dutchess
Don't Slam The Door	Skatalites	Coxsone
Down Beat Burial (Johnny Dark)	Don Drummond	Blue Beat
Down Beat Burial (Johnny Dark)	Don Drummond	Prince Buster
Down Beat Burial (Johnny Dark)	Don Drummond	Wildbells
Downtown Gal	Joe White	Treasure Isle
Downtown Gal	Joe White	Island
Dr. Decker	Baba Brooks & Don Drummond	Treasure Isle
Dr. Kildare	Skatalites	All Stars
Dr. No (La Paloma)	Baba Brooks	King Edwards
Dr. No (La Paloma)	Baba Brooks	Rio
Dreadnaught	Baba Brooks	Beverley's
Dreadnaught	Baba Brooks	Black Swan
Drop Your Sword	Eric Monty	Morris Treasure Isle
Drop Your Sword	Eric Monty	Morris Island
Eastern Standard Time	Skatalites	Treasure Isle
Eastern Standard Time	Skatalites	Island

Discography by Michael Turner

Song Title	A Side Artist	Label
Elusive Baby	Charley Organaire & Anette	Organaire's
Emmanuel Road	Baba Brooks	Sir Mike The Musical Dragon
Ethiopia	Baba Brooks & Beverley's All Stars	Black Swan
Ever Loving Feeling	Delroy Wilson	Studio 1
Every Mouth Must Be Fed	Delroy Wilson	Ska Beat/R&B
Every Mouth Must Be Fed	Delroy Wilson	Coxsone
Every Night	Joe White	Prince Buster Voice of the People
Exodus	Skatalites	Muzik City
Exodus	Skatalites	Port-O-Jam
Fast Mouth	Eric Monty Morris	Treasure Isle
Feeling Fine	Roland Alphonso & Frank Anderson	Treasure Isle
Feeling Fine	Roland Alphonso & Frank Anderson	Island
Festival	Don Drummond	Ska Beat/R&B
Festival	Don Drummond	Studio 1
Fidel Castro	Don Drummond	C&N
The Fits Is On Me	Owen Silvera & Leon Silvera	Treasure Isle
The Fits Is On Me	Owen Silvera & Leon Silvera	Island
Fly Flying Dove (Wings of a Dove) (Flying Ska)	Prince Buster	Blue Beat
Fly Flying Dove (Wings of a Dove) (Flying Ska)	Prince Buster	Prince Buster Voice of the People
Fly Flying Dove (Wings of a Dove) (Flying Ska)	Prince Buster	Dragon's Breath
Fly Right	Baba Brooks	Beverley's
Fly Right	Baba Brooks	Black Swan
Forest Flowers	Roland Alphonso	Coxsone
Freedom Ska	Skatalites	Randy's
Full Dread	Skatalites	Rolando & Powie
Garden of Love	Don Drummond	Treasure Isle
Garden of Love	Don Drummond	Island
Go Home	Beverley's All Stars	Beverley's
Go Home	Charley Organaire	Black Swan
Going West (Driving West)	Prince Buster All Stars	Prince Buster Voice of the People
Gonna Tell You My Mind	Joe White	Ska Beat/R&B
Good Collie Bud	Skatalites	Randy's
Good from Bad	Owen Silvera & Leon Silvera	Blue Beat
Good from Bad	Owen Silvera & Leon Silvera	Prince Buster Voice of the People
Good News	Skatalites	Treasure Isle
Good News	Skatalites	Island
Goodbye	Delroy	Wilson D Darling

Song Title	A Side Artist	Label
Goodbye	Delroy	Wilson Black Swan
Guns of Navarone	Skatalites	Muzik City
Hanging the Beam (Roland Plays Prince)	Skatalites	Islam
He Who Feels It Knows It	Stranger Cole	Treasure Isle
He Who Feels It Knows It	Stranger Cole	Island
Healing in the Balm Yard	Prince Buster	Wildbells
Healing in the Balm Yard (Healing)	Prince Buster	Blue Beat
Hello Mother	Skatalites	Randy's
Hill & Gully Ride	Charmers	Treasure Isle
Hill & Gully Ride	Charmers	Island
Hog in a Cocoa	Joe White	Treasure Isle
Hog in a Cocoa	Joe White	Island
Hot Cargo	Lester Sterling	Ska Beat/R&B
Hot Cargo	Lester Sterling	N D Records
How Many Times	Owen Silvera & Leon Silvera	Treasure Isle
How Many Times	Owen Silvera & Leon Silvera	Island
Hucklebuck	Roland Alphonso	Rio
Hucklebuck	Roland Alphonso	King Edwards
I Don't Need Your Love	Bob Marley & Wailers	Studio 1
I Need Your Loving	Delroy Wilson	Studio 1
I Want Justice	Delroy Wilson	Studio 1
Indian Summer	Skatalites	Ska Beat/R&B
Indian Summer	Skatalites	Coxsone
Irene	Joe White	Treasure Isle
Iron Bar	Skatalites	Studio 1
Islam (Africa Is Calling My People)	Don Drummond	Islam
Jack Ruby (Crime Wave)	Roland Alphonso	Ska Beat/R&B
Jack Ruby (Crime Wave)	Roland Alphonso	Studio 1
Jack The Ripper	Prince Buster	All Stars
Jam Rock	Skatalites	Muzik City
Jam Rock	Tommy McCook	Port-O-Jam
Jet 707	Prince Buster All Stars	Blue Beat
Jet 707	Prince Buster All Stars	Wildbells
JFK's Memory	Don Drummond	Treasure Isle
JFK's Memory	Don Drummond	Island
Jingle Bell	Ska Skatalites	Islam
Jordan River	Justin Hinds	Treasure Isle
Jordan River	Justin Hinds	Ska Beat
Just in Time	Beverley's All Stars	Beverley's
Key to the City	Baba Brooks	Dutchess
Key to the City	Baba Brooks	Black Swan
King & Queen	Lord Creator	Randy's
King Samuel	Justin Hinds	Treasure Isle
King Samuel	Justin Hinds	Ska Beat

Song Title	A Side Artist	Label
King Solomon	Skatalites	Ska Beat/R&B
King Solomon	Skatalites	N D Records
Last Love (Lost Love)	Stranger Cole	Sir Mike The Musical Dragon
Last Love (Lost Love)	Stranger Cole	Rio
Latin Goes Ska	Skatalites	Treasure Isle
Latin Goes Ska	Skatalites	Ska Beat
Lee Harvey Oswald	Skatalites	Studio 1
Little Flea (Nobody Knows) (Flea War)	Maytals	Wildbells
Little Flea (Nobody Knows) (Flea War)	Maytals	Island
Little Flea (Nobody Knows) (Flea War) mistitled Little Slea	Maytals	Blue Beat
Little Holiday (It Happens on a Holiday)	Charley Organaire	Organaire's
Little Holiday (It Happens on a Holiday)	Charley Organaire	Ska Beat/R&B
Little Holiday (It Happens on a Holiday)	Charley Organaire	Rio
Little Village	Charley Organaire	Organaire's
Little Village	Charley Organaire	Giant
Little Village	Charley Organaire	Ska Beat/R&B
Little Village	Charley Organaire	Rio
Look at Me	Lord Creator	Studio 1
Love in the Afternoon	Don Drummond	Top Sound
Love Won't Be Mine	Bob Marley & Wailers	Coxsone
Lover Mouth (Lover Man)	Delroy Wilson	Ska Beat/R&B
Lover Mouth (Lover Man)	Delroy Wilson	Coxsone
Low Minded Hypocrite	Delroy Wilson	Studio 1
Low Minded People	Joe White & Chuck Joseph	Treasure Isle
Make Hay	Cornel Campbell	Black Swan
Man in the Street	Don Drummond	Coxsone
Marcus Junior	Don Drummond	Top Deck
Melody Jamboree	Baba Brooks	Dutchess
Melody Jamboree	Baba Brooks	Black Swan
The Mill Man	Jackie Opel	Studio 1
Miss Lulu	Derrick Morgan	Blue Beat
Miss Lulu	Derrick Morgan	Wildbells
Miss Lulu	Derrick Morgan	Prince Buster
Mr. Talkative	Bob Marley & Wailers	Coxsone
More Wood (Push Wood)	Jackie Opel	Studio 1
Morning Star	Stranger Cole	Ska Beat/R&B
Motoring (Take Five)	Baba Brooks	Beverley's
Mule Train	Skatalites	Islam
Musical Storeroom Roland	Alphonso & Frank Anderson	Treasure Isle

Song Title	A Side Artist	Label
Musical Storeroom Roland	Alphonso & Frank Anderson	Island
Musical Workshop	Baba Brooks & Ron Wilson	King Edwards
Musical Workshop	Baba Brooks & Ron Wilson	Black Swan
My Business	Lord Tanamo	Treasure Isle
My Business	Lord Tanamo	Ska Beat
My Daily Food	Maytals	Kentone
Next Door Neighbor Owen	Silvera & Leon Silvera	Treasure Isle
Next Door Neighbor Owen	Silvera & Leon	Silvera Island
Night Food Ska	Lord Tanamo	Ska Beat
Night Food Ska	Lord Tanamo	Treasure Isle
Nimble Foot Roland	Alphonso	Studio 1
Non Stop	Skatalites	Top Deck
Nothing Tried	Stranger Cole	Ska Beat/R&B
Occupation	Skatalites	Treasure Isle
Occupation	Skatalites	Ska Beat
One Look	Maytals	Kentone
One More Time	Lloyd Brevett	Black Swan
One Two Three	Delroy Wilson	Rolando & Powie
Oppression	Delroy Wilson	Coxsone
Out of Fire (Out De Fire)	Royals	Blue Beat
Out of Fire (Out The Fire)	Royals	Islam
Out of Many	One Stranger Cole	Ska Beat/R&B
Over the River	Justin Hinds	Treasure Isle
Passing Through (Coconut Rock)	Skatalites	Rolando & Powie
Peace & Love	Lester Sterling	Ska Beat/R&B
Peanut Vendor	Tommy McCook & Frank Anderson	Ska Beat/R&B
Peanut Vendor	Tommy McCook & Frank Anderson	N D Records
Penny Reel	Eric Monty Morris	Treasure Isle
Penny Reel	Eric Monty Morris	Island
Pick Up the Pieces	Delroy Wilson	Coxsone
Pomps & Pride (Squeeze You Toe) (mistitled Come Down from Your Palms & Pray)	Delroy Wilson	R&B
Prince Is Back (instrumental)	Prince Buster All Stars	Prince Buster
The Reburial	Don Drummond	Top Deck
Red Hot Skatalites	Randy's	
Reincarnation (Prince Royal)	Skatalites	Blue Beat
Reincarnation (Prince Royal)	Skatalites	Wildbells
Return of Paul Bogle	Roland Alphonso	Top Sound
Road Block	Skatalites	Port-O-Jam

Song Title	A Side Artist	Label
Road Block	Skatalites	Rolando & Powie
Road Block	Skatalites	Port-O-Jam
Roll On Sweet Don	Don Drummond	Port-O-Jam
Roll On Sweet Don	Don Drummond	Studio 1
Royal Charley Charley	Organaire	Island
Royal Charley Charley	Organaire	Randy's
Rude Boy	Roland Alphonso	Treasure Isle
Rude Boy	Roland Alphonso	Island
Running Around	Owen Silvera & Leon Silvera	Treasure Isle
Running Around	Owen Silvera & Leon Silvera	Island
Russian Ska Fever	Skatalites	Studio 1
Salt Lane	Ska Skatalites	C&N
Sammy Dead	Delroy Wilson	Ska Beat/R&B
Sammy Dead	Delroy Wilson	Coxsone
Sampson	Skatalites	C&N
Sampson	Tommy McCook	Ska Beat/R&B
Sands of the Sea Dragon	Alton Ellis	Sir Mike The Musical
Sandy Gully	Roland Alphonso	Treasure Isle
Sandy Gully	Roland Alphonso	Island
Santa Lucia	Roland Alphonso & Frank Anderson	Treasure Isle
Santa Lucia	Roland Alphonso & Frank Anderson	Island
Sauvitt	Skatalites	Studio 1
Save Mama	Royals	Blue Beat
Save Mama	Royals	B R A
Save Mama	Royals	Prince Buster
Say Say Business	Jackie Opel	Studio 1
Searching for You	Delroy Wilson	Studio 1
Senorita	Senor Pablo (Lord Brynner?)	Coxsone
Shenk I Sheck	Baba Brooks	King Edwards
Shuffle Duck	Roland Alphonso	King Edwards
Silver Dollar	Skatalites	Treasure Isle
Silver Dollar	Tommy McCook	Ska Beat
Simmer Down	Bob Marley & Wailers	Coxsone
Sit Down Servant	Jackie Opel	Studio 1
Ska La Parisienne	Skatalites	Muzik City
Ska Portrait (Portrait of My Love)	Skatalites	Randy's
Ska Portrait (Portrait of My Love)	Skatalites	Island
Sleep Walk	Beverley's	All Stars Beverley's
Smiling	Don Drummond	Top Deck
Solid Rock	Jackie Opel	Ska Beat/R&B
Solid Rock	Jackie Opel	N D Records

Song Title	A Side Artist	Label
Somebody Stolen (Somebody's Stolen My Baby)	Delroy Wilson	Studio 1
Spider	Tommy McCook & Baba Brooks	Dutchess
Spider	Tommy McCook & Baba Brooks	Black Swan
Spit in the Sky (Remember Your Nest)	Delroy Wilson	N D Records
Spitfire	Don Drummond	Black Swan
Straight & Narrow Way	Bob Marley & Wailers	Coxsone
Street Corner	Skatalites	Treasure Isle
Sucu Sucu	Roland Alphonso	Muzik City
Sudden Attack	Skatalites	Wildbells
Sudden Destruction	Skatalites	Muzik City
Sugar Pie	Delroy Wilson & Dimples	R&B
Summer Day	Dotty & Clive Bonnie	Black Swan
Sun Rises in the East	Dotty & Clive Bonnie	Treasure Isle
Sun Rises in the East	Dotty & Clive Bonnie	Island
Sundown	Roland Alphonso	Top Sound
Supercharge (Walk Along)	Skatalites	Blue Beat
Surplus	Don Drummond	C&N
Sweet Eileen	Baba Brooks	Black Swan
Sweet Jamaica (Jamaican's a Sweet Place)	Charley Organaire	Organaire's
Take Five	Baba Brooks	Black Swan
Take Five	Baba Brooks	Beverley's
Tear Up	Skatalites	Studio 1
Tear Up	Skatalites	W I R L
Tear Us Apart	Delroy Wilson	Coxsone
Teenager in Love	Bob Marley & Wailers	Coxsone
Tell Them Lord	Bob Marley & Wailers	Muzik City
Things Come to Those Who Wait	Stranger Cole	Island
Three Blind Mice	Baba Brooks	Sir Mike The Musical Dragon
The Tickler	Prince Buster All Stars	Blue Beat
The Tickler	Prince Buster All Stars	Prince Buster Voice of the People
Til My Dying Days	Stranger Cole	Island
Tom, Dick & Harry	Stranger Cole & Patsy Todd	Dutchess
Tom, Dick & Harry	Stranger Cole & Patsy Todd	Island
Treat Me Right (Treat Me Good)	Delroy Wilson	D Darling
Treat Me Right (Treat Me Good)	Delroy Wilson	Black Swan

Song Title	A Side Artist	Label
Tribute to Kennedy (President Kennedy) (The president)	Roland Alphonso & Lester Sterling	Coxsone
Tribute to Kennedy (President Kennedy) (The President)	Roland Alphonso & Lester Sterling	R&B
Tribute to Nehru	Skatalites	Randy's
Trip to Mars (Corner Stone)	Skatalites	Treasure Isle
Trip to Mars (Corner Stone)	Skatalites	Island
Turn Your Lamp Down Low (Turn the Light Down Low)	Jackie Opel	Studio 1
Twilight Zone	Lord Inventor	Islam
Two for One	Tommy McCook	D Darling
Two for One	Tommy McCook	Black Swan
Ungrateful People	Theophilus Beckford	Black Swan
Ungrateful People	Theophilus Beckford	Beverley's
unknown	Delroy Wilson	
unknown instrumental	Skatalites	
unknown ska instrumental	Roland Alphonso	Top Sound
Vacation	Melodies	Treasure Isle
Vacation	Melodies	Ska Beat
Wayward Ska	Lloyd Brevett	S E P
We Two Happy People	Stranger Cole & Patsy Todd	Dutchess
We Two Happy People	Stranger Cole & Patsy Todd	Island
Welcome You Back Home (Welcome Home)	Jackie Opel & Doreen Schaeffer	Studio 1
Well Charge	Skatalites	Studio 1
What A Man Doeth	Eric Monty Morris	Treasure Isle
What A Man Doeth	Eric Monty Morris	Island
When First I Heard the Ska	Delroy Wilson & Paulette	Muzik City
Whole World Doing the Ska	Melodies	Treasure Isle
Wolverton Mountain (Twin Double)	Skatalites	C&N
Woman a Come	Marguerita & Baba Brooks	Dutchess
Woman a Come (Woman Come)	Marguerita	Black Swan
Words of My Mouth	Eric Monty Morris	Dutchess
Words of My Mouth	Eric Monty Morris	Black Swan
Words of Wisdom	Eric Monty Morris & Baba Brooks	Black Swan
Your Love	Bob Marley & Wailers	Coxsone
You're No Good	Jackie Opel	Black Swan
You're The Beat	Delroy Wilson & Paulette	Studio 1
You're Too Bad	Jackie Opel	Studio 1
You're Wondering Now	Reuben Anderson & Joanne Dennis	C&N

Song Title	A Side Artist	Label
You're Wondering Now	Reuben Anderson & Joanne Dennis	Ska Beat/R&B

1965

Song Title	A Side Artist	Label
African Chant (Timothy Junior)	Skatalites	Studio 1
African Chant (Timothy Junior)	Skatalites	Ska Beat
African Queen	Don Drummond	King Edwards
Ally Pon (Allepon)	Don Drummond	Treasure Isle
Ally Pon (Allepon)	Don Drummond	Ska Beat
Ananias	Delroy Wilson	Studio 1
The Ark	Justin Hinds	Treasure Isle
The Ark	Justin Hinds	Island
Around The Corner	Derrick Morgan	Treasure Isle
Around The Corner	Derrick Morgan	Ska Beat
Baby Elephant Walk	Baba Brooks	Black Swan
Baby Face Nelson	Prince Buster	All Stars
Bajan Girl	Theophilus Beckford	King Pioneer
Bajan Girl	Theophilus Beckford	Island
Ball O Fire	Skatalites	Island
Ball O Fire	Skatalites	Fire
Beardman Ska	Skatalites	Studio 1
Beardman Ska	Skatalites	Island
Beggars Have No Choice	Leonard Dillon	Supreme
Bellevue Special	Don Drummond	Caribou
Blackhead Chinaman	Prince Buster	Prince Buster Voice of the People
Blues Market	Prince Buster All Stars	Blue Beat
Blues Market	Prince Buster All Stars	Prince Buster Voice of the People
Boderation Diah (Botheration)	Justin Hinds	Treasure Isle
Boderation Diah (Botheration)	Justin Hinds	Island
Burke's Law	Prince Buster	Blue Beat
Burke's Law	Prince Buster	Prince Buster Voice of the People
Captain Burke	Prince Buster All Stars	Blue Beat
China Clipper	Skatalites	Tuneico
China Jacket	Prince Buster	Prince Buster Voice of the People
Christine Keeler	Skatalites	Coxsone
Cleopatra	Roland Alphonso	Port-O-Jam
Cleo's Back	Skatalites	Top Deck
Come Bail Me	Justin Hinds	Treasure Isle
Come Bail Me	Justin Hinds	Island

Song Title	A Side Artist	Label
Congo Revolution	Prince Buster All Stars	Blue Beat
Cool Smoke	Don Drummond	Island
Coolie Boy	Don Drummond	Island
Dan De Lion	Skatalites	Treasure Isle
Dan De Lion	Skatalites	Ska Beat
Determination	Skatalites	Top Deck
Devil's Daffodil	Prince Buster All Stars	Blue Beat
Devil's Daffodil	Prince Buster All Stars	Prince Buster Voice of the People
Devoted to You	Roland Alphonso	Tuneico
Dick Tracy	Skatalites	Studio 1
Dick Tracy	Skatalites	Island
Dr. Decker	Baba Brooks & Don Drummond	Ska Beat
Dr. Decker	Baba Brooks & Don Drummond	Island
Dr. Kildare	Skatalites	Island
Don's Special	Don Drummond	Black Swan
Don's Special	Don Drummond	Beverley's
Don't Call Me Daddy	Derrick Morgan	Treasure Isle
Don't Call Me Daddy	Derrick Morgan	Ska Beat
Down Beat Burial (Johnny Dark)	Don Drummond	Blue Beat
Dragon Weapon	Don Drummond	Beverley's
Dragon Weapon	Don Drummond	Island
Drums of Fueman Tru (Nimrod)	Roland Alphonso	Studio 1
Duck Soup	Baba Brooks	Treasure Isle
Duck Soup	Baba Brooks	Island
El Cid	Roland Alphonso & King Sporty	Top Deck
El Pussy Cat Ska	Roland Alphonso	Studio 1
El Pussy Cat Ska	Roland Alphonso	Island
Fast Mouth	Eric Monty Morris	Island
1st Session	Baba Brooks	Gay Feet
Forest Flowers	Roland Alphonso	Coxsone
Four Seasons of the Year	Skatalites & Sir Lord Comic	King Edwards
From Russia with Love	Roland Alphonso	Studio 1
The Fugitive	Prince Buster	Blue Beat
The Fugitive	Prince Buster	Prince Buster Voice of the People
Ghost Town	Skatalites	Top Deck
Girls Town Ska	Baba Brooks	Treasure Isle
Girls Town Ska	Baba Brooks	Ska Beat
Going West (Driving West)	Prince Buster All Stars	Blue Beat
Green Island	Don Drummond	Coxsone

Song Title	A Side Artist	Label
Greenfield Ska	Baba Brooks & Frank Anderson	Treasure Isle
Greenfield Ska	Baba Brooks & Frank Anderson	Island
Gun Fever (Guns Fever)	Baba Brooks	Treasure Isle
Gun Fever (Guns Fever)	Baba Brooks	Island
Guns of Navarone	Skatalites	Island
Hairy Mango	Jackie Opel	Coxsone
Hanging the Beam (Roland Plays Prince)	Skatalites	Blue Beat
Hanging the Beam (Roland Plays Prince)	Skatalites	Blue Beat
The Harder They Come	Eric Monty Morris	Treasure Isle
The Harder They Come	Eric Monty Morris	Island
Haunted Room	Prince Buster All Stars	Blue Beat
Haunted Room	Prince Buster All Stars	Prince Buster Voice of the People
Heart of Stone	Derrick Morgan & Naomi	Treasure Isle
Heart of Stone	Derrick Morgan & Naomi	Ska Beat
Holy Dove	Justin Hinds	Treasure Isle
Holy Dove	Justin Hinds	Island
The Hunter (Happy Hunter)	Prince Buster All Stars	Prince Buster Voice of the People
I Don't Need Your Love	Bob Marley & Wailers	Ska Beat
I Feel Good	Delroy Wilson	Studio 1
I Should Have Known Better	Roland Alphonso	Studio 1
I Want My Cock (Woman)	Owen Silvera & Leon Silvera	Treasure Isle
I Want My Cock (Woman)	Owen Silvera & Leon Silvera	Ska Beat
I Want My Cock (Woman)	Owen Silvera & Leon Silvera	Island
I Wish I Were An Apple	Derrick Morgan & Naomi	Treasure Isle
I Wish I Were An Apple	Derrick Morgan & Naomi	Ska Beat
Ice Water	Leonard Dillon	Studio 1
Independence '65 (Happy Independence)	Prince Buster All Stars	Blue Beat
Independence Ska (Pussy Cat)	Baba Brooks	Treasure Isle
Independence Ska (Pussy Cat)	Baba Brooks	Island
Irene	Joe White	Island
Islam (Africa Is Calling My People)	Prince Buster All Stars	Blue Beat
James Bond Girl	Roland Alphonso	C&N
James Bond Girl	Roland Alphonso	Island
Jazz Ska	Roland Alphonso	Rio
Jazz Ska	Roland Alphonso	King Edwards
Jerk All Night	Delroy Wilson	Studio 1
Jerk Town	Skatalites	Sound Deck

Song Title	A Side Artist	Label
Joe Snow Cone	Baba Brooks	Treasure Isle
Jump Out of Frying Pan	Justin Hinds	Treasure Isle
Jump Out of Frying Pan	Justin Hinds	Island
King Size	Baba Brooks	Gay Feet
Koo Koo Do Stranger	Cole & Owen Silvera & Leon Silvera	Treasure Isle
Koo Koo Do (Cow in a Pasture)	Stranger Cole & Owen & Leon Silvera	Island
Lawless Street	Skatalites	Tuneico
Lee Harvey Oswald Jr.	Skatalites	Coxsone
Let Me Go	Derrick Morgan	Treasure Isle
Let Me Go	Derrick Morgan	Ska Beat
Linger On	Prince Buster All Stars	Prince Buster Voice of the People
Little Did You Know	Techniques	Treasure Isle
Little Did You Know	Techniques	Island
Live Wire	Skatalites	Top Deck
Look Into That	Justin Hinds	Treasure Isle
Love & Affection	Bob Marley & Wailers	Coxsone
Love & Affection	Bob Marley & Wailers	Ska Beat
Low Minded People	Joe White & Chuck Joseph	Island
Lucky Seven	Don Drummond	Treasure Isle
Lucky Seven	Don Drummond & Baba Brooks	Island
Magic Star	Roland Alphonso	Studio 1
Malika	Lord Brynner & Norma Fraser	Studio 1
Man in the Street	Don Drummond	Island
Maria Elena	Roland Alphonso	Studio 1
Mattie Rag Pt. 2 (instrumental)	Baba Brooks	Ska Beat
Mattie Rag Pt. 2 (instrumental)	Baba Brooks	S E P
Miss Ska Culation	Roland Alphonso	Doctor Bird
More Wood (Push Wood)	Jackie Opel	Ska Beat
Mother Banner	Justin Hinds	Treasure Isle
Mother Banner	Justin Hinds	Ska Beat
Mr. Talkative	Bob Marley & Wailers	Island
Mule Train (Mules Mules Mules)	Skatalites	Blue Beat
My Girl	Jackie Opel	Coxsone
My Lover Derrick	Morgan & Naomi	Treasure Isle
Never Too Young	Justin Hinds	Treasure Isle
Never Too Young	Justin Hinds	Island
Nimble Foot	Roland Alphonso	Ska Beat
No More	Don Drummond	Caribou
Nuclear Weapon	Stanley Ribbs & Skatalites	Treasure Isle

Song Title	A Side Artist	Label
Nuclear Weapon	Stanley Ribbs & Skatalites	Ska Beat
One Eyed Giant	Baba Brooks	Treasure Isle
One Eyed Giant	Baba Brooks	Ska Beat
One Love	Bob Marley & Wailers	Coxsone
One Minute to Zero	Keith Walker	Soft Touch
One Minute to Zero	Keith Walker	Soft Touch
One Step Beyond	Prince Buster All Stars & King Sporty	Blue Beat
One Step Beyond	Prince Buster All Stars & King Sporty	Prince Buster Voice of the People
Oppression	Delroy Wilson	Island
Pain in My Heart	Derrick Morgan & Naomi	Treasure Isle
Pain in My Heart	Derrick Morgan & Naomi	Island
Peace & Love	Justin Hinds	Treasure Isle
Peace & Love	Justin Hinds	Island
Perhaps	Skatalites	Blue Beat
Perhaps	Skatalites	Prince Buster Voice of the People
Phoenix City	Roland Alphonso	Studio 1
Phoenix City	Roland Alphonso	Tuneico
Pick Up the Pieces	Delroy Wilson	Island
Prince of Peace	Prince Buster All Stars	Prince Buster Voice of the People
Provocation	Roland Alphonso	Studio 1
Red Is Danger	Skatalites	Sound Deck
Renegade	Zodiacs	Treasure Isle
Renegade	Zodiacs	Island
Ringo	Skatalites	Tuneico
Ringo's Theme (This Boy) (Ringo's Ska) (Ska With Ringo)	Roland Alphonso	Coxsone
Riverton City	Tommy McCook	Jontom
Rocket Ship	Tommy McCook & Baba Brooks	Treasure Isle
Rocket Ship	Tommy McCook & Baba Brooks	Island
Rollie Pollie	Roland Alphonso	Supreme
Rub Up Push Up	Justin Hinds	Treasure Isle
Rub Up Push Up	Justin Hinds	Island
Rude Boy (Rude Boy Ska) (Rule Them Rudie)	Bob Marley & Wailers	Coxsone
Rude Rude Rudee (Rude Rude Rudie) (Don't Throw Stones)	Prince Buster the People	Prince Buster Voice of
Ryging (Watch Your Head)	Prince Buster All Stars	Blue Beat
Ryging (Watch Your Head)	Prince Buster All Stars	Prince Buster Voice of the People

Song Title	A Side Artist	Label
Ryging (Watch Your Head)	Prince Buster All Stars	Soulsville Centre
Satan	Justin Hinds	Treasure Isle
Satan	Justin Hinds	Island
Scambalena (Sca-Balena)	Roland Alphonso	Studio 1
Scattered Lights	Skatalites	Top Deck
Seven Days a Week	Stranger Cole & Claudelle Clarke	Treasure Isle
Seven Days a Week	Stranger Cole & Claudelle Clarke	Island
Seven Guns Alive	Baba Brooks	Treasure Isle
Shame & Scandal	Peter Tosh & Wailers	Studio 1
Shame & Scandal	Peter Tosh & Wailers	Island
Shenk I Sheck	Baba Brooks	Rio
Shot in the Dark	Skatalites	Top Deck
Si Senor	Ossie & Upsetters	Beverley's
Si Senor	Ossie & Upsetters	Island
Simmer Down	Bob Marley & Wailers	Ska Beat
Ska Boo Ba Da	Skatalites	Top Deck
Ska in Vienna Woods	Skatalites	Studio 1
Ska in Vienna Woods	Skatalites	Island
Ska Jam	Tommy McCook	Caltone
Ska Jerk	Bob Marley & Wailers	Studio 1
Ska Town	Don Drummond	Blue Beat
Ska Town	Don Drummond	Prince Buster Voice of the People
Skahara	Skatalites	Prince Buster Voice of the People
Skahara (Skara)	Skatalites	Blue Beat
Skalarama	Lyn Taitt & Baba Brooks	Treasure Isle
Skalarama	Lyn Taitt & Baba Brooks	Island
Skaravan	Roland Alphonso	Top Deck
Smoking Ska	Baba Brooks	Treasure Isle
Smooth Sailing	Tommy McCook	Caltone
So Good (Rinky Dink)	Roland Alphonso	Studio 1
Something Special	Roland Alphonso	Coxsone
Sometimes I Wonder	Jackie Opel	Tuneico
Song of Love	Roland Alphonso	Studio 1
South China Sea	Skatalites	Top Deck
South Virginia	Prince Buster All Stars	Blue Beat
Spread Satin	Roland Alphonso	Studio 1
Stampede	Baba Brooks & Don Drummond	Treasure Isle
Stampede	Baba Brooks & Don Drummond	Island
Sting Like a Bee	Prince Buster All Stars	Blue Beat
Sting Like a Bee	Prince Buster All Stars	Prince Buster Voice of the People

Song Title	A Side Artist	Label
Street Corner	Skatalites	Ska Beat
Sucu Sucu	Roland Alphonso	Island
Sudden Destruction	Skatalites	Ska Beat
Sufferer's Choice	Roland Alphonso	Studio 1
Supercharge (Walk Along)	Skatalites	Prince Buster Voice of the People
Surftide Seven	Skatalites	Tuneico
Surprise	Skatalites	Top Deck
Sweeter Than Honey	Derrick Morgan & Naomi	Blue Beat
Sweeter Than Honey	Derrick Morgan & Naomi	Treasure Isle
Take Your Time	Jackie Opel	Top Deck
Tall in The Saddle	Roland Alphonso	Coxsone
Teenage Ska	Baba Brooks	Treasure Isle
Teenage Ska	Baba Brooks	Island
Teenager in Love	Bob Marley & Wailers	Ska Beat
Toy Cat (Pussy Cat)	Stranger Cole	Treasure Isle
Toy Cat (Pussy Cat)	Stranger Cole	Ska Beat
Train to Skaville	Roland Alphonso	Supreme
Train to Skaville	Roland Alphonso	Ska Beat
Treasure Isle (Thoroughfare)	Don Drummond	Treasure Isle
Treasure Isle (Thoroughfare)	Don Drummond	Island
Trenchtown People	Theophilus Beckford	King Pioneer
Trenchtown People	Theophilus Beckford	Island
Trip to Mars	Prince Buster All Stars	Prince Buster Voice of the People
Trip to Mars (next version)	Prince Buster All Stars	Prince Buster Voice of the People
Try Me	Jackie Opel	Studio 1
Tuff Talk	Skatalites	Tuneico
Turn Them Back	Justin Hinds	Treasure Isle
Turn Them Back	Justin Hinds	Island
Turn to the Almighty	Jackie Opel	Top Deck
Twilight Zone	Baba Brooks	Treasure Isle
Two of a Kind	Derrick Morgan & Naomi	Treasure Isle
Two of a Kind	Derrick Morgan & Naomi	Island
University Goes Ska	Don Drummond & Baba Brooks	Treasure Isle
University Goes Ska	Don Drummond & Baba Brooks	Island
unknown instrumental	Skatalites	Top Deck
unknown instrumental (dark destroyer?)	Prince Buster	All Stars
unknown title	Justin Hinds	
V C 10 (Shake a Lady)	Skatalites	Tuneico
Valley of Green	Jackie Opel	Top Deck
Vat 7	Don Drummond	Beverley's
Vera Cruz	Prince Buster All Stars	Blue Beat

Discography by Michael Turner

Song Title	A Side Artist	Label
Vera Cruz	Prince Buster All Stars	Prince Buster Voice of The People
Verona	Justin Hinds	Treasure Isle
Virginia Ska	Baba Brooks	Treasure Isle
Virginia Ska	Baba Brooks	Island
Vitamin A	Baba Brooks	Treasure Isle
Vitamin A	Baba Brooks	Island
Warlock	Skatalites	Top Deck
Wayward Ska	Lloyd Brevett	Ska Beat
Welcome You Back Home (Welcome Home)	Jackie Opel & Doreen Schaeffer	Ska Beat
What a Woe	Theophilus Beckford	King Pioneer
What a Woe	Theophilus Beckford	Island
What's New Pussycat	Bob Marley & Wailers	Supreme
What's New Pussycat	Bob Marley & Wailers	Island
When I Realize	Stranger Cole & Patsy Todd	Prince Buster Voice of the People
When You Are Wrong	Techniques	Treasure Isle
When You Are Wrong	Techniques	Island
Where's The Girl for Me	Bob Marley & Wailers	Coxsone
Willow Weep (Look Away Ska)	Skatalites	Studio 1
Wolverton Mountain (Twin Double)	Skatalites	Ska Beat
Worlds Fair Stranger	Cole & Ken Boothe	Coxsone
Yard Broom	Skatalites	Ska Beat
Yard Broom	Skatalites	Treasure Isle
Yeah Yeah	Prince Buster All Stars	Prince Buster Voice of the People
Yeah Yeah (Everybody Say Yeah) (Stubborn Kind of Fellow)	Charmers	Blue Beat
Yeah Yeah (Everybody Say Yeah) (Stubborn Kind of Fellow)	Charmers	Blue Beat
Yeah Yeah (Everybody Say Yeah) (Stubborn Kind of Fellow)	Charmers	Prince Buster Voice of the People
Yeah Yeah Yeah	Techniques	Treasure Isle
Yeah Yeah Yeah	Techniques	Island
Yogi Man	Skatalites	Sound Deck
You Are So Delightful	Skatalites	Studio 1
You Don't Know	Techniques	Treasure Isle
You Don't Know	Techniques	Island
Your Love	Bob Marley & ailers	Island

Song Title	A Side Artist	Label
1966		
African Chant (Timothy Junior)	Skatalites	Coxsone
African Queen	Don Drummond	Rio
After a Storm	Justin Hinds	Treasure Isle
Alcatraz	Baba Brooks & King Sporty	Treasure Isle
Back to Normal	Skatalites	Soft Touch
Black Joe	Skatalites	Pat's
Blues Market Prince Buster	All Stars	Blue Beat
Bond Street Special Roland	Alphonso	Treasure Isle
Bugle Boy	Baba Brooks	Gay Feet
Call Me Master	Prince Buster All Stars	Blue Beat
Call Me Master	Prince Buster All Stars	Prince Buster Voice of the People
Cleopatra	Roland Alphonso	Doctor Bird
The Clock	Baba Brooks	Doctor Bird
The Clock	Baba Brooks	Treasure Isle
Contact	Baba Brooks & Roy Richards	Doctor Bird
Dance	Cleopatra	Prince Buster Olive Blossom
Devoted to You	Roland Alphonso	Island
Down in My Heart	Delroy Wilson	All Stars
Eighth Games	Baba Brooks	Doctor Bird
Eighth Games	Baba Brooks	Gay Feet
Faberge (Sailing)	Baba Brooks	Gay Feet
Fight for Your Right	Justin Hinds	Dutchess
1st Session	Baba Brooks	Doctor Bird
1st Session	Baba Brooks	Gay Feet
Froggy	Baba Brooks	Treasure Isle
From Russia with Love	Roland Alphonso	Doctor Bird
Give Me A Chance	Delroy Wilson	Studio 1
Goldfinger	Tommy McCook	Treasure Isle
Green Moon	Don Drummond	Island
Green Moon	Don Drummond	Studio 1
Hard Man Fe Dead	Prince Buster	Blue Beat
Hard Man Fe Dead	Prince Buster	Prince Buster
Hard Man Fe Dead	Prince Buster	Soulsville Center
Here Comes the Heartaches	Delroy Wilson	Studio 1
The Higher the Monkey Climbs	Justin Hinds	Doctor Bird
The Higher the Monkey Climbs	Justin Hinds	Dutchess
Hooligans	Count Lasher	Dutchess
The Hunter (Happy Hunter)	Prince Buster	All Stars Dice
I Found My Love	Sensations	Treasure Isle

Song Title	A Side Artist	Label
I Should Have Known Better (Independent Anniversary Ska)	Skatalites	Island
Ice Water	Leonard Dillon	Doctor Bird
Jam Session	Baba Brooks	Doctor Bird
Jam Session	Baba Brooks	Gay Feet
James Bond Girl	Roland Alphonso	Ska Beat
James Bond Girl	Roland Alphonso	Muzik City
Jump Indpendently	Count Lasher	Dutchess
Juvenile Delinquent	Sensations	Treasure Isle
Ki Salaboca	Baba Brooks	Gay Feet
King Size	Baba Brooks	Doctor Bird
Know Your Friend	Derrick Morgan	Treasure Isle
Last Call	Don Drummond	Studio 1
The Last Time (You Turn Me Down)	Sensations	Treasure Isle
Life in Living Colours	Roland Alphonso	Prince Buster
Lion of Judah	Prince Buster All Stars	Blue Beat
Lion of Judah	Prince Buster All Stars	Prince Buster Voice of the People
Looking Through the Window	Don Drummond	Island
Looking Through the Window	Don Drummond	Coxsone
Love Not to Brag	Sensations	Treasure Isle
Love Won't Be Mine	Bob Marley & Wailers	Island
Mad World	Baba Brooks	Dutchess
Magic Star	Roland Alphonso	Island
Maureen	Baba Brooks & Roy Richards	Doctor Bird
Maureen	Baba Brooks & Roy Richards	Gay Feet
Me Mama Told Me	Justin Hinds	Treasure Isle
Miss Ska Culation	Roland Alphonso	Doctor Bird
Miss Ska Culation	Roland Alphonso	Doctor Bird
More Love	Tommy McCook	Doctor Bird
More Love	Tommy McCook	Treasure Isle
More Love (Take 2)	Tommy McCook	Treasure Isle
Mouth A Massey	Alton Ellis	Pat's
Musical Sermon	Baba Brooks	Gay Feet
My Girl	Melodies	Treasure Isle
Naked City	Tommy McCook	Doctor Bird
Naked City	Tommy McCook	Coxsone
Nightfall	Baba Brooks	Treasure Isle
Nightmare	Baba Brooks	Treasure Isle
One Nation	Joe White & Chuck Joseph	Gay Feet
Open The Door	Baba Brooks	Gay Feet
Party Time	Baba Brooks	P E P
Phoenix City	Roland Alphonso	Doctor Bird

Song Title	A Side Artist	Label
Picket Line	Prince Buster All Stars	Blue Beat
Portrait to Don	Tommy McCook	Treasure Isle
Prince of Peace	Prince Buster All Stars	Blue Beat
Ringo's Theme (This Boy) (Ringo's Ska) (Ska With Ringo)	Roland Alphonso	Doctor Bird
Ringo's Theme (This Boy) (Ringo's Ska) (Ska With Ringo)	Roland Alphonso	Coxsone
Riverton City	Tommy McCook	Rio
Riverton City	Tommy McCook	Caltone
Rude Boy (Rude Boy Ska) (Rule Them Rudie)	Bob Marley & Wailers	Doctor Bird
Rude Rude Rudee (Rude Rude Rudie) (Don't Throw Stones)	Prince Buster	Blue Beat
Say Boss Man	Prince Buster All Stars	Blue Beat
The Scratch	Baba Brooks & Granville Williams	Gay Feet
Set Me Free	Don Drummond	Blue Beat
Shake It (Music Keep On Playing) (Let the Music Play)	Sensations	Treasure Isle
Shame & Scandal	Peter Tosh & Wailers	Ska Beat
Shanty Town	Baba Brooks	Gay Feet
Ska Beat	Alton Ellis	Randy's
Ska Jam	Tommy McCook	Rio
Ska-ing West	Sir Lord Comic	Doctor Bird
Ska-ing West	Sir Lord Comic	B M N
Ska-Lite (Roll Call) (Call Off) (Cast Off)	Baba Brooks	Gay Feet
Ska-Lite (Roll Call) (Call Off) (Cast Off)	Baba Brooks	Gay Feet/ Excel
Skaramouche	Charley Organaire	S E P
Smooth Sailing	Tommy McCook	Rio
So Good (Rinky Dink)	Roland Alphonso	Ska Beat
So Long	Baba Brooks & Lester Sterling	Treasure Isle
So Wonderful	Derrick Morgan & Naomi	Treasure Isle
Song of Love	Roland Alphonso	Doctor Bird
Special Event	Baba Brooks	Treasure Isle
Strong Man Sampson	Eric Monty Morris	Treasure Isle
Sufferer's Choice	Roland Alphonso	Doctor Bird
Temptation	Eric Monty Morris	Dutchess
10:30 with Tony V	Baba Brooks	Gay Feet
10:30 with Tony V (Our Man Flint)	Baba Brooks	Gay Feet
Third Man Ska	Skatalites	Supreme

Song Title	A Side Artist	Label
This Is Thunder	Baba Brooks	Doctor Bird
This Is Thunder	Baba Brooks	Gay Feet
Thunderball	Tommy McCook	Treasure Isle
The Toughest	Prince Buster All Stars	Prince Buster
The Toughest	Prince Buster All Stars	Rio
Trotting	Skatalites	Coxsone
Try Me	Justin Hinds	Treasure Isle
unknown instrumental	Skatalites	
V C 10 (Shake A Lady)	Roland Alphonso	Doctor Bird
Western Flyer	Baba Brooks	Treasure Isle
What You're Gonna Do	Techniques	Treasure Isle
You Should Have Known	Sensations	Treasure Isle
1967		
Dance Cleopatra	Prince Buster	Blue Beat
Faberge (Sailing)	Baba Brooks	Doctor Bird
Marcus Junior	Don Drummond	Pyramid
One Eyed Giant	Baba Brooks	Ska Beat
Open the Door	Baba Brooks	Doctor Bird
Open the Door	Baba Brooks	Doctor Bird
Party Time	Baba Brooks	Doctor Bird
The Scratch	Baba Brooks & Granville Williams	Doctor Bird
Ska-Lite (Roll Call) (Call Off) (Cast Off)	Baba Brooks	Doctor Bird
Willow Weep (Look Away Ska)	Skatalites	Studio 1
1968		
Blues (Lavender Blue)	Baba Brooks	P E P
Dance Cleopatra	Prince Buster Blue	Elephant
Dreadnaught	Baba Brooks	Pyramid
Motoring (Take Five)	Baba Brooks & Beverley's	All Stars Pyramid
Sly Mongoose	Baba Brooks	Pyramid
Watermelon Man	Baba Brooks	W & C
1969		
Bridgeview Shuffle	Roland Alphonso	Doctor Bird
Bridgeview Shuffle	Roland Alphonso	Matador
Cool Shade	Don Drummond	Studio 1
Faberge (Sailing)	Baba Brooks	High Note
Ki Salaboca	Baba Brooks	Gay Feet
10:30 With Tony V (Our Man Flint)	Baba Brooks	High Note
When You Call My Name	Stranger Cole & Patsy Todd	Treasure Isle
1970		
Bridge View Shuffle (mistitled Red Cow)	Roland Alphonso	Pama

Song Title	A Side Artist	Label
Carry Go Bring Come	Justin Hinds	Duke Reid Greatest Hits
Dog War (Broadway Jungle)	Maytals	Prince Buster
Elevator Rock	Don Drummond	Studio 1
River to the Bank	Skatalites	Randy's
River to the Bank	Skatalites	Randy's
The Rocket (mislabeled Royal Flush)	Don Drummond	Bamboo
Ruff & Tuff (Rough & Tough)	Stranger Cole	Duke Reid Greatest Hits
Simmer Down	Bob Marley & Wailers	Coxsone
When You Call My Name	Stranger Cole & Patsy Todd	Duke Reid Greatest Hits

1971

Dog War (Broadway Jungle)	Maytals	Prince Buster
Man To Man	Lord Creator	Randy's

1972

Blue Dot (Hot Rod)	Roland Alphonso	Bongo Man
Hard Man Fe Dead	Prince Buster	Prince Buster
Little Flea (Nobody Knows) (Flea War)	Maytals	Prince Buster
One Love	Bob Marley & Wailers	Coxsone
Something Special	Roland Alphonso	Studio 1
You're Wondering Now	Reuben Anderson & Joanne Dennis	Coxson

1973

Blues (Lavender Blue) (mislabeled Together)	Baba Brooks	Gay Feet
Eastern Standard Time	Skatalites	Duke Reid Greatest Hits
Little Did You Know	Techniques	Treasure Isle
Little Did You Know	Techniques	Treasure Isle
Occupation	Skatalites	Treasure Isle

1974

Eastern Standard Time	Skatalites	Treasure Isle
One Eyed Giant	Baba Brooks	Torpedo

1976

Jumbo Malt	Skatalites	Tropical
Jumbo Malt	Skatalites	Planit
Middle East	Skatalites	Planit

1977

Gun Fever (Guns Fever)	Baba Brooks	Trojan
Guns Of Navarone	Skatalites	Trojan
Guns Of Navarone	Skatalites	Trojan

Song Title	A Side Artist	Label	
Phoenix City	Roland Alphonso	Trojan	
Shockers Rock	Skatalites	Studio 1	
1978			
One Love	Bob Marley & Wailers	Studio 1	
Peace With Your Neighbor	Delroy Wilson	Coxsone	
You're Wondering Now	Reuben Anderson & Joanne Dennis	Studio 1	
1979			
Burke's Law	Prince Buster	Blue Beat	
City Riot	Prince Buster All Stars	Blue Beat	
El Pussy Cat Ska	Roland Alphonso	Island	
Phoenix City	Roland Alphonso	Trojan	
Phoenix City	Roland Alphonso	Island	
1980			
Beardman	Ska Skatalites	Island	
Devil's Triangle	Skatalites	Deep Groove	
Rub Up Push Up	Justin Hinds	Island	
Others			
Away From it All (Ska Train, Siberia)	Skatalites	Randy's	196–
Going Downtown Ska	Prince Buster All Stars	Prince Buster	196–
Memphis Ska	Skatalites	Randy's	196–
Pig Pen Sound	Baba Brooks	Top Deck	196–
Portrait of My Love	Baba Brooks	Dutchess	196–
Ska Ta Shot	Roland Alphonso	Top Deck	196–
Willow Weep (Look Away Ska)	Skatalites	Studio 1	198–
Practice What You Preach	Owen Silvera & Leon Silvera	Treasure Isle	
What Have I Done	Owen Silvera & Leon Silvera	Treasure Isle	

Essential Albums

There are many collections of music featuring Don Drummond, but below is a selective listing of some essential albums.

The Best of Don Drummond	Studio One
Skatalites and Friends at Randy's	VP Records
Foundation Ska (Studio One Presents The Ska-Talites)	Heartbeat
Don Drummond Memorial	Treasure Isle
In Memory of Don Drummond	Studio One
Jazz Ska Attack 1964	Jet Set Records
Don Drummond Memorial Album	Studio One
Tribute to the Ska-Talites	Treasure Isle/ Lagoon
Ska Bonanza: The Studio One Ska Years	Studio One/ Heartbeat
Jazz Jamaica from the Workshop	Studio One
The Birth of Ska	Trojan
Ska-Boo-Da-Ba: Sounds from Top Deck Vol. 3	Top Deck/ Warner Bros.
100 Years After	Studio One
Don Drummond Greatest Hits	Treasure Isle

Bibliography

Alphonso, Roland. Interview by Heather Augustyn. May 17, 1997.

Barrett, Leonard. *The Rastafarians*. Boston: Beacon Press, 1997.

_____. *The Sun and the Drum*. Kingston: Sangster's Book Stores, 1976.

Barrow, Steve. "Ska Boo-Da-Ba. Top Sounds from Top Deck" [CD booklet]. London: Westside, 1998.

_____. "Tougher Than Tough: The Story of Jamaican Music" [CD booklet]. London: Mango Records, 1993.

Bennett, Headley. Interview with Heather Augustyn. March 7, 2011.

Bennett, JoJo. Interview with Heather Augustyn. February 7, 2011.

Bent, Suzanne. Interview with Heather Augustyn. March 3, 2011, March 19, 2011.

Bongo Jerry (Robin Small). "Roll on Sweet Don." *Abeng*. May 17, 1969.

Bradley, Lloyd. "The Graduates." *MOJO*, August 2002.

_____. *This Is Reggae Music: The Story of Jamaica's Music*. New York: Grove Press, 2000.

Brevett, Lloyd. Interview by Heather Augustyn. May 17, 1997.

Bryan, Karl. Interview with Heather Augustyn. January 25, 2012.

Cameron, Charley. Interview with Heather Augustyn. November 14, 2011.

Campbell, Howard. "The Legendary Don Drummond." *Jamaica Observer*, August 25, 1996.

_____. "Strains of praise for Sister Mary." *Jamaica Observer*, February 14, 2003.

Cane-Honeysett, Laurence. "Don Drummond Memorial Album" [CD booklet]. London: Trojan Records, May, 2009.

Carney, Joseph. "Splash and Ripple from Green island: The Musical Legacy of Don Drummond." lightmillennium. org/2006_17th/jcarney_drummond_part2.html. Accessed October 21, 2012.

Chin, Clive. Interview with Heather Augustyn. November 11, 2011.

Chin, Norma Faye. Interview with Heather Augustyn. March 21, 2011.

Clarke, Sebastian. *Jah Music: The Evolution of the Popular Jamaican Song*. London: Heinemann Educational Books, 1980.

Cullen, Miguel. "The Skatalites — Ska Legends." *The Independent*, November 24, 2010.

Daily Gleaner. Numerous articles accessed at Jamaica-gleaner.com.

de Koningh, Michael, and Laurence Cane-Honeysett. *Young Gifted and Black: The Story of Trojan Records*. London: Sanctuary House, 2003.

Edwards, Nadi. "Iconic Drummond: The Musician as Muse in Four Jamaican Poems." *Small Axe*, No. 1. 1997.

Escoffery, Dr. Carlos. Correspondence with Heather Augustyn. December 2011–February 2012.

Foster, Chuck. *Roots Rock Reggae: An Oral History of Reggae Music from Ska to Dancehall*. New York: Billboard, 1999.

_____. *The Small Axe Guide to Rock Steady*. London: Muzik Tree & I Am the Gorgon, 2009.

Goodall, Graeme. Interview with Heather Augustyn. June 23, 2011, July 13, 2011.

Goodison, Vaughn "Bunny." Interview

with Heather Augustyn, February 6, 2012.

Gordon, Vin. Interview with Heather Augustyn. March 15, 2011, April 29, 2012.

Grey, Owen. Interview by Heather Augustyn. January 11, 2011.

Griffiths, Marcia. Interview with Heather Augustyn. May 21, 2011.

Heart Foundation of Jamaica. "Heart Disease." *Jamaica Journal*, September, 1972.

Hebdige, Dick. *Cut 'n' Mix: Culture, Identity and Caribbean Music*. London: Routledge, 1987.

Hickling, Dr. Frederick. Interview with Heather Augustyn. July 9, 2011.

Hussey, Dermot. Interview with Heather Augustyn. June 27, 2011.

_____. "Requiem to Don Drummond." RJR radio show, 1969.

Hutton, Clinton. "Oh Rudie: Jamaican Popular Music and the Narrative of Urban Badness in the Making of Postcolonial Society." *Caribbean Quarterly*, December, 2010. 22.

Irons, Dr. Aggrey. Interview with Heather Augustyn. June 27, 2011.

Jamaica Gleaner. Numerous articles accessed at Jamaica-gleaner.com.

Katz, David. *Solid Foundation: An Oral History of Reggae*. New York: Bloomsbury, 2003.

Keyo, Brian. "Foundation Ska: A Brief History of the Skatalites" [CD booklet]. Burlington, MA: Heartbeat Records, 1996.

King, Herman. Interview with Heather Augustyn. March 29, 2011.

Knibb, Lloyd. Interview by Heather Augustyn. May 17, 1997.

Knight, Ronald. Interview with Heather Augustyn. January 11, 2011.

Lee, Helene. *The First Rasta: Leonard Howell and the Rise of Rastafarianism*. Chicago: Chicago Review Press, 2004.

Mahfood, Paul Jad. Interview with Heather Augustyn. October 21, 2011.

Malcolm, Carlos. Interview with Heather Augustyn. April 25, 2011.

Martin, Winston "Sparrow." Interview with Heather Augustyn. June 15, 2011.

McDonald, Larry. Interview with Heather Augustyn. February 8, 2011.

McKenzie, Earl. "Don Drummond and the Philosophy of Music." *Caribbean Quarterly*, Vol. 56, No. 4, December 2010.

Miller, Herbie. "Brown Girl in the Ring: Margarita and Malungu." *Caribbean Quarterly*, December 2007.

_____. "Creative Resistance: The Life and Music of Don Drummond." *Jamaica Observer*, May 25, 2007.

_____. "Don Drummond, Jazz and Black Nationalism." *Jamaica Observer*, May 23, 2007.

_____. "Don Drummond's Mania: Myth or Reality?" *Jamaica Observer*, May 13, 2007.

Morgan, Derrick. Interview with Heather Augustyn. February 25, 2011.

Murray, Robin, et al. *The Epidemiology of Schizophrenia*. Cambridge: Cambridge University Press, 2003.

Murray, Robin, and David Castle. *Marijuana and Madness: Psychiatry and Neurobiology*. Cambridge: Cambridge University Press, 2004.

Patterson, P.J. Interview with Heather Augustyn. June 13, 2011.

Perrone, Pierre. "Obituary: Sister Mary Ignatius Davies." *The Independent*, March 3, 2003.

Poole, Rob. "'Kind of Blue': Creativity, Mental Disorder and Jazz." *The British Journal of Psychiatry*, Vol. 18, No. 9, September 2003.

Prince, Raymond, et al. "Cannabis or Alcohol? Observations on Their Use in Jamaica." United Nations Office on Drug Crimes Bulletin on Narcotics, 1972.

Ranglin, Ernest. Interview with Heather Augustyn. September 8, 2011.

Robinson, Greg. "The Skatalites: Playing the Jamaican Sound." *Windplayer*, No. 51.

Rodriguez, Rico. Interview with Heather

Augustyn. January 13, 2011, February 11, 2011, February 19, 201.

Rohlehr, Gordon. "Jamaica Blues Play serenade in Sound." *Cipriani Labour Review*, 1970.

_____. "Some Problems of Assessment: A Look at new expressions in the Arts of the Contemporary Caribbean." *Caribbean Quarterly*, September 1971.

_____. "Sounds and Pressure." *My Strangled City and Other Essays*. Port-of-Spain: Longman Trinidad Limited, 1992, 86–94.

Royes, Gillian. Interview with Heather Augustyn. March 30, 2011.

Royes, Heather. Interview with Heather Augustyn. March 4, 2011, March 10, 2011, June 14, 2011, June 27, 2011.

Royes, Dr. K.C. "Bellevue Hospital, Kingston, Jamaica: Yesterday, Today, Tomorrow?" *The Jamaican Nurse*, 1966.

Sang, Herman. Interview with Heather Augustyn. February 15, 2011, April 10, 2011.

Seaton, B.B. Interview with Heather Augustyn. February 3, 2011.

Selim. "The Instrumentalist." *The Jamaica Daily News*, August 20, 1976.

Sergi, Zola Buckland. Interview with Heather Augustyn. November 18, 2011.

Smith, Winston. Interview with Heather Augustyn. March 7, 2011.

Spence, Patricia Ann. "The Roots of Reggae." *New York Amsterdam News*, May 1, 1976.

Sterling, Lester. Recorded interview with Heather Augustyn, May 17, 1997.

Stewart, Ken. Interview with Heather Augustyn. May 20, 2011.

Taitt, Lyn. Interview by Heather Augustyn. June 11, 2009.

Tanna, Laura. "Don Drummond: That Broken Music." *Jamaica Gleaner*, jamaica-gleaner.com/gleaner/20000517/Cleisure/Cleisure5.html. Accessed October 21, 2012.

Thornton, Eddie "Tan Tan." Interview with Heather Augustyn. February 22, 2011, February 26, 2011, February 27, 2011.

Walker, Klive. *dubwise*. Toronto, Ontario: Insomniac Press, 2005.

Walters, Basil. "The Immortal Trombonist." *Daily News*, April 30, 1982.

White, Cathy. "Personally and Socially: The Jamaica Ska Takes Over!" *New York Amsterdam News*, May 30, 1964.

White, Garth. "Patriarchs of Sound: Popular Music's Early Instrumentalists." *The Jamaican*, December 1986.

_____. "Rudie, Oh Rudie!" *Caribbean Quarterly*, September 1967

White, Timothy. *Catch a Fire*. New York: Henry Holt, 1983.

Williams, Mark. "Alpha Boys' School: Music in Education" [CD booklet]. London: Trojan, 2006.

Wills, Geoffrey. "Forty Lives in the Bebop Business: Mental Health in a Group of Eminent Jazz Musicians." *The British Journal of Psychiatry*, 183, 2003.

Index